Structural Holes

Structural Holes

The Social Structure of Competition

RONALD S. BURT

Harvard University Press
Cambridge, Massachusetts, and London, England

This book has been digitally reprinted. The content remains
identical to that of previous printings.

First Harvard University Press paperback edition, 1995

Library of Congress Cataloging-in-Publication Data

Burt, Ronald S.
  Structural holes : the social structure of competition / Ronald S. Burt.
    p. cm.
  Includes bibliographical references and index.
  ISBN 0–674–84372–X (cloth)
  ISBN 0–674–84371–1 (pbk.)
  1. Competition—Social aspects. 2. Competition, Imperfect—Social
  aspects. 3. Entrepreneurship—Social aspects. 4. Social networks.
  I. Title.
HD41.B88   1992
338.6'048—dc20
91–43396
    CIP

Contents

Acknowledgments

Work on this book was facilitated by support from the National Science Foundation (SES-7925728, SES-8208203), support from Columbia University's Center for the Social Sciences, and consulting revenues of the Strategy Laboratory at the Center. Most of the manuscript was drafted in May and June of 1990 while I was a Fellow at the Netherlands Institute for Advanced Study (NIAS) and revised in the summer of 1991 at Columbia's Center for the Social Sciences. Charles Corbin, Miguel G. Guilarte, and Larry Jacobs helped me assemble the market data. Andrej Rus, working with Rick Brunner, Maurice Coleman, Hajdeja Iglic, and Elisa Weiss, helped me prepare the data on manager networks. Portions of the argument were presented at the 1983 Sunbelt Social Networks Conference, the 1989 European Conference on Social Network Analysis, the 1990 NIAS symposium "Interdisciplinary Perspectives on Organization Studies," the 1990 Harvard Business School conference "Networks and Organizations," the 1991 Theodore Standing Lecture at the State University of New York, Albany, and colloquia at the University of California, Irvine (1982), the University of North Carolina, Chapel Hill (1983), Cornell University (1986), Stanford University (1989), the University of California, Berkeley (1990), and the Russell Sage Foundation (1990).

I am grateful to my colleagues for their helpful suggestions. Paul DiMaggio, Linton Freeman, Noah Friedkin, David Knoke, Peter Marsden, Thomas Schøtt, and Douglas White made influential comments on my 1983 first-draft manuscript on the *tertius gaudens* in negotiated relations. Paul DiMaggio kindly shared the insights of students and faculty who discussed an early version of this book in the Yale Complex Organization Workshop. Charles Perrow and Richard Swedberg influenced the final form of sections discussed at the Russell Sage Foundation. Chapter 6 was much improved in response to comments from Glenn Carroll and

John Freeman on population ecology and Harrison White on the interface model of markets. I owe a special debt to students in my network analysis class, organization research seminar, and social leverage class. In particular, Donald Nagle and Ilan Talmud gave me detailed critiques that influenced the manuscript. Bernard Barber, Robert Eccles, Hendrik Flap, John Freeman, and Peter Marsden did me the honor and service of working through a complete draft of the manuscript. Their comments resulted in substantial changes to the presentation of the argument in Chapters 1 and 2. My final debt is to Michael Aronson and Elizabeth Gretz of Harvard University Press: to Michael for his encouragement over eight years and to Elizabeth for her editing. Remaining thistles and burrs in the text index my obstinacy.

Manhattan
November 1991

Structural Holes

Introduction

"This," my colleague smiled, "is what we call a home run." I was in a well-appointed conference room at the top of the building. Panoramic view. State-of-the-art audiovisual. Nice chairs. Good wood. Intense audience. My colleague and I had just explained to the CEO and his senior staff how a former manager, a political entrepreneur of the first order, had seized control of the firm many years earlier by strategically handing out jobs in an area desperate for jobs. Deep cleavages now existed between employees obligated to the entrepreneur and those hoping to make the firm work. The situation had deteriorated to the point of shootings and bomb threats. My colleague and I had ideas for bringing the firm back, but the ideas would have to wait for another day. Today was captive to the history and depth of the problem. The CEO kept turning back to our graphics describing the social structure of his firm. He knew the players. He understood what had happened. "You know," he mused, "they just seemed like waves of turtles coming over the hill; hired as they made it to our door."

He was a skilled engineer and a good administrator. He understood supply and demand in the market for his product. He had been blindsided by a man who better understood the social structure of competition.

That is the subject of this book: how competition works when players have established relations with others. My argument is that much of competitive behavior and its results can be understood in terms of player access to "holes" in the social structure of the competitive arena. Players are connected to certain others, trusting of certain others, obligated to support certain others, dependent on exchange with certain others. Push here and someone over there moves. By dint of who is connected to whom, holes exist in the social structure of the competitive arena. The holes in social structure, or, more simply, structural holes, are disconnections or nonequivalencies between players in the arena. Structural holes are entrepreneurial opportunities for information access, timing, referrals, and control. The argument presented in Chapter 1 (with formal details in Chapter 2) explains how players with networks rich in structural holes—players with networks that provide high structural autonomy— enjoy high rates of return on investments. These players know about, take part in, and exercise control over more rewarding opportunities. Competitive advantage is a matter of access to holes.

The conclusions of Chapters 1 and 2 are tested in Chapters 3 and 4. Structural holes turn out to be an advantage in the predicted ways. In Chapter 3, structural holes in product networks are shown to be an advantage for producers negotiating price, an advantage visible in higher profit margins. In Chapter 4, structural holes in the contact networks of senior managers are an advantage in negotiating work, an advantage visible in the speed of manager promotions past one another.

I return to the argument in Chapter 5, where I unpack the connection between player and structure. The unit of analysis in which structural holes have their causal effect is the network of relations that intersect in a player. The intersection is known by various names, depending on the context; it may be termed a role, a market, or a position in social structure. The players in which relations intersect are physical and legal entities: a person, an organization, or a broader aggregation of physical and legal entities. Where an intersection occurs is merely an empirical curiosity; causation resides in the intersection of relations. The distribution of structural holes around the relations that intersect in a person or an organization determines the player's entrepreneurial opportunities and thus the player's competitive advantage. Holes create inequality between organizations as they create inequality between people.

Chapter 1, in focusing on the way in which structural holes are responsible for player differences *between* markets, provides one view of the player-structure duality. Chapters 6 and 7 provide two other views, examining, respectively, player differences *within* and *around* markets as positions in social structure.

In Chapter 6, I argue that structural holes are responsible for heterogeneity and survival within a market. The commit hypothesis is that low autonomy players conform more closely, under threat of being excluded from relationships, to behavior characteristic of their location in social structure. This is a bridge to the interface model of markets (White, 1981a; Leifer, 1985). Empirical evidence on American markets illustrates the point: the lower the structural autonomy of players in a market, the more they conform to the market schedule characteristic of their market. The corollary survival hypothesis is that higher rates of change—new players replacing old—occur where there is little structural autonomy because there is little room for error. This is a bridge to population ecology analysis (Hannan and Freeman, 1989). The network image of a market is the population ecology image of a niche. Structural autonomy is analogous to niche width. The greater the structural autonomy of a market, the wider the niche, and the more likely that diverse organization forms can survive in the market niche. Illustrative data show that firms survive longer as leaders in more autonomous markets, and structural autonomy decreases the mortality of organizations new to a market.

In Chapter 7, I argue that structural holes are responsible for social and emotional organization as a kind of residue that accumulates in the wake of entrepreneurial players navigating around the constrained relations that define a market. This is a strategy hypothesis: players develop ways to manage their low control in constraint relations and protect their control advantage in opportunity relations. When the constrained player is an organization, the strategy hypothesis is a theory of the firm; the firm is the social residue that results when managers try to ease the constraint of certain market transactions. This is a bridge to the neoclassical theory of the firm (Coase, 1937), resource dependence theory (Pfeffer and Salancik, 1978), and transaction cost economics (Williamson, 1975, 1985). Illustrative data show how corporate hierarchy ties span constraint transactions and avoid opportunity transactions. When the constrained player is a person, the strategy hypothesis is a description of personality as the emotional residue of a person who is trying to manage the loss of control in constrained relationships. The argument is here at its most speculative, developed with illustrations from Sullivan's interpersonal theory of psychiatry, Freudian identification as a defense mechanism, and Bott images of segregated conjugal roles.

This account provides a distant view of the argument. The structural hole is an element of social structure simple in concept, powerful in describing empirical data, with integrating implications for diverse lines of social science theory. The chapter summaries provide a closer view. But before I get into the substance of the argument, let me provide a final orienting view to put the argument in broader comparative perspective.

The structural hole argument has four signature qualities. First, competition is a matter of relations, not player attributes. Second, competition is a relation emergent, not observed. Third, competition is a process, not just a result. Fourth, imperfect competition is a matter of freedom, not just power. These four qualities are not individually unique to the structural hole argument. They are jointly characteristic of it.

First, competition is a matter of relation, not player attributes. The structural hole argument escapes the debilitating social science practice of using player attributes for explanation. The relations that intersect to create structural holes give a player entrepreneurial opportunities to get higher rates of return. The player in whom the relations intersect—black, white, female, male, old, young, rich, poor—is irrelevant to the explanation. Competition is not about being a player with certain physical attributes; it is about securing productive relationships. Physical attributes are a correlate, not a cause, of competitive success. Holes can have different effects for people with different attributes or for organizations of different kinds, but these differences in effect occur because the attributes and organization forms are correlated with different positions in social structure. The manner in which a structural hole is an entrepreneurial opportunity for information benefits and control benefits is the bedrock explanation that carries across player attributes, populations, and time. The task for the analyst is to cut past the spurious correlation between attributes and outcomes to reach the underlying social structural factors that cause the outcome. This point is developed in Chapter 5.

Second, competition is a relation emergent, not observed. The structural holes in which competition develops are invisible relations of nonredundancy, relations visible only by their absence. Consider the atavistic driver experiment. You're on the freeway. There is a car ahead of you going 65. Pull up so your front wheels are parallel to his. Stay there. This won't take long. If he speeds up, speed up. If he slows down, slow down. You feel the tension, which you know is also building in the next car. He looks over. Is this a threat? He may slow down, hoping you'll go away. If that doesn't work, and he doesn't feel that his car can escape yours, his anger will only be apparent on his face. If he is more confident, he'll accelerate to get away from you. Let him.

For the moment when you two stood in common time and place, you were competitors. Break the parallelism, and the competition is gone. There is no behavioral relationship between the drivers that is competition. Competition is an intense, intimate, transitory, invisible relationship created between players by their visible relations with others. It is being cheek by jowl with respect to the passing environment that makes the drivers competitors.

The task of analyzing competition is made more difficult by the fact that the structural holes in which competition thrives do not connect the players we see. The holes connect invisible pieces of players, the pieces we see in any one of the many roles and markets in which the person or firm is a player. I see one piece of you in the office, another on the street, another at home. Each piece has an attendant network of relations with relevant others. The causal force of structural holes resides in the pattern of relations that intersect in each network. That intersection happens in players, but where it occurs is distinct from the causal force released by its occurrence. This is another view of my first point, that people and organizations are not the source of action so much as they are the vehicles for structurally induced action.

These qualities make it difficult to capture competition without conceptual and research tools to represent the social structure of the competitive arena. A growing understanding of competition is one of the important returns on the network analysis ideas developed during the 1970s and 1980s. The social structure of competition is not about the structure of competitive relations. It is about the social structure of the relations for which players compete. The structural hole argument is not a theory of competitive relationships. It is a theory about competition for the benefits of relationships. To explain variation in competitive success, I look beyond the competitors themselves to the circumstances of the relations for which they compete. The terrain on which competition plays out lies beyond the competitors themselves. It lies in their efforts to negotiate relations with other players. When those relations are positioned in social structure such that there is little room to negotiate, the margin between success and failure is slim. The social structure of competition is about the negotiability of the relationships on which competitors survive. This is the essence of the structural autonomy concept.

Third, competition is a process, not just a result. With important exceptions, most theories of competition concern what is left when competition is over. They are an aside in efforts to answer the practical question of how to maximize producer profit. Answering the question requires a definition of how price varies with output. It is convenient to assume that there is a condition of "competition" such that price is constant with output. The presumed competition exists when: (a) there are an infinite number of buyers and sellers known to one another, (b) goods can be divided for sale to any number of buyers, and (c) buyers and sellers are free to exchange without interference from third parties. When goods are exchanged under these conditions, conditions of "perfect" competition, equilibrium prices can be derived that will clear the market. An architecture of powerful theory about price and production follows.[1]

The alternative is to start with the process of competition and work toward its results. This is a less elegant route for theory, but one that veers closer to the reality of competition as we experience it. The structural hole argument is not about the flow of goods. No mechanism is proposed to define the prices that "clear" the imperfectly competitive market. Such a mechanism could be proposed, but it is not my concern here. This book is about the competitive process by which the price and occurrence of transactions is decided. It is about initiating and sculpting the deal, about the process of negotiating the relationships on which competitors survive. Structural holes determine the extent and nature of a player's competitive advantage in that negotiation.

Fourth, imperfect competition is a matter of freedom, not just power. The structural hole argument is a theory of competition made imperfect by the freedom of individuals to be entrepreneurs. In this the theory cuts across the usual axis of imperfect competition.

In the perfectly competitive arena, any party to a transaction has an unlimited choice of partners. Numerous alternatives exist and players are free to choose. The fact of that choice drives price to a minimum. The significance of any one player as an entrepreneur is zero. The structural image is one of relational chaos. Players are free to withdraw from existing relations to join with anyone who better serves their interests. Obligation stops with the execution of the transaction.

Deviations from this image measure imperfect competition, usually defined by the extent to which choice is concentrated in the hands of the strongest player. Stigler (1957:262) concludes his historical review: "If we were free to redefine competition at this late date, a persuasive case could be made that it should be restricted to meaning the absence of monopoly power in a market." At the extreme of perfect competition, every player has an unlimited choice among possible relationships. At the other extreme, choice is concentrated in the hands of a dominant player. Everyone else is assigned to relations by the dominant player. Familiar images include monopolies, cults, village kinship systems, political machines, and fascist bureaucracies. The structural image is one of a completely and rigidly interconnected system of people and establishments within a market. High-obligation relations, with obligation enforced by authority or convention, allow neither negotiation nor the strategic replacement of partners.

Observed behavior lies between these extremes. Control is never absolute; it is negotiated—whether exercised through competitive price, bureaucratic authority, or some other control mechanism. In the most regulated arena, there are special relations through which certain players are able to get around the dicta of the governing mechanism. In the most competitive of arenas, there are relations between certain players that provide them special advantages. Competition is omnipresent and everywhere imperfect.

The extremes of perfect and regulated competition are more similar on one critical point than either is to the reality of observed behavior between them. They are both images of dominance. Players are homogeneously trivial under competitive market pricing and, at the other extreme, homogeneously trivial under the dicta of the dominant player. The dominant player defines fair exchange in the regulated market. Buyer and seller are locked into exchange relations by the dicta of the dominant player. The press of numbers defines fair exchange in the perfectly competitive market. Competition between countless buyers and sellers involves negotiation between alternative relations, not within a relationship. Any single partner in a relationship is a faceless cog, readily replaced with someone else. At either extreme, the lack of negotiation within a relationship denies the individuality of buyer and seller.

But their individuality is the key to understanding competition. The substantive richness of competition lies in its imperfections, the jostling of specific players against one another, each looking for a way to make a difference. In the substantive details of imperfect competition lie the defining parameters of competition. They are the parameters of player individuality. Competition is imperfect to the extent that any player can affect the terms of any relationship. Oligopoly, the extent to which multiple players together dominate a market, is an insufficient answer. The central question for imperfect competition is how players escape domination, whether it is domination by the market or domination by another player.

This is the focus of the structural hole argument—a theory of freedom instead of power, of negotiated instead of absolute control. It is a description of the extent to which the social structure of a competitive arena creates entrepreneurial opportunities for certain players to affect the terms of their relationships.

1

The Social Structure
of Competition

A player brings capital to the competitive arena and walks away with profit determined by the rate of return where the capital was invested. The market production equation predicts profit: invested capital, multiplied by the going rate of return, equals the profit to be expected from the investment. You invest a million dollars. The going rate of return is 10 percent. The profit is one hundred thousand dollars. Investments create an ability to produce a competitive product. For example, capital is invested to build and operate a factory. Rate of return is an opportunity to profit from the investment.

The rate of return is keyed to the social structure of the competitive arena and is the focus here. Each player has a network of contacts in the arena. Something about the structure of the player's network and the location of the player's contacts in the social structure of the arena provides a competitive advantage in getting higher rates of return on investment. This chapter is about that advantage. It is a description of the way in which social structure renders competition imperfect by creating entrepreneurial opportunities for certain players and not for others.[1]

Opportunity and Capital

A player brings at least three kinds of capital to the competitive arena. Other distinctions can be made, but three are sufficient here. First, the player has financial capital: cash in hand, reserves in the bank, investments coming due, lines of credit. Second, the player has human capital. Your natural qualities—charm, health, intelligence, and looks—combined with the skills you have acquired in formal education and job experience give you abilities to excel at certain tasks.

Third, the player has social capital: relationships with other players.

You have friends, colleagues, and more general contacts through whom you receive opportunities to use your financial and human capital. I refer to opportunities in a broad sense, but I certainly mean to include the obvious examples of job promotions, participation in significant projects, influential access to important decisions, and so on. The social capital of people aggregates into the social capital of organizations. In a firm providing services—for example, advertising, brokerage, or consulting—there are people valued for their ability to deliver a quality product. Then there are "rainmakers," valued for their ability to deliver clients. Those who deliver the product do the work, and the rainmakers make it possible for all to profit from the work. The former represent the financial and human capital of the firm. The latter represent its social capital. More generally, property and human assets define the firm's production capabilities. Relations within and beyond the firm are social capital.

DISTINGUISHING SOCIAL CAPITAL

Financial and human capital are distinct in two ways from social capital. First, they are the property of individuals. They are owned in whole or in part by a single individual defined in law as capable of ownership, typically a person or corporation. Second, they concern the investment term in the market production equation. Whether held by a person or the fictive person of a firm, financial and human capital gets invested to create production capabilities. Investments in supplies, facilities, and people serve to build and operate a factory. Investments of money, time, and energy produce a skilled manager. Financial capital is needed for raw materials and production facilities. Human capital is needed to craft the raw materials into a competitive product.

Social capital is different on both counts. First, it is a thing owned jointly by the parties to a relationship. No one player has exclusive ownership rights to social capital. If you or your partner in a relationship withdraws, the connection, with whatever social capital it contained, dissolves. If a firm treats a cluster of customers poorly and they leave, the social capital represented by the firm-cluster relationship is lost. Second, social capital concerns rate of return in the market production equation. Through relations with colleagues, friends, and clients come the opportunities to transform financial and human capital into profit.

Social capital is the final arbiter of competitive success. The capital invested to bring your organization to the point of producing a superb product is as rewarding as the opportunities to sell the product at a profit. The investment to make you a skilled manager is as valuable as the opportunities—the leadership positions—you get to apply your managerial skills. The investment to make you a skilled scientist with state-of-the-art research facilities is as valuable as the opportunities—the projects—you get to apply those skills and facilities.

More accurately, social capital is as important as competition is imperfect and investment capital is abundant. Under perfect competition, social capital is a constant in the production equation. There is a single rate of return because capital moves freely from low-yield to high-yield investments until rates of return are homogeneous across alternative investments. When competition is imperfect, capital is less mobile and plays a more complex role in the production equation. There are financial, social, and legal impediments to moving cash between investments. There are impediments to reallocating human capital, both in terms of changing the people to whom you have a commitment and in terms of replacing them with new people. Rate of return depends on the relations in which capital is invested. Social capital is a critical variable. This is all the more true when financial and human capital are abundant—which in essence reduces the investment term in the production equation to an unproblematic constant.

These conditions are generic to the competitive arena, which makes social capital a factor as routinely critical as financial and human capital. Competition is never perfect. The rules of trade are ambiguous in the aggregate and everywhere negotiable in the particular. The allocation of opportunities is rarely made with respect to a single dimension of abilities needed for a task. Within an acceptable range of needed abilities, there are many people with financial and human capital comparable to your own. Whatever you bring to a production task, there are other people who could do the same job—perhaps not as well in every detail, but probably as well within the tolerances of the people for whom the job is done. Criteria other than financial and human capital are used to narrow the pool down to the individual who gets the opportunity. Those other criteria are social capital. New life is given to the proverb that says success is determined less by what you know than by whom you know. As a senior colleague once remarked (and Cole, 1992: chaps. 7–8, makes into an intriguing research program), "Publishing high-quality work is important for getting university resources, but friends are essential." Of those who are equally qualified, only a select few get the most rewarding opportunities. Of the products that are of comparably high quality, only some come to dominate their markets. The question is how.

WHO AND HOW

The competitive arena has a social structure: players trusting certain others, obligated to support certain others, dependent on exchange with certain others, and so on. Against this backdrop, each player has a network of contacts—everyone the player now knows, everyone the player has ever known, and all the people who know the player even though he or she doesn't know them. Something about the structure of the player's network and the location of the player's contacts in the social structure of the arena provides a competitive advantage in getting higher rates of return on investment.

Who

There are two routes into the social capital question. The first describes a network as your access to people with specific resources, which creates a correlation between theirs and yours. This idea has circulated as power, prestige, social resources, and more recently, social capital. Nan Lin and his colleagues provide an exemplar of this line of work, showing how the occupational prestige of a person's job is contingent on the occupational prestige of a personal contact leading to the job (Lin, 1982; Lin, Ensel, and Vaughn, 1981; Lin and Dumin, 1986). Related empirical results appear in Campbell, Marsden, and Hurlbert (1986), De Graaf and Flap (1988), Flap and De Graaf (1989), and Marsden and Hurlbert (1988). Coleman (1988) discusses the transmission of human capital across generations. Flap and Tazelaar (1989) provide a thorough review with special attention to social network analysis.

Empirical questions in this line of work concern the magnitude of association between contact resources and the actor's own resources, and variation in the association across kinds of relationships. Granovetter's (1973) weak tie metaphor, discussed in detail shortly, is often invoked to distinguish kinds of relationships.[2]

Network analysts will recognize this as an example of social contagion analysis. Network structure is not used to predict attitudes or behaviors directly. It is used to predict similarity between attitudes and behaviors (compare Barber, 1978, for a causal analysis). The research tradition is tied to the Columbia Sociology survey studies of social influence conducted during the 1940s and 1950s. In one of the first well-known studies, for example, Lazarsfeld, Berelson, and Gaudet (1944) show how a person's vote is associated with the party affiliations of friends. Persons claiming to have voted for the presidential candidate of a specific political party tend to have friends affiliated with that party. Social capital theory developed from this line of work describes the manner in which resources available to any one person in a population are contingent on the resources available to individuals socially proximate to the person.

Empirical evidence is readily available. People develop relations with people like themselves (for example, Fischer, 1982; Marsden, 1987; Burt, 1990b). Wealthy people develop ties with other wealthy people. Educated people develop ties with one another. Young people develop ties with one another. There are reasons for this. Socially similar people, even in the pursuit of independent interests, spend time in the same places. Relationships emerge. Socially similar people have more shared interests. Relationships are maintained. Further, we are sufficiently egocentric to find people with similar tastes attractive. Whatever the etiology for strong relations between socially similar people, it is to be expected that the resources and opinions of any one individual will be correlated with the resources and opinions of his or her close contacts.

How

A second line of work describes social structure as capital in its own right. The first line describes the network as a conduit; the second line describes how networks are themselves a form of social capital. This line of work is less developed than the first. Indeed, it is little developed beyond intuitions in empirical research on social capital. Network range, indicated by size, is the primary measure. For example, Boxman, De Graaf, and Flap (1991) show that people with larger contact networks obtain higher-paying positions than people with small networks. A similar finding in social support research shows that persons with larger networks tend to live longer (Berkman and Syme, 1979).

Both lines of work are essential to a general definition of social capital. Social capital is at once the resources contacts hold and the structure of contacts in a network. The first term describes whom you reach. The second describes how you reach.

For two reasons, however, I ignore the question of who to concentrate on how. The first is generality. The question of who elicits a more idiographic class of answers. Predicting rate of return depends on knowing the resources of a player's contacts. There will be interesting empirical variation from one kind of activity to another, say, job searches versus mobilizing support for a charity, but the empirical generalization is obvious. Doing business with wealthy clients, however wealth is defined, has a higher margin than doing business with poor clients. I want to identify parameters of social capital that generalize beyond the specific individuals connected by a relationship.

The second reason is correlation. The two components in social capital should be so strongly correlated that I can reconstruct much of the phenomenon from whichever component more easily yields a general explanation. To the extent that people play an active role in shaping their relationships, then a player who knows how to structure a network to provide high opportunity knows whom to include in the network. Even if networks are passively inherited, the manner in which a player is connected within social structure says much about contact resources. I will show that players with well-structured networks obtain higher rates of return. Resources accumulate in their hands. People develop relations with people like themselves. Therefore, how a player is connected in social structure indicates the volume of resources held by the player and the volume to which the player is connected.[3]

The nub of the matter is to describe network benefits in the competitive arena in order to be able to describe how certain structures enhance those benefits. The benefits are of two kinds, information and control.

Information

Opportunities spring up everywhere: new institutions and projects that need leadership, new funding initiatives looking for proposals, new jobs for which you know of a good candidate, valuable items entering the market for which you know interested buyers. The information benefits of a network define who knows about these opportunities, when they know, and who gets to participate in them. Players with a network optimally structured to provide these benefits enjoy higher rates of return to their investments, because such players know about, and have a hand in, more rewarding opportunities.

ACCESS, TIMING, AND REFERRALS

Information benefits occur in three forms: access, timing, and referrals. Access refers to receiving a valuable piece of information and knowing who can use it. Information does not spread evenly across the competitive arena. It isn't that players are secretive, although that too can be an issue. The issue is that players are unevenly connected with one another, are attentive to the information pertinent to themselves and their friends, and are all overwhelmed by the flow of information. There are limits to the volume of information you can use intelligently. You can only keep up with so many books, articles, memos, and news services. Given a limit to the volume of information that anyone can process, the network becomes an important screening device. It is an army of people processing information who can call your attention to key bits—keeping you up to date on developing opportunities, warning you of impending disasters. This second-hand information is often fuzzy or inaccurate, but it serves to signal something to be looked into more carefully.

Related to knowing about an opportunity is knowing whom to bring into it. Given a limit to the financing and skills that we possess individually, most complex projects will require coordination with other people as staff, colleagues, or clients. The manager asks, "Whom do I know with the skills to do a good job with that part of the project?" The capitalist asks, "Whom do I know who would be interested in acquiring this product or a piece of the project?" The department head asks, "Who are the key players needed to strengthen the department's position?" Add to each of these the more common question, "Whom do I know who is most likely to know the kind of person I need?"

Timing is a significant feature of the information received by network. Beyond making sure that you are informed, personal contacts can make you one of the people who is informed early. It is one thing to find out that the stock market is crashing today. It is another to discover that the price of your stocks will plummet tomorrow. It is one thing to learn the names of the two people referred to the board for the new vice-presidency. It is another to discover that the job will be created and that your credentials could make you a serious candidate for the position. Personal contacts get significant information to you before the average person receives it. That early warning is an opportunity to act on the information yourself or to invest it back into the network by passing it on to a friend who could benefit from it.

These benefits involve information flowing from contacts. There are also benefits in the opposite flow. The network that filters information coming to you also directs, concentrates, and legitimates information about you going to others.

In part, this network does no more than alleviate a logistics problem. You can only be in a limited number of places within a limited amount of time. Personal contacts get your name mentioned at the right time in the right place so that opportunities are presented to you. Their referrals are a positive force for future opportunities. They are the motor expanding the third category of people in your network, the players you don't know who are aware of you. Consider the remark so often heard in recruitment deliberations: "I don't know her personally, but several people whose opinion I trust have spoken well of her."

Beyond logistics, there is the issue of legitimacy. Even if you know about an opportunity and can present a solid case for why you should get it, you are a suspect source of information. The same information has more legitimacy when it comes from someone inside the decision-making process who can speak to your virtues. Candidates offered the university positions with the greatest opportunity, for example, are people who have a strong personal advocate in the decision-making process, a person in touch with the candidate to ensure that both favorable information and responses to any negative information get distributed during the decision.

BENEFIT-RICH NETWORKS

A player with a network rich in information benefits has contacts: (a) established in the places where useful bits of information are likely to air, and (b) providing a reliable flow of information to and from those places.

Selecting Contacts

The second criterion is as ambiguous as it is critical. It is a matter of trust, of confidence in the information passed and the care with which contacts look out for your interests. Trust is critical precisely because competition is imperfect. The question is not whether to trust, but whom to trust. In a perfectly competitive arena, you can trust the system to provide a fair return on your investments. In the imperfectly competitive arena, you have only your personal contacts. The matter comes down to a question of interpersonal debt. If I do for her, will she for me? There is no general answer. The answer lies in the match between specific people. If a contact feels that he is somehow better than you—a sexist male dealing with a woman, a racist white dealing with a black, an old-money matron dealing with an upwardly mobile ethnic—your investment in the relationship will be taken as proper obeisance to a superior. No debt is incurred. We use whatever cues can be found for a continuing evaluation of the trust in a relation, but we never know a debt is recognized until the trusted person helps us when we need it. With this kind of uncertainty, players are cautious about extending themselves for people whose reputation for honoring interpersonal debt is unknown. The importance of this point is illustrated by the political boundary around senior management discussed in Chapter 4. The more general point of trust as people meeting your expectations is illustrated in Barber's (1983) analysis of competence and duty as dimensions of trust relations in diverse institutions in American society.

Theory and research exist to identify trustworthy contacts. Strong relationships and mutual acquaintances tend to develop between people with similar social attributes such as education, income, occupation, and age (for example, Fischer, 1982; Burt, 1986, 1990b; Marsden, 1987; and see note 4 below). Both factors are linked to trust. Trust is a component in the strong relationships, and mutual acquaintances are like an insurance policy through which interpersonal debt is enforced such that the other person can be deemed trustworthy. (Nohria, 1991). Whether egocentrism, cues from presumed shared background and interests, or confidence in mutual acquaintances to enforce interpersonal debt, the operational guide to the formation of close, trusting relations seems to be that a person more like me is less likely to betray me. For the purposes here, I set the whole issue to one side as person-specific and presume that it is resolved by the able player.

Siting Contacts

That leaves the first criterion, establishing contacts where useful bits of information are likely to air. Everything else constant, a large, diverse network is the best guarantee of having a contact present where useful information is aired. This is not to say that benefits must increase linearly with size and diversity, a point to which I will return (Figure 1.5), but only that, other things held constant, the information benefits of a large, diverse network are more than the information benefits of a small, homogeneous network.

Size is the more familiar criterion. Bigger is better. Acting on this understanding, people can expand their networks by adding more and more contacts. They make more cold calls, affiliate with more clubs, attend more social functions. Numerous books and self-help groups can assist them in "networking" their way to success by putting them in contact with a large number of potentially useful, or helpful, or like-minded people. The process is illustrated by the networks in Figure 1.1. The four-contact network at the left expands to sixteen contacts at the right. Relations are developed with a friend of each contact in network A, doubling the contacts to eight in network B. Snowballing through friends of friends, there are sixteen contacts in network C, and so on.

Size is a mixed blessing. More contacts can mean more exposure to valuable information, more likely early exposure, and more referrals.

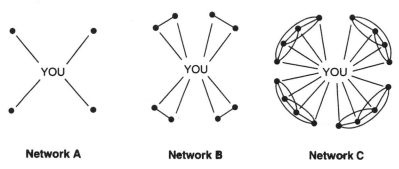

Network A   **Network B**   **Network C**

Figure 1.1   Network expansion

But increasing network size without considering diversity can cripple a network in significant ways. What matters is the number of nonredundant contacts. Contacts are redundant to the extent that they lead to the same people, and so provide the same information benefits.

Consider two four-contact networks, one sparse, the other dense. There are no relations between the contacts in the sparse network, and strong relations between every contact in the dense network. Both networks cost whatever time and energy is required to maintain four relationships. The sparse network provides four nonredundant contacts, one for each relationship. No single one of the contacts gets the player to the same people reached by the other contacts. In the dense network, each relationship puts the player in contact with the same people reached through the other relationships. The dense network contains only one nonredundant contact. Any three are redundant with the fourth.

The sparse network provides more information benefits. It reaches information in four separate areas of social activity. The dense network is a virtually worthless monitoring device. Because the relations between people in that network are strong, each person knows what the other people know and all will discover the same opportunities at the same time.

The issue is opportunity costs. At minimum, the dense network is inefficient in the sense that it returns less diverse information for the same cost as that of the sparse network. A solution is to put more time and energy into adding nonredundant contacts to the dense network. But time and energy are limited, which means that inefficiency translates into opportunity costs. If I take four relationships as an illustrative limit on the number of strong relations that a player can maintain, the player in the dense network is cut off from three fourths of the information provided by the sparse network.

Structural Holes

I use the term structural hole for the separation between nonredundant contacts. Nonredundant contacts are connected by a structural hole. A structural hole is a relationship of nonredundancy between two contacts. The hole is a buffer, like an insulator in an electric circuit. As a result of the hole between them, the two contacts provide network benefits that are in some degree additive rather than overlapping.

EMPIRICAL INDICATORS
Nonredundant contacts are disconnected in some way—either directly, in the sense that they have no direct contact with one another, or indirectly, in the sense that one has contacts that exclude the others. The respective empirical conditions that indicate a structural hole are cohesion and structural equivalence. Both conditions define holes by indicating where they are absent.

Under the cohesion criterion, two contacts are redundant to the extent that they are connected by a strong relationship. A strong relationship indicates the absence of a structural hole. Examples are father and son, brother and sister, husband and wife, close friends, people who have been partners for a long time, people who frequently get together for social occasions, and so on. You have easy access to both people if either is a contact. Redundancy by cohesion is illustrated at the top of Figure 1.2. The three contacts are connected to one another, and so provide

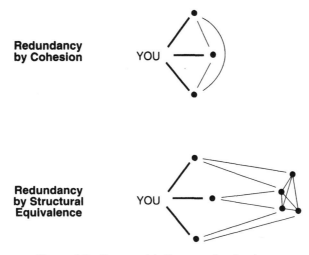

Figure 1.2   Structural indicators of redundancy

the same network benefits. The presumption here—routine in network analysis since Festinger, Schachter, and Back's (1950) analysis of information flowing through personal relations and Homans's (1950) theory of social groups—is that the likelihood that information will move from one person to another is proportional to the strength of their relationship. Empirically, strength has two independent dimensions: frequent contact and emotional closeness (see Marsden and Hurlbert, 1988; Burt, 1990b).

Structural equivalence is a useful second indicator for detecting structural holes. Two people are structurally equivalent to the extent that they have the same contacts. Regardless of the relation between structurally equivalent people, they lead to the same sources of information and so are redundant. Cohesion concerns direct connection; structural equivalence concerns indirect connection by mutual contact. Redundancy by structural equivalence is illustrated at the bottom of Figure 1.2. The three contacts have no direct ties with one another. They are nonredundant by cohesion. But each leads you to the same cluster of more distant players. The information that comes to them, and the people to whom they send information, are redundant. Both networks in Figure 1.2 provide one nonredundant contact at a cost of maintaining three.

The indicators are neither absolute nor independent. Relations deemed strong are only strong relative to others. They are our strongest relations. Structural equivalence rarely reaches the extreme of complete equivalence. People are more or less structurally equivalent. In addition, the criteria are correlated. People who spend a lot of time with the same other people often get to know one another. The mutual contacts responsible for structural equivalence set a stage for the direct connection of cohesion. The empirical conditions between two players will be a messy combination of cohesion and structural equivalence, present to varying degrees, at varying levels of correlation.

Cohesion is the more certain indicator. If two people are connected with the same people in a player's network (making them redundant by structural equivalence), they can still be connected with different people beyond the network (making them nonredundant). But if they meet frequently and feel close to one another, then they are likely to communicate and probably have contacts in common. More generally, and especially for field work informed by attention to network benefits, the general guide is the definition of a structural hole. There is a structural hole between two people who provide nonredundant network benefits. If the cohesion and structural equivalence conditions are considered together, redundancy is most likely between structurally equivalent people connected by a strong relationship. Redundancy is unlikely, indicating a structural hole, between total strangers in distant groups. I will return to this issue again, to discuss the depth of a hole, after control benefits have been introduced.

THE EFFICIENT-EFFECTIVE NETWORK
Balancing network size and diversity is a question of optimizing structural holes. The number of structural holes can be expected to increase with network size, but the holes are the key to information benefits. The optimized network has two design principles.

Efficiency
The first design principle of an optimized network concerns efficiency: Maximize the number of nonredundant contacts in the network to maximize the yield in structural holes per contact. Given two networks of equal size, the one with more nonredundant contacts provides more benefits. There is little gain from a new contact redundant with existing contacts. Time and energy would be better spent cultivating a new contact to unreached people.[4] Maximizing the nonredundancy of contacts maximizes the structural holes obtained per contact.[5]

Efficiency is illustrated by the networks in Figure 1.3. These reach the same people reached by the networks in Figure 1.1, but in a different way. What expands in Figure 1.1 is not the benefits, but the cost of maintaining the network. Network A provides four nonredundant contacts. Network B provides the same number. The information benefits provided by the initial four contacts are redundant with benefits provided by their close friends. All that has changed is the doubled number of relationships maintained in the network. The situation deteriorates even further with the sixteen contacts in network C. There are still only four

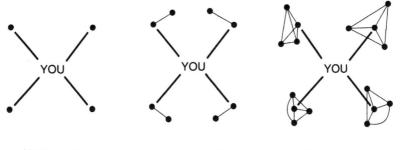

Network A'   Network B'   Network C'

Figure 1.3 Strategic network expansion

nonredundant contacts in the network, but their benefits are now obtained at a cost of maintaining sixteen relationships.

With a little network surgery, the sixteen contacts can be maintained at a fourth of the cost. As illustrated in Figure 1.3, select one contact in each cluster to be a primary link to the cluster. Concentrate on maintaining the primary contact, and allow direct relationships with others in the cluster to weaken into indirect relations through the primary contact. These players reached indirectly are secondary contacts. Among the redundant contacts in a cluster, the primary contact should be the one most easily maintained and most likely to honor an interpersonal debt to you in particular. The secondary contacts are less easily maintained or less likely to work for you (even if they might work well for someone else). The critical decision obviously lies in selecting the right person to be a primary contact. The importance of trust has already been discussed. With a trustworthy primary contact, there is little loss in information benefits from the cluster and a gain in the reduced effort needed to maintain the cluster in the network.

Repeating this operation for each cluster in the network recovers effort that would otherwise be spent maintaining redundant contacts. By reinvesting that saved time and effort in developing primary contacts to new clusters, the network expands to include an exponentially larger number of contacts while expanding contact diversity. The sixteen contacts in network C of Figure 1.1, for example, are maintained at a cost of four primary contacts in network C' of Figure 1.3. Some portion of the time spent maintaining the redundant other twelve contacts can be reallocated to expanding the network to include new clusters.

Effectiveness

The second design principle of an optimized network requires a further shift in perspective: Distinguish primary from secondary contacts in order to focus resources on preserving the primary contacts. Here contacts are not people on the other end of your relations; they are ports of access to clusters of people beyond. Guided by the first principle, these ports should be nonredundant so as to reach separate, and therefore more diverse, social worlds of network benefits. Instead of maintaining relations with all contacts, the task of maintaining the total network is delegated to primary contacts. The player at the center of the network is then free to focus on properly supporting relations with primary contacts and expanding the network to include new clusters. The first principle concerns the average number of people reached with a primary contact; the second concerns the total number of people reached with all primary contacts. The first principle concerns the yield per primary contact. The second concerns the total yield of the network. More concretely, the first principle moves from the networks in Figure 1.1 to the corresponding networks in Figure 1.3. The second principle moves from left to right in Figure 1.3. The target is network C′ in Figure 1.3: a network of few primary contacts, each a port of access to a cluster of many secondary contacts.

Figure 1.4 illustrates some complexities in unpacking a network to maximize structural holes. The "before" network contains five primary contacts and reaches a total of fifteen people. However, there are only two clusters of nonredundant contacts in the network. Contacts 2 and 3 are redundant in the sense of being connected with each other and reaching the same people (cohesion and structural equivalence criteria). The same is true of contacts 4 and 5. Contact 1 is not connected directly to contact 2, but he reaches the same secondary contacts; thus contacts 1 and 2 provide redundant network benefits (structural equivalence crite-

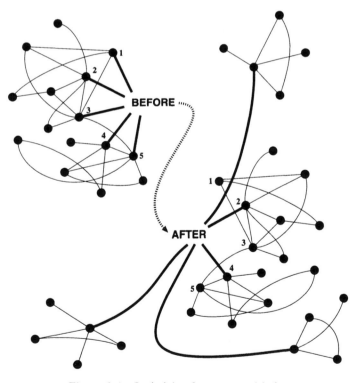

Figure 1.4   Optimizing for structural holes

rion). Illustrating the other extreme, contacts 3 and 5 are connected directly, but they are nonredundant because they reach separate clusters of secondary contacts (structural equivalence criterion). In the "after" network, contact 2 is used to reach the first cluster in the "before" network and contact 4 is used to reach the second cluster. The time and energy saved by withdrawing from relations with the other three primary contacts is reallocated to primary contacts in new clusters. The "before" and "after" networks are both maintained at a cost of five primary relationships, but the "after" network is dramatically richer in structural holes, and so network benefits.

Network benefits are enhanced in several ways. There is a higher volume of benefits, because more contacts are included in the network. Beyond volume, diversity enhances the quality of benefits. Nonredundant contacts ensure exposure to diverse sources of information. Each cluster of contacts is an independent source of information. One cluster, no matter how numerous its members, is only one source of information, because people connected to one another tend to know about the same things at about the same time. The information screen provided by multiple clusters of contacts is broader, providing better assurance that you, the player, will be informed of opportunities and impending disasters. Further, because nonredundant contacts are only linked through the central player, you are assured of being the first to see new opportunities created by needs in one group that could be served by skills in another group. You become the person who first brings people together, which gives you the opportunity to coordinate their activities. These benefits are compounded by the fact that having a network that yields such benefits makes you even more attractive as a network contact to other people, thus easing your task of expanding the network to best serve your interests.

Growth Patterns

A more general sense of efficiency and effectiveness is illustrated with network growth. In Figure 1.5, the number of contacts in a player's network increases from left to right on the horizontal axis. The number who are nonredundant increases up the vertical axis. Observed network size increases on the horizontal, effective size up the vertical. Networks can be anywhere in the gray area. The maximum efficiency line describes networks in which each new contact is completely nonredundant with other contacts. Effective size equals actual size. Efficient-effective networks are in the upper right of the graph. The minimum efficiency line

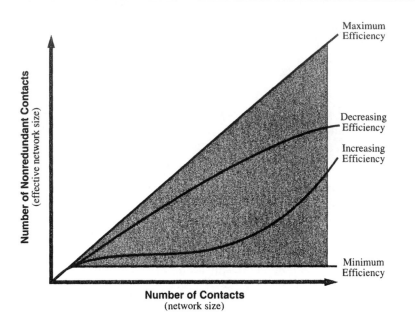

Figure 1.5 Efficiency and effectiveness

describes networks in which each new contact is completely redundant with other contacts; effective size equals one, regardless of multiple contacts in the network.

The two lines between the extremes illustrate more probable growth patterns. The decreasing efficiency line shows players building good information benefits into their initial network, then relaxing to allow increasing redundancy as the network gets large. Friends of friends begin to be included. Comparisons across networks of different sizes suggest that this is the growth pattern among managers (see Figure 4.15), though controls for time would be necessary to make the suggestion an inference.

The increasing efficiency line illustrates a different growth pattern. Initial contacts are redundant with one another. A foundation is established with multiple contacts in the same cluster. After the foundation is established, the player's network expands to include contacts in other clusters and effective size begins to increase. There are two kinds of clusters in which optimizing for saturation is wiser than optimizing for efficiency. The first is obvious. Leisure and domestic clusters are a congenial environment of low-maintenance, redundant contacts. Efficiency mixes poorly with friendship. Judging friends on the basis of efficiency is an interpersonal flatulence from which friends will flee. The second exception is a cluster of contacts where resources are dense. For the CEO, the board of directors is such a cluster. The university provost is similarly tied to the board of trustees. For the more typical manager, the immediate work group is such a cluster, especially with respect to funding authority within the group. These clusters are so important to the vitality of the rest of the network that it is worth treating each person in them as a primary contact, regardless of redundancy. Saturation minimizes the risk of losing effective contact with the cluster and minimizes the risk of missing an important opportunity anywhere in the cluster.

The more general point is that the probability of receiving network benefits from a cluster has two components, the probability that a contact will transmit information to you and the probability that it will be transmitted to the contact. I count on dense ties within a cluster to set the second probability to one. The probability of having a benefit transmitted to you therefore depends only on the strength of your relationship with a contact in the cluster. However, where the density of ties in an opportunity-rich cluster lowers the probability that your contact will know about an opportunity, there is value in increasing the number, and thus the redundancy, of contacts in the cluster so that total coverage of the cluster compensates for imperfect transmission within it.

STRUCTURAL HOLES AND WEAK TIES
Discontinuities in social structure have long been a subject of study in sociology. Fitting the structural hole argument into the history of sociological thought is not the task of this book, but one piece of contemporary history adds value to the argument here. Mark Granovetter's weak tie argument provides an illuminating aside on the information benefits of structural holes.

History
In the late 1960s and early 1970s at Harvard University, Harrison White, with a cluster of exceptional sociology graduate students, was engaged in studying the importance of gaps, as opposed to the ties, in social structure. First came his celebrated work on chains of mobility (White, 1970), and later his work with colleagues, most notably Ronald Breiger and Scott Boorman, on concrete network models—blockmodels—of social structure (White, Boorman, and Breiger, 1976; see Burt, 1982:63–69, for review). The usual analysis of mobility describes patterns of mobility, or careers, created by people moving between positions in a social struc-

ture. White (1970) shifted perspective to focus on the hole, or opportunity, created when a person leaves a position. As people move up the hierarchy, they create opportunities for people below them. Chains of promotion move up a hierarchy. Chains of opportunity move down. Looking at social structure more generally, White, Boorman, and Breiger (1976, esp. pp. 732n, 737–740) stressed the structural hole metaphor as a substantive motivation for their network blockmodels. They focused on "zeroblocks" as an especially significant component in the relation pattern defining a position in social structure. It is clear from their analysis that they meant structural holes to be important for understanding network contingent action as well as the task they addressed of clustering network elements into blocks (for example, see pp. 763ff. on the low rate of change in zeroblocks).

One of the students, Mark Granovetter, found a troubling result in his dissertation research. Hoping to link network structure to job searches, he interviewed men about how they found their current jobs and included sociometric items asking for the names of close contacts. The troubling result was that the men almost never found work through close contacts. When information on a job opportunity came through a personal contact, the contact was often distant, such as a high school acquaintance met by accident at a recent social event. He developed the point in a widely cited article, "The Strength of Weak Ties" (Granovetter, 1973), and in a book, *Getting a Job* (Granovetter, 1974).

Connecting the Two Arguments
The weak tie argument is elegantly simple. The stage is set with results familiar from the social psychology of Festinger and Homans circa 1950, discussed above with respect to cohesion indicators of structural holes. People live in a cluster of others with whom they have strong relations. Information circulates at a high velocity within these clusters. Each person tends to know what the other people know. The spread of information on new ideas and opportunities, therefore, must come through the weak ties that connect people in separate clusters. The weak ties so often ignored by social scientists are in fact a critical element of social structure. Hence the strength of weak ties. Weak ties are essential to the flow of information that integrates otherwise disconnected social clusters into a broader society.

The idea and its connection with structural holes is illustrated in Figure 1.6. There are three clusters of players. Strong ties, indicated by solid lines, connect players within clusters. Dashed lines indicate two weak

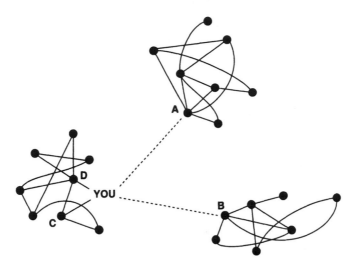

Figure 1.6   Structural holes and weak ties

ties between players in separate clusters. One of the players, you, has a unique pattern of four ties: two strong ties within your cluster and a weak tie to a contact in each in the other clusters. There are three classes of structural holes in your network: (a) holes between the cluster around contact A and everyone in your own cluster, for example, the hole between contacts A and C; (b) holes between the cluster around contact B and everyone in your own cluster, for example, the hole between contacts B and C; and (c) the hole between contacts A and B.

Weak ties and structural holes seem to describe the same phenomenon. In Figure 1.6, for example, they predict the same ranking of information benefits. You are best positioned for information benefits, contacts A and B are next, followed by everyone else. You have two weak ties, contacts A and B have one each, and everyone else has none. You have the largest volume of structural holes between your contacts, contacts A and B have fewer, and everyone else has few or none.

The Strength of Structural Holes

The weak tie argument is simpler and already well known. Why complicate the situation with the structural hole argument? There are two reasons.

First, the causal agent in the phenomenon is not the weakness of a tie but the structural hole it spans. Tie weakness is a correlate, not a cause. The structural hole argument captures the causal agent directly and thus provides a stronger foundation for theory and a clearer guide for empirical research. Second, by shifting attention away from the structural hole responsible for information benefits, to the strength of the tie providing them, the weak tie argument obscures the control benefits of structural holes. Control benefits augment and in some ways are more important than the information benefits of structural holes. Building both benefits into the argument speaks more clearly to the generality of the phenomenon under study. I will elaborate the first point, then move to the second in the next section.

The weak tie argument is about the strength of relationships at the same time that it is about their location. The two dashed lines in Figure 1.6 are bridges. They are the only connection between two otherwise separate clusters of strongly interconnected players (compare Granovetter, 1973:1065, on weak ties as bridges). A bridge is at once two things. It is a chasm spanned and the span itself. By title and subsequent application, the weak tie argument is about the strength of relationships that span the chasm between two social clusters. The structural hole argument is about the chasm spanned. It is the latter that generates information benefits. Whether a relationship is strong or weak, it generates information benefits when it is a bridge over a structural hole.

Consider a crosstabulation of ties by their strength and location. Your relationships can be sorted into two categories of strength. Strong ties are your most frequent and close contacts. Weak ties are your less frequent, less close contacts. Between these two categories, you have a few strong ties and many weak ties.

Now sort, by location, redundant ties within your social cluster versus nonredundant ties to people in other clusters. The nonredundant ties are your bridges to other clusters. From what we know about the natural etiology of relationships, bridges are less likely to develop than ties within clusters. The category of redundant ties includes your strong ties to close friends and colleagues, whom you see often, but it also includes their friends, and friends of friends, whom you meet only occasionally if at all. As you expand your inventory from your closest, most frequent contacts to your more distant, contacts tend to be people like yourself before you reach a sufficiently low level of relationship to include people from completely separate social worlds. This tendency varies from one person to the next, but it is in the aggregate the substance of the well-documented tendency already discussed for relations to develop between socially similar people. In Figure 1.6, you are one of nine people in your social cluster. You have strong ties to two people. Through those two, you have weak ties to the other six people in the cluster. To keep the sociogram simple, I deleted the dashed lines for those ties and their equivalent inside the other clusters. The other six people in your cluster are friends of friends whom you know and sometimes meet but don't have the time or energy to include among your closest contacts. The cluster is clearly held together by strong ties. Everyone has two to five strong ties to others within the cluster. All nine people are likely to know about the same opportunities as expected in a cohesive cluster. Of the 36 possible connections among the nine people in the cluster, however, only 12 are solid line strong ties. The remaining two thirds are weak ties between redundant friends of friends.

Now crosstabulate the two classifications and take expected values. The result is given in Table 1.1. Information benefits vary across the columns of the table and are higher through nonredundant ties. This is accurately represented in both the weak tie and the structural hole argument. But a quick reading of the weak tie argument, with its emphasis on the strength of a relationship, has led some to test the idea that information benefits covary inversely with the strength of ties. This is a correlation between the rows and columns of Table 1.1, which is no correlation at all. In fact, the typical tie in Table 1.1 is weak and provides redundant information. The correlation in a study population depends on the distribution of ties in the table, but there is no theoretical reason to expect a strong correlation between the strength of a relationship and the information benefits it provides.

The weak tie argument is about the two cells in the second column of the table. It predicts that nonredundant ties, the bridges that provide information benefits, are more likely weak than strong. In the second column of Table 1.1, weak tie bridges are more likely than strong tie bridges. To simplify his argument, Granovetter makes this tendency absolute by ruling out strong tie bridges (the "rare" cell in Table 1.1, the

Table 1.1 The natural distribution of relationships

Strength	Location in social structure		TOTAL
	Redundant tie within cluster	Nonredundant tie beyond cluster	
Weak tie	many	some	MORE
Strong tie	some	rare	LESS
TOTAL	MORE	LESS	

"forbidden triad" in Granovetter's argument, 1973:1063). He (1973:1064) says, "A strong tie can be a bridge, therefore, only if neither party to it has any other strong ties, unlikely in a social network of any size (though possible in a small group). Weak ties suffer no such restriction, though they are certainly not automatically bridges. What is important, rather, is that all bridges are weak ties."

Bridge strength is an aside in the structural hole argument. Information benefits are expected to travel over all bridges, strong or weak. Benefits vary between redundant and nonredundant ties, the columns of Table 1.1. Thus structural holes capture the condition directly responsible for the information benefits. The task for a strategic player building an efficient-effective network is to focus resources on the maintenance of bridge ties. Otherwise, and this is the correlative substance of the weak tie argument, bridges will fall into their natural state of being weak ties.

Control and the Tertius Gaudens

I have described how structural holes can determine who knows about opportunities, when they know, and who gets to participate in them. Players with a network optimized for structural holes, in addition to being exposed to more rewarding opportunities, are also more likely to secure favorable terms in the opportunities they choose to pursue. The structural holes that generate information benefits also generate control benefits, giving certain players an advantage in negotiating their relationships. To describe how this is so, I break the negotiation into structural, motivational, and outcome components (corresponding to the textbook distinction between market structure, market conduct, and market performance; for example, Caves, 1982). The social structure of the competitive arena defines opportunities, a player decides to pursue an opportunity, and is sometimes successful. I will begin with the outcome.

TERTIUS GAUDENS

Sometimes you will emerge successful from negotiation as the *tertius gaudens*. Taken from the work of Georg Simmel, the *tertius* role is useful here because it defines successful negotiation in terms of the social structure of the situation in which negotiation is successful. The role is the heart of Simmel's (1922) later analysis of the freedom an individual derives from conflicting group affiliations (see Coser, 1975, for elaboration).[6] The *tertius gaudens* is "the third who benefits" (Simmel, 1923:154, 232).[7] The phrase survives in an Italian proverb, *Far i due litiganti, il terzo gode* (Between two fighters, the third benefits), and, to the north, in a more jovial Dutch wording, *de lachende derde* (the laughing third).[8] *Tertius, terzo,* or *derde,* the phrase describes an individual who profits from the disunion of others.

There are two *tertius* strategies: being the third between two or more players after the same relationship, and being the third between players in two or more relations with conflicting demands. The first, and simpler, strategy is the familiar one that occurs in economic bargaining between buyer and seller. When two or more players want to buy something, the seller can play their bids against one another to get a higher price. The strategy extends directly: a woman with multiple suitors or a professor with simultaneous offers of positions in rival institutions.

The control benefits of having a choice between players after the same relationship extends directly to choice between the simultaneous demands of players in separate relationships. The strategy can be seen between hierarchical statuses in the enterprising subordinate under the authority of two or more superiors: for example, the student who strikes her own balance between the simultaneous demands of imperious faculty advisors.[9] The bargaining is not limited to situations of explicit competition. In some situations, emerging as the *tertius* depends on creating competition. In proposing the concept of a role-set, for example, Merton (1957:393–394) identifies this as a strategy to resolve conflicting role demands. Make simultaneous, contradictory demands explicit to the people posing them, and ask them to resolve their—now explicit—conflict. Even where it doesn't exist, competition can be produced by defining issues such that contact demands become contradictory and must be resolved before you can meet their requests. Failure is possible. You might provide too little incentive for the contacts to resolve their differences. Contacts drawn from different social strata need not perceive one another's demands as carrying equal weight. Or you might provide too much incentive. Now aware of one another, the contacts could discover sufficient reason to cooperate in forcing you to meet their mutually agreed-upon demands (Simmel, 1902:176, 180–181, calls attention to such failures). But if the strategy is successful, the pressure on you is alleviated and is replaced with an element of control over the negotiation. Merton (1957:430) states the situation succinctly: the player at the center of the network, "originally at the focus of the conflict, virtually becomes a more or less influential bystander whose function it is to high-light the conflicting demands by members of his role-set and to make it a problem for them, rather than for him, to resolve *their* contradictory demands."

The strategy holds equally well with large groups. Under the rubric "divide and rule," Simmel (1902:185–186) describes institutional mechanisms through which the Incan and Venetian governments obtained advantage by creating conflict between subjects. The same point is illustrated more richly in Barkey's (1991) comparative description of state control in early seventeenth-century France and Turkey. After establishing the similar conditions in the two states at the time, Barkey asks why peasant-noble alliances developed in France against the central state while no analogous or substitutable alliances developed in Turkey. The two empires were comparable with respect to many factors that scholars have cited to account for peasant revolt. They differed in one significant factor correlated with revolt—not in the structure of centralized state control, but in control strategy. In France, the king sent trusted representatives as agents to collect taxes and to carry out military decisions in provincial populations. These outside agents, *intendants,* affected fundamental local decisions and their intrusion was resented by the established local nobility. Local nobility formed alliances with the peasantry against the central state. In Turkey, the sultan capitalized on conflict among leaders in the provinces. When a bandit became a serious threat to the recognized governor, a deal was struck with the bandit to make him the legitimate governor. Barkey (1991:710) writes: "At its extreme, the state could render a dangerous rebel legitimate overnight by striking a bargain that ensured new sources of revenue for the rebel and momentary relief from internal warfare and, perhaps, an army or two for the state." The two empires differed in their use of structural holes. The French king, assuming he had absolute authority, ignored them. The Turkish sultan, promoting competition between alternative leaders, strategically exploited them. Conflict within the Turkish empire remained in the province, rather than being directed against the central state. As is characteristic of the control obtained via structural holes, the resulting Turkish control was more negotiated than was the absolute control exercised in France. It was also more effective.

THE ESSENTIAL TENSION

There is a presumption of tension here. Control emerges from *tertius* brokering tension between other players. No tension, no *tertius.*

It is easy to infer that the tension presumed is the tension between combatants. There is certainly a *tertius*-rich tension between combatants. Governors and bandits in the Turkish game played for life or death stakes. A corporate executive listening to the control argument illustrates the problem. Her colleagues, she explained, took pride in working together in a spirit of partnership and goodwill. The *tertius* imagery rang true for many firms she knew of, but not her own.

The reasoning is good. The conclusion is wrong. I referred the skeptical executive to Chapter 4, which by coincidence is an analysis of managers at her level, in her firm. Promotions in the firm are strongly correlated, and illuminatingly so for women, with the structural holes in a manager's network.

The tension essential to the *tertius* is merely uncertainty. Separate the uncertainty of control from its consequences. The consequences can be life or death, in the extreme, or merely a question of embarrassment. Everyone knows you made an effort to get that job, but it went to someone else. The *tertius* strategies can be applied to control with severe consequences or to control of little consequence. What is essential is that control is uncertain, that no one can act as if he or she has absolute authority. Where there is any uncertainty about whose preferences should dominate a relationship, there is an opportunity for the *tertius* to broker the negotiation for control by playing demands against one another. There is no long-term contract that keeps a relationship strong, no legal binding that can secure the trust necessary to a productive relationship. Your network is a pulsing swirl of mixed, conflicting demands. Each contact wants your exclusive attention, your immediate response when a concern arises. All, to warrant their continued confidence in you, want to see you measure up to the values against which they judge themselves. Within this preference webwork, where no demands have absolute authority, the *tertius* negotiates for favorable terms.

THE CONNECTION WITH INFORMATION BENEFITS

Structural holes are the setting for *tertius* strategies. Information is the substance. Accurate, ambiguous, or distorted information is moved between contacts by the *tertius*. One bidder is informed of a competitive offer in the first *tertius* strategy. A player in one relationship is informed of demands from other relationships in the second *tertius* strategy.

The two kinds of benefits augment and depend on one another. Application of the *tertius* strategies elicits additional information from contacts interested in resolving the negotiation in favor of their own preferences. The information benefits of access, timing, and referrals enhance the application of strategy. Successful application of the *tertius* strategies involves bringing together players who are willing to negotiate, have sufficiently comparable resources to view one another's preferences as valid, but won't negotiate with one another directly to the exclusion of the *tertius*. Having access to information means being able to identify where there will be an advantage in bringing contacts together and is the key to understanding the resources and preferences being played against one another. Having that information early is the difference between being the one who brings together contacts versus being just another person who hears about the negotiation. Referrals further enhance strategy. It is one thing to distribute information between two contacts during negotiation. It is another thing to have people close to each contact endorsing the legitimacy of the information you distribute.

Entrepreneurs

I have described how the information and control benefits that are relevant to gaining an advantage in negotiating relationships are multiplicative. They augment and depend on one another, and together emerge from the wellspring of structural holes in a network. But what prompts a player to pursue these benefits? Negotiation contains a motivational component.

THE ISSUE OF MOTIVATION
Behavior of a specific kind converts opportunity into higher rates of return. The information benefits of structural holes might come to a passive player, but control benefits require an active hand in the distribution of information. Motivation is now an issue. Knowing about an opportunity and being in a position to develop it are distinct from doing something about it. The *tertius* plays conflicting demands and preferences against one another and builds value from their disunion. You enter the structural hole between two players to broker the relationship between them. Such behavior is not to everyone's taste. A player can respond in ways ranging from fully developing the opportunity to ignoring it. When you take the opportunity to be the *tertius,* you are an entrepreneur in the literal sense of the word—a person who generates profit from being between others. Both terms will be useful in these precise meanings; entrepreneur refers to a kind of behavior, the *tertius* is a successful entrepreneur.[10]

Both are distinct from behavior subsequent to emerging as the *tertius.* The *tertius* can choose to extract value from negotiated relations, or to add value, strengthening the relations for later profit. Some reinvestment is to be expected if the player's network is to remain intact. A nonprofit player, pursuing entrepreneurial opportunities just for the pleasure of being the one who brings others together to build value, could choose to reinvest it all. The issue at hand is not the uses to which profit is put. It is who chooses to have a hand in the distribution of profit.

Motivation can be traced to cultural images of good and evil. In *The Protestant Ethic and the Spirit of Capitalism,* Weber (1905, esp. pp. 166ff.) describes the seventeenth-century bourgeois Protestant as an individual seeking—in his religious duty, his Calvinist "calling"—the profit of sober, thrifty, diligent exploitation of opportunities for usury and trade. Kilby (1971) provides a review and criticism of research on culturally induced entrepreneurs.

Psychological need is another motive. McClelland (1961) describes the formation in childhood of a need to achieve as critical to later entrepreneurial behavior (a need that can also be cultivated later if desired, McClelland, 1975). Without going into the etiology of motive, Schumpeter (1912:93) stresses nonutilitarian motives for entrepreneurship: "First of all, there is the dream and the will to found a private kingdom, usually, though not necessarily, also a dynasty . . . Then there is the will to conquer: the impulse to fight, to prove oneself superior to others, to succeed for the sake, not of the fruits of success, but of the success itself . . . Finally, there is the joy of creating, of getting things done, or simply of exercising one's energy and ingenuity."[11]

OPPORTUNITY AND MOTIVATION

These are powerful frameworks for understanding competition, but I don't wish to detour into the beliefs behind entreprencurial behavior. I propose to leap over the motivation issue by taking the network as simultanously an indicator of entrepreneurial opportunity and of motivation. Psychological and cultural motives for entrepreneurial behavior have been conceptualized and studied without data on the social network surrounding the entrepreneur. Such data are the substance of the structural hole argument and, in three ways, carry their own answer to the question of motivation.

First, there is the clarity of an opportunity. The above are "push" explanations. Players are pushed by psychological need or cultural imperative to be entrepreneurs. There is also a "pull" explanation. Players can be pulled to entrepreneurial action by the promise of success. I do not mean that players are rational creatures expected to calculate accurately and act in their own interest. Nor do I mean to limit the scope of the argument to situations in which players act as if they are rational in that way. I mean simply that given two opportunities, any player is more likely to act on the one with the clearer path to success. The clarity of opportunity is its own motivation. As the number of entrepreneurial opportunities in a network increases, the odds of some being clearly defined by deep structural holes increases, and therefore the odds of entrepreneurial behavior increase. To be sure, a person whose abilities or values proscribe entrepreneurial behavior is unlikely to act, and someone inclined to entrepreneurial behavior is more likely to act or even to take the initiative to create opportunities.[12] Regardless of ability or values, however, within the broad range of acceptable behaviors, a person is unlikely to take entrepreneurial action if the probability of success is low. An observer might question the propriety of a scholar who negotiates with several universities offering a position, but the question is not an issue for the player with one offer.

There are also network analogues to the push explanations of motive. A person with a psychological need for entrepreneurial behavior is prone to building a network configured around such behavior. If I find a player with a network rich in the structural holes that make entrepreneurial behavior possible, I have a player willing and able to act entrepreneurially. But it is the rare person who is the sole author of a network. Networks are more often built in the course of doing something else. If your work, for example, involves meeting people from different walks of life, your network will end up composed of contacts who without you have no contact with one another. Even so, the network is its own explanation of motive. As the volume of structural holes in a player's network increases—regardless of the process that created them—the entrepreneurial behavior of making and negotiating relations between others becomes a way of life. This is a network analogue to the cultural explanation of motive. If all you know is entrepreneurial relationships, the motivation question is a nonissue. Being willing and able to act entrepreneurially is how you understand social life.

I will treat motivation and opportunity as one and the same. For reasons of a clear path to success, or the tastes of the player as the network's author, or the nature of the player's environment as author of the network, a network rich in entrepreneurial opportunity surrounds a player motivated to be entrepreneurial. At the other extreme, a player innocent of entrepreneurial motive lives in a network devoid of entrepreneurial opportunity.[13]

MEASUREMENT IMPLICATIONS

This detour into the issue of entrepreneurial motivation highlights a complexity that might otherwise obscure the association between structural holes and rates of return. Consider Figure 1.7. Players are defined by their rate of return on investments (vertical axis) and the entrepreneurial opportunities of structural holes in their networks (horizontal axis).

The sloping line in the graph describes the hole effect of players rich in structural holes (horizontal axis) getting higher rates of return on investments (vertical axis). The increasingly positive slope of the line captures the increasing likelihood of *tertius* profit. A player invests in certain relationships. They need not all be high-yield relationships. The higher the proportion of relationships enhanced by structural holes, the more likely and able the entrepreneurial player, and so the more likely it is that the player's investments are in high-yield relationships. The result is a higher aggregate rate of return on investments.

I have shaded the area in the graph to indicate how I expect data to be distributed around the line of association. There is no imperative that says players have to take advantage of the benefits provided by structural holes. Players rich in entrepreneurial opportunity may choose to develop opportunities (and so appear in the upper right corner of the graph) or ignore them (and so appear in the lower right corner of the graph). Some players in Figure 1.7 are above the line. Some are below. If players

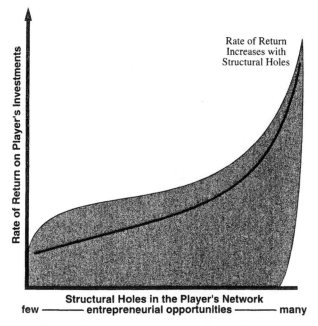

Figure 1.7   Rate of return and structural holes

were perfectly rational, observations would be clustered around the line. Players would take advantage of any entrepreneurial opportunity presented to them. A control for differences in player motivation, such as a McClelland measure of need for achievement, would have the same effect. The point is not the degree of deviation from the line of association; it is the greater deviation below the line. Variable motivation creates deviations below the true hole effect on rate of return.

This emphasizes the relative importance for empirical research of deviations above and below the line of association. Observations in the lower right corner of the graph, players underutilizing their entrepreneurial opportunities, might be due to variation in motivation. Observations in the upper left corner are a severe test of the argument. Players who have opportunities can choose whether to develop them. Players without opportunities do not have that choice. Within the limits of measurement error, there should be no observations in the upper left corner of the graph.

Secondary Holes

This brings me to the third component in the negotiation: the social structural conditions that constitute entrepreneurial opportunity. I have linked opportunity to structural holes, but not with respect to the whole domain of relevant holes. Thus far, a network optimized for entrepreneurial opportunity has a vine-and-cluster structure. As illustrated in Figures 1.3 and 1.4, a player has direct relations with primary contacts, each a port of access to a cluster of redundant secondary contacts. Structural holes between the primary contacts, a primary structural holes, provide information and control benefits. But the benefits they provide are affected by structural holes just beyond the border of the network. Structural holes among the secondary contacts within the cluster around each primary contact play a role in the *tertius* strategies. These are secondary structural holes.

CONTROL BENEFITS AND SECONDARY STRUCTURAL HOLES
The ultimate threat in negotiating a relationship is withdrawal: either severing your link to a former contact's cluster or transferring the primary relationship to a new person in the cluster. This threat depends on two things. First, there must be alternatives, secondary contacts who are redundant with your primary contact and capable of replacing the primary contact in your network. Examples include an alternative spouse in the case of negotiating a conjugal relationship, an alternative job in the case

of negotiating with a truculent supervisor, or an alternative supplier in the case of a firm renewing a contract with a past supplier. Second, there must be structural holes among the secondary contacts. If there are no contacts substitutable for your current primary contact, he or she is free to impose demands—up to the limit of structural holes between primary contacts. If your current primary contact is in collusion with whatever substitutes exist, which eliminates structural holes you might exploit, he or she is free to impose demands—again, up to the limit of structural holes between primary contacts.

Consider Figure 1.8. You are negotiating with a primary contact in a cluster of redundant contacts indicated by dots enclosed by a gray circle. Situation A illustrates the familiar negotiation between buyer and seller. You use the offer from one buyer to raise the other's offer.

Situation B illustrates the exact opposite condition. Here the redundant contacts are all connected by strong relations. This is the situation of negotiating with a member of a social clique or cult. In the absence of holes over which you can broker the connection between redundant contacts, your only recourse is to live with your contact's demands, dominate the cluster, or cut the cluster from your network.

Network density is not the issue here. Situation C is a relatively low

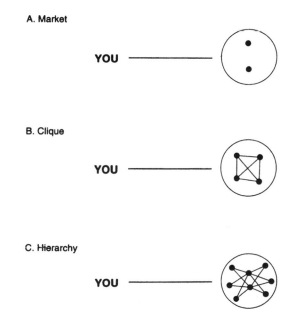

A. Market

YOU

B. Clique

YOU

C. Hierarchy

YOU

Figure 1.8   Contact clusters with and without secondary structural holes

density cluster (43% of the 28 relations within the cluster are marked with a line as strong), but contacts within the cluster are coordinated through their joint ties to two leaders in the center. It doesn't make sense to negotiate the price of a purchase in a department store by playing one sales clerk against another. They both answer to a higher authority. You have to make a purchase sufficiently large that is allows you to deal with someone higher in the organization. Then, as in Situation C, you can develop the structural hole between the two leaders at the center of the circle and play one leader against the other.

CLUSTER BOUNDARIES

Secondary contacts are a cluster of redundant players in the competitive arena beyond any one player's network. Players in the cluster are redundant by cohesion (strongly connected within the cluster) or structural equivalence (connected with the same players beyond the cluster). Given redundancy within clusters, the more general statement is that players are redundant contacts in the same cluster to the extent that they are connected with the same clusters of redundant contacts.

The idea is illustrated in Figure 1.9. Four identical networks are displayed at the top of the figure. Lines are relations, each gray circle indicates a cluster of redundant contacts, and the dark circle at the center is the player responsible for the network. Each network includes a primary contact in each of the six clusters.

The four central players are redundant. They are connected to the same clusters of redundant contacts, and so have the same information and control benefits. They might be connected to different people in each cluster, but their contacts are ports of access into the same six clusters. Rather than representing the four players with separate networks, it is more accurate to represent them as four redundant contacts within the dark circle in the network at the bottom of Figure 1.9. Contacts are aggregated similarly within each of the clusters identified by letter.

The same comparison illustrates nonredundancy. Notice the two bold curved lines between the player and two clusters, B and E. Clusters B and E are rich in structural holes, so relations with any contact in them will be more easily negotiated than relations with the better-organized clusters, such as A, D and F. Suppose that one of the central players decides to focus on these relations, leaving the other three to deal with clusters A, C, D, and E. The three are then no longer redundant with the first. The first is connected to clusters different from the ones in their networks.

This image of redundancy is analogous to the concept of substitutable producers in input-output economics. Two producers are substitutable in an economic network to the extent that they purchase similar volumes of the same kinds of supplies to make the commodity they sell. Suppliers are in turn substitutable to the extent that their product requires similar volumes of the same kinds of supplies. Two bakers are substitutable to the extent that they use the same kinds of ingredients. They might purchase their flour and sugar from different vendors, but they are substitut-

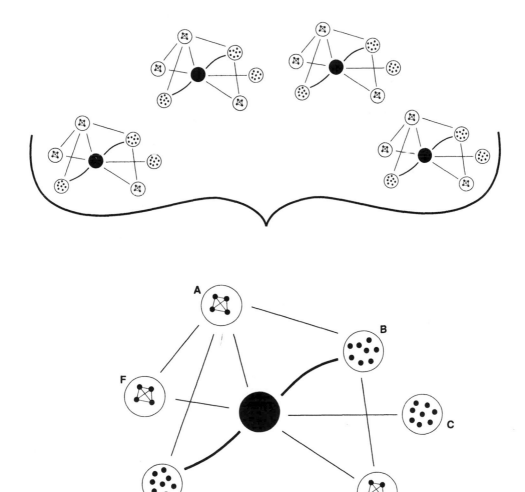

Figure 1.9   Four redundant networks pooled as one network surrounding four substitutable players

able to the extent that they similarly purchase flour from one of the alternative flour vendors and sugar from one of the alternative sugar vendors. Two auto manufacturers are substitutable to the extent that they use the same proportions of metal, glass, rubber, and plastic to produce the cars they sell. Each manufacturer might purchase glass from a different vendor, but they similarly purchase glass from one or another of the available glass vendors to make their cars. I will return to this point in the analysis of markets in Chapter 3 (Figure 3.2).

Redundancy as substitutability is analogous to the equivalence concept in network analysis, but different from the often-used variations of structural and role equivalence. Structurally equivalent people have identical relations with the same people. This is too narrow a definition of redundancy. The dark circles in the four networks in Figure 1.9 can have relations with completely different people within each cluster, which would make them redundant, but not structurally equivalent. At the other extreme, role equivalent people have identically structured relations, regardless of the specific individuals with whom they have relations. This is too broad a definition of redundancy. For example, a person connected only to cluster A in Figure 1.9 would be role equivalent to a person only connected to clusters D and F. They would be role equivalent in the sense of being an outsider connected to a clique; however, they are nonredundant because they are connected with different clusters of redundant contacts. Operationally, I am left with cluster boundaries defined a priori by some criterion, as I will illustrate in Chapter 3.

THE DEPTH OF A STRUCTURAL HOLE

Secondary only refers to the remove of a hole from the central player. Primary holes are between a player's direct contacts, secondary holes between indirect contacts. Of the two kinds of holes, the latter are the more intense.

Let the depth of a structural hole be the ease with which it can be developed for control and information benefits. When the hole is deep between two individuals, it is easy to play them against one another with *tertius* strategies.

Depth is characterized in Table 1.2 with combinations of the two indicators of holes: cohesion and equivalence. The columns contrast players who have no relationship with one another with players who meet frequently and feel emotionally close to one another (in other words, have a strong relationship). The rows contrast players in completely separate clusters with those who have equivalent ties to the same clusters (in other words, are close together in the same cluster).

Much of the table is clear from the cohesion and structural equivalence indicators for defining structural holes already discussed. There is a structural hole of some depth between the players in all conditions except the "no hole" cell. Redundancy is most likely between structurally equivalent people connected by a strong relationship. At the other extreme, there is a structural hole where both indicators show no connection: the "hole" cell in the upper left of Table 1.2. Redundancy is unlikely between total strangers in distant clusters.

Cohesion is a good indicator. Where cohesion is low, there is a hole between the players. There is no hole where cohesion is high between players equivalently connected to the same clusters. There is also a hole between players in distant clusters connected by a strong relationship. The two players are ports into different clusters of information, but their strong tie means a strong flow of information between them. Playing them against one another turns on the extent to which their cluster interests override their commitment to each other.

Cohesion is an especially good indicator relative to equivalence. The first row of the table shows a hole between players in separate clusters. But the second row shows that the widest extremes of hole depth occur between players in the same cluster. The second row of the table is the usual axis of imperfect market competition. Players connected to the same clusters are redundant, and so could replace one another in their respective networks. What I bring to your network, a contact connected to the same clusters that I reach could also bring to your network. I and the contact are substitutable producers; we are competitors in the same market. If I have strong relations with my colleagues, we collude to avoid people playing us against one another, and you face a cluster like the one in Figure 1.8B. If the relations are poor among my colleagues and myself, we are easy prey to being played against one another because we are so readily substitutable, and you face a cluster like the one in Figure 1.8A.

Equivalence is the frame and cohesion the indicator. Equivalent ties to the same clusters frame two players as competitors in the same market.

Table 1.2   Depth of a structural hole between players

Equivalent ties to clusters	Cohesion between players	
	None	Strong
None	HOLE	SHALLOW
Strong	DEEP	NO HOLE

Cohesion defines the depth of the hole between them. In terms of a regression model, the depth of the hole between two players increases with their equivalence, decreases with the strength of relation between them, and decreases sharply with the extent to which they are equivalent and strongly connected.

Structural Autonomy

The argument can now be summarized with a concept defining the extent to which a player's network is rich in structural holes, and thus rich in entrepreneurial opportunity, and thus rich in information and control benefits. The concept is structural autonomy. I will present the concept in a general way here, postponing detailed discussion for Chapter 2.

The argument began with a generic production equation. Profit equals an investment multiplied by a rate of return. The benefits of a relationship can be expressed in an analogous form: time and energy invested to reach a contact multiplied by a rate of return. A player's entrepreneurial opportunities are enhanced by a relationship to the extent that: (a) the player has invested substantial time and energy to secure a connection with the contact, and (b) there are many structural holes around the contact ensuring a high rate of return on the investment. More specifically, rate of return concerns how and whom you reach with the relationship. Time and energy invested to reach a player with more resources generates more social capital. For the sake of argument, as explained in the discussion of social capital, I assume that a player with a network optimized for structural holes can identify suitably endowed contacts. My concern is the how of a relationship, defined by the structure of a network and its connection with the social structure of the competitive arena. Thus the rate of return keyed to structural holes is a product of the extent to which there are: (a) many primary structural holes between the contact and others in the player's network, and (b) many secondary structural holes between the contact and others outside the network who could replace the contact.

There is also the issue of structural holes around the player. As the holes around contacts provide information and control benefits to the player, holes around the player can be developed by contacts for their benefit. Consider your position as one of four disconnected players at the center of the network at the bottom of Figure 1.9. Your contacts have the option of replacing you with one of your colleagues who provides the same network benefits that you do. To manage this uncertainty, you might develop relationships with your colleagues so that it would be difficult to play them off against you (an oligopoly strategy), or you might specialize in some way so that they no longer provide network benefits redundant with your own (a differentiation strategy). The issue of strategic response is the subject of Chapter 7. The point here is that your negotiating position is weaker than expected from the distribution of structural holes around contacts. Developing entrepreneurial opportunities depends on having numerous structural holes around your contacts and none attached to yourself.

These considerations come together in the concept of structural autonomy. Players with relationships free of structural holes at their own end and rich in structural holes at the other end are structurally autonomous. These are the players best positioned for the information and control benefits that a network can provide. These are the players to the far right of the graph in Figure 1.7. Structural autonomy summarizes the action potential of the *tertius*'s network. The budget equation for optimizing structural autonomy has an upper limit set by the time and energy of the *tertius*, and a trade-off between the structural holes a new contact provides versus the time and energy required to maintain a productive relationship with the contact.[14]

Summary

This chapter contains the core argument of the book. Structural holes are introduced and the manner in which they are a competitive advantage is explained.

The argument begins with the task of profit. Profit is generated by a production equation in which player investments are multiplied by the going rate of return. A million dollars invested at a 10 percent rate of return yields a hundred thousand dollar profit. Investments create an ability to produce a competitive product. Capital is invested, for example, to build and operate a factory. Rate of return is an opportunity to profit from the investment.

The rate of return is keyed to the social structure of the competitive arena. Each player has a network of contacts in the competitive arena. Certain players are connected to certain others, trusting of certain others, obligated to support certain others, dependent on exchange with certain others. Something about the structure of the player's network and the location of the player's contacts in the social structure of the arena defines the player's chances of getting higher rates of return on investment.

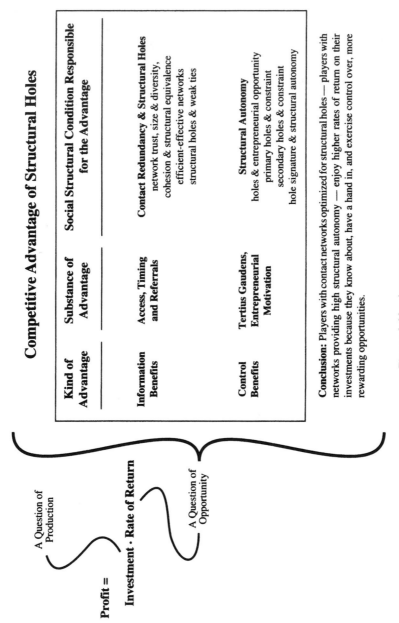

Competitive Advantage of Structural Holes

Kind of Advantage	Substance of Advantage	Social Structural Condition Responsible for the Advantage
Information Benefits	**Access, Timing and Referrals**	**Contact Redundancy & Structural Holes** network trust, size & diversity, cohesion & structural equivalence efficient-effective networks structural holes & weak ties
Control Benefits	**Tertius Gaudens, Entrepreneurial Motivation**	**Structural Autonomy** holes & entrepreneurial opportunity primary holes & constraint secondary holes & constraint hole signature & structural autonomy

Conclusion: Players with contact networks optimized for structural holes — players with networks providing high structural autonomy — enjoy higher rates of return on their investments because they know about, have a hand in, and exercise control over, more rewarding opportunities.

Profit =

Investment · **Rate of Return**

A Question of Production

A Question of Opportunity

Figure 1.10 Argument

The chances are enhanced by two kinds of network benefits, information and control, distinguished by the rows of the box in Figure 1.10.

The substance of information benefits are access, timing, and referrals. The player's network provides access to information well beyond what the player could process alone. The network also provides that information early, which gives the player an advantage in acting on the information. These benefits concern information coming to the player from contacts. Referral benefits involve the opposite flow. The network that filters information coming to the player also directs, concentrates, and legitimates information received by others about the player. Referrals get the player's interests represented in a positive light, at the right time, in the right places.

Information benefits are maximized in a large, diverse network of trusted contacts. Trust is important with respect to the honoring of interpersonal debt by contacts, but is an idiographic question answered by the social match between player and each contact individually. Network size and diversity under a presumption of trust are the general parameters to be optimized. The effective size of a network can be less than its observed size. Size is the number of primary contacts in a network; effective size is the number of nonredundant contacts. Two contacts are redundant to the extent that they provide the same information benefits to the player. Cohesion is an empirical indicator of redundancy. Contacts strongly connected to each other are likely to have similar information and so provide redundant benefit to the player. Structural equivalence is a second indicator. Contacts who, regardless of their relationship with one another, link the player to the same third parties have the same sources of information, and so provide redundant benefit to the player. Structural holes are the gaps between nonredundant contacts. As a result of the hole between them, the two contacts provide network benefits that are in some degree additive rather than overlapping. A network optimized for information benefits can be described with respect to its contacts or its connections between contacts. A network rich in nonredundant contacts is rich in structural holes.

The structural holes that generate information benefits also generate control benefits, giving certain players an advantage in negotiating their relationships. Sociological theory offers a role describing people who derive control benefits from structural holes. It is the *tertius gaudens,* the third who benefits: a person who derives benefit from brokering relationships between other players. There are two *tertius* strategies. People can be played against one another when they compete for the same relationship: for example, two buyers after the same purchase. Second, people can be played against one another when they make conflicting demands on the same individual in separate relationships: a science professor's course demands, for example, being played by a student against the course demands of a humanities professor. There is a presumption of tension here, but the essential tension is not the hostility of combatants; it is merely uncertainty. Separating the uncertainty of control from its consequences, *tertius* strategies apply similarly to negotiating control that has severe consequences or to negotiating control that is of little consequence. What is essential is that the control is uncertain, that no one can act as if he or she has absolute authority in the relationship under negotiation. In the swirling mix of preferences characteristic to social networks, where no demands have absolute authority, the *tertius* negotiates for favorable terms.

The information and control benefits are multiplicative, augmenting and dependent on one another, together emerging from the wellspring of structural holes in a network. Structural holes are the setting for *tertius* strategies. Information is the substance. Accurate, ambiguous, or distorted information is moved between contacts by the *tertius*. One bidder is informed of a competitive offer in the first strategy. A player in one relationship is informed of demands from other relationships in the second strategy.

The final task is to bring the argument together in a definition, relevant to empirical research, of the extent to which a player's network is rich in structural holes, and so entrepreneurial opportunity, and so information and control benefits. Each of a player's relationships is treated as an investment on which structural holes determine the rate of return. A player's entrepreneurial opportunities are enhanced by a relationship to the extent that: (a) the player has invested substantial time and energy to secure a connection with the contact, and (b) there are many structural holes around the contact ensuring a high rate of return on the investment. The rate of return keyed to structural holes is a product of the extent to which there are: (a) many primary structural holes between the contact and others in the player's network, and (b) many secondary structural holes between the contact and others outside the network who could replace the contact. There are also the structural holes around the player. As the holes around contacts provide information and control benefits to the player, holes around the player can be developed by contacts for their benefit.

These considerations come together in the concept of structural autonomy. Players with relationships free of structural holes at their own end and rich in structural holes at the other end are structurally autonomous. These are the players best positioned for the information and control benefits that a network can provide. Structural autonomy summarizes the action potential of the *tertius*'s network. The budget equation for optimizing structural autonomy has an upper limit set by the *tertius*'s time and energy, and a trade-off between the structural holes a new contact provides versus the time and energy required to maintain a productive relationship with the contact. The summary conclusion is that players with networks optimized for structural holes—players with networks providing high structural autonomy—enjoy higher rates of return on their investments because they know about, have a hand in, and exercise control over, more rewarding opportunities.

The reasoning isn't new. The argument draws on social psychological studies of negotiation, economic studies of imperfect competition, and, most especially, sociological studies of roles and statuses in social structure.

What is new is the expression of competitive advantage—in economic, political, or social arenas—in terms of structural holes as an elemental unit clearly defined in theory and readily operationalized for empirical research.

2

Formalizing the Argument

The next task is to define structural autonomy for empirical research. The formal details are an important component in the argument, but some readers may prefer to skip to the summary at the end of this chapter; the calculations are readily available in the network analysis program STRUCTURE.[1]

Network Data

Network data are needed on the strength of relations between each pair of players. The data are often one of three kinds. Sociometric choices are binary data in which a person cites another as the object of some kind of relationship. For example, "Who are your most important contacts?" These are the data used in Chapter 4 to analyze manager networks. Joint involvement data are counts of the times that two players are involved in the same events. For example, the interlocking directorate tie between two firms is the number of people who serve on the board of directors in both firms. There are also direct measures of interaction. For example, Chapter 3 is an analysis of dollars flowing between supplier and customer markets. These three kinds of data are transformed in various ways to define a relationship variable z_{ij}. The subscripts are needed to indicate the source and object of the relationship. Magnitude indicates the strength of the relationship. A high value of z_{ij} indicates a strong relationship from player i to player j.[2]

The patterns of z_{ij} that connect players define the empirical indicators of structural holes. A high value of z_{ij} indicates a cohesive tie between players i and j. Players i and j are structurally equivalent to the extent that they have identical relations with every other player q. That definition is sufficient for the moment.[3] As explained in Chapter 1, both indicators measure the lack of a structural hole, and cohesion is the more certain indicator. There is no certain indicator that a structural hole is present. The hole itself is an invisible seam of nonredundancy waiting to be discovered by the able entrepreneur. It would be difficult to develop a structural hole between structurally equivalent players connected by a strong relationship. The assumption in the following discussion is that the probability of being able to develop a hole decreases in proportion to the strength of direct and indirect connection between players.

Redundancy

I will begin with the number of nonredundant contacts in a network. Consider the setting at the top of Figure 2.1, in which you as player i evaluate the extent to which a contact j is redundant with your other contacts. The information access, timing, and referrals you get through j are redundant to the extent that: (a) you have a substantial investment of time and energy in a relationship with another contact, q, (b) to whom j has a strong tie:

(2.1) $p_{iq} m_{jq}$,

where p_{iq} is the proportion of i's network time and energy invested in the relationship with q (interaction with q divided by the sum of i's relations),

$$(z_{iq} + z_{qi}) \Big/ \left[\sum_j (z_{ij} + z_{ji}) \right], \qquad i \neq j,$$

and m_{jq} is the marginal strength of contact j's relation with contact q (interaction with q divided by the strongest of j's relationships with anyone), and

$$(z_{jq} + z_{qj})/\max(z_{jk} + z_{kj}), \qquad j \neq k,$$

where $\max(z_{jk})$ is the largest of j's relations with anyone (so $0 \leq m_{jq} \leq 1$), and z_{jq} is the network variable measuring the strength of the relation from j to q.[4] Aggregating the product in Eq. (2.1) across all contacts q (excluding i and the contact j under evaluation) measures the portion of

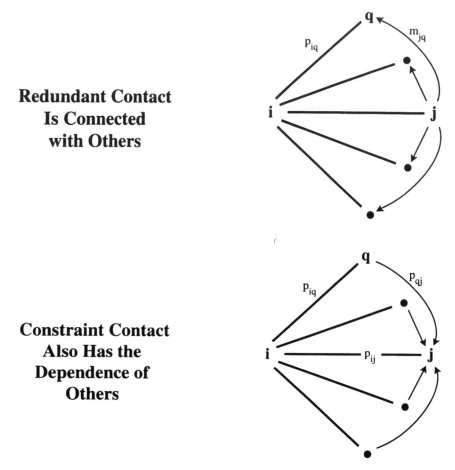

**Redundant Contact
Is Connected
with Others**

**Constraint Contact
Also Has the
Dependence of
Others**

Figure 2.1   Hole conditions of redundancy and constraint

i's relationship with j that is redundant to i's relations with other primary contacts:

$$\sum_q p_{iq} m_{jq}, \qquad q \neq i, j.$$

One minus this expression is the nonredundant portion of the relationship. The sum across relationships of the nonredundant portion in each is the number of nonredundant contacts, or effective size, of your network:

$$(2.2) \qquad \text{Effective size of } i\text{'s network} = \sum_j \left[1 - \sum_q p_{iq} m_{jq} \right], \qquad q \neq i, j,$$

where the first summation is across all N primary contacts j in your network. If contact j is completely disconnected from all other primary contacts, then the bracketed term equals one, indicating that j provides one nonredundant contact in the network. As relations between j and the other contacts strengthen, the bracketed term approaches p_{ij}, indicating that j is completely redundant with other contacts in i's network. The sum in Eq. (2.2) across contacts varies from one, indicating that the network only provides a single contact, up to the observed number of contacts in the network, N, indicating that every contact in the network is nonredundant.[5] With respect to structural holes, the index measures a network's effective size. The ratio of this number divided by N measures efficiency. The efficiency ratio varies from a maximum of one, indicating that every contact in the network is nonredundant, down to a minimum approaching zero, indicating high contact redundancy and therefore low efficiency.

Table 2.1 contains the size, effective size, and efficiency of each network in Figures 1.1, 1.3, and 1.4. For this illustration, I have treated the networks as sociometric choice data, setting all relations to 1 where there is a line in a sociogram and 0 otherwise. The networks in Figures 1.1 and 1.3 all have an effective size of four contacts, however, the increasing contacts in Figure 1.1 are redundant and so lower efficiency.

The results also highlight what is not captured. Network C' in Figure 1.3 reaches 16 people, four primary contacts and 12 secondary contacts, but its effective size of four contacts computed from the above measure is no different from network A', which only reaches a total of four con-

Table 2.1 Size, effective size, and efficiency

	Number of contacts		Effective size	Efficiency
	Primary	Secondary		
Figure 1.1				
Network A	4	0	4.0	1.00
Network B	8	0	4.0	0.50
Network C	16	0	4.0	0.25
Figure 1.3				
Network A'	4	0	4.0	1.00
Network B'	4	4	4.0	1.00
Network C'	4	12	4.0	1.00
Figure 1.4				
BEFORE	5	10	3.4	0.68
AFTER	5	24	5.0	1.00

tacts. I have limited the measure to primary contacts because these are typically the only relations on which network data are obtained. Ideally, network data would be snowballed to include secondary contacts so that effective size could be measured in terms of primary and secondary contacts.

Constraint

Connection is the key to redundant benefits; dependence is the key to constrained benefits more generally. I will discuss the constraint of holes missing within the network, dependence and exclusion, then the constraint of holes missing beyond the network.

THE CONSTRAINT OF ABSENT PRIMARY HOLES

Consider the setting at the bottom of Figure 2.1, in which you are player *i* evaluating the role of contact *j* in your network. Your entrepreneurial opportunities are constrained to the extent that: (a) another of your contacts *q*, in whom you have invested a large proportion of your network time and energy, has (b) invested heavily in a relationship with contact *j*:

(2.3) $p_{iq}p_{qj}$,

where p_{qj} is the proportional strength of *q*'s relationship with *j*, as p_{ij} is the proportional strength defined above of *i*'s relation with *j*. When the product in Eq. (2.3) is high, investment in your relationship with *q* leads back to *j*, augmenting your investment in direct contact with *j*, and making it difficult to develop a structural hole between the two contacts. Aggregating the product in Eq. (2.3) across all contacts *q* (excluding *i*) and adding *i*'s direct connection with *j* defines the proportion of *i*'s network time and energy that directly or indirectly involves *j:*

$$p_{ij} + \sum_q p_{iq}p_{qj}, \qquad q \neq i,j.$$

This defines constraint. Contact *j* constrains your entrepreneurial opportunities to the extent that: (a) you've made a large investment of time and energy to reach *j*, and (b) *j* is surrounded by few structural holes with which you could negotiate to get a favorable return on the investment. Both conditions are measured by the above expression. Measuring investment, the expression is the proportion of your network time and energy that leads you back to contact j. Even if you withdrew from your direct relationship with j, portions of your other relations lead you back to j (to the extent that the sum across q in the expression is greater than zero). The expression also measures the lack of structural holes with which you could negotiate j's demands. As sum approaches its maximum of one, you have no one to turn to within the network to support you against a demand from j. With constraint the product of investment multiplied by the lack of structural holes, the expression squared, defines the constraint on you from a lack of primary holes around contact j:

$$(2.4) \qquad \left(p_{ij} + \sum_q p_{iq} p_{qj} \right)^2, \qquad q \neq i, j.$$

Your entrepreneurial opportunities are constrained to the extent that you have invested the bulk of your network time and energy in relationships that lead back to a single contact. Constraint in Eq. (2.4) varies from a minimum of p_{ij} squared (j disconnected from all other contacts), up to a maximum of one (if j is your only contact). The sum of Eq. (2.4) across contacts j measures the aggregate constraint on your entrepreneurial opportunities within the network.

The calculation is illustrated in Figure 2.2. Constraint is evaluated for the player represented by the dark circle at the center of the network. Relations are symmetric and only primary contacts are presented. There are six contacts in the network, few of whom have relations with one another, so the observed and effective size are similar and the structure is efficient. The level of constraint posed by each contact is listed (these are typically small numbers), and sums across contacts to the 0.400 aggregate level of constraint on the central player. Contact A is the strongest constraint because A is most connected with other players in the network. A's demands would be the most difficult to avoid or negotiate. Contact C poses the least constraint because he is completely isolated from the other contacts. His demands would be the most negotiable. Constraint from the other contacts lie between these extremes. A final point to note is the slightly higher Eq. (2.4) constraint, 0.0493, posed by contact D relative to the constraint, 0.0434, from contacts E and F. The difference is trivial, but instructive. All three contacts D, E, and F have a relation with one other contact in the network. However, E and F are connected to the dominant contact, A, and their relation with A is less important to A ($p_{EA} = p_{FA} = 0.25$) than B's relation is with D

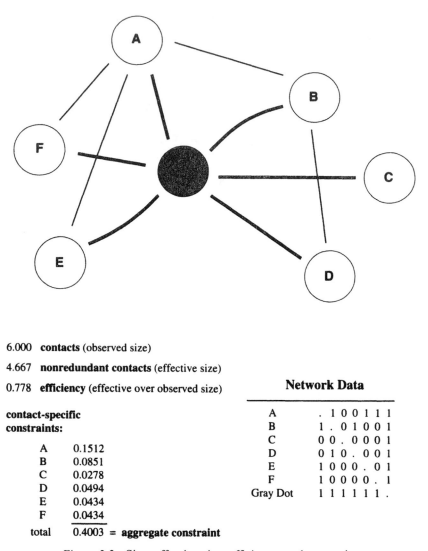

6.000   **contacts** (observed size)

4.667   **nonredundant contacts** (effective size)

0.778   **efficiency** (effective over observed size)

contact-specific
constraints:

A	0.1512
B	0.0851
C	0.0278
D	0.0494
E	0.0434
F	0.0434
total	0.4003 = **aggregate constraint**

Network Data

A	.	1 0 0 1 1 1
B	1	. 0 1 0 0 1
C	0 0	. 0 0 0 1
D	0 1 0	. 0 0 1
E	1 0 0 0	. 0 1
F	1 0 0 0 0	. 1
Gray Dot	1 1 1 1 1 1	.

Figure 2.2   Size, effective size, efficiency, and constraint

(p_{DB} = 0.33). In other words, E and F have less ability to negotiate through their relation with A than D has ability to negotiate through his relation with B.

EXCLUSIVE ACCESS AND CONSTRAINT
The constraint and redundancy measures are closely related. It might seem appropriate to use just one or the other. However, they differ in an

important way with respect to an unanswered question. What is it about a strong relationship between two contacts that spans a structural hole? The redundancy measure is based on connection. The constraint measure is based on dependence, indicated by exclusive access. The difference merits elaboration to clarify empirical tests in the next two chapters.

The redundancy of contact j is measured by the strength of j's connections to other contacts. I look at the strength of j's connection to other contacts q—m_{jq} in Eq. (2.1) and at the top of Figure 2.1—under the presumption that information access, timing, and referrals from j are to some extent second-hand from the contacts with whom j has strong relations. The result is that effective size increases linearly with the observed number of contacts in a sparse network and is constant with increasing contacts in a dense network. The point is illustrated in the graph at the top of Figure 2.3. The dashed line shows how effective size increases linearly with number of contacts in a zero density network. No contact has any connection with any other contact, so each addition is another nonredundant contact in the network. The solid line shows how effective size is constant in networks where every contact has a maximum strength connection with every other contact. Effective size is constant at a value of one regardless of the number of contacts. Completely interconnected contacts are completely redundant.

Constraint is different. The constraint from contact j is measured with proportional relations from other contacts q—p_{qj} in Eq. (2.3) and at the bottom of Figure 2.1. I look at the extent to which the relationship between j and q is a large proportion of all relations available to q. The presumption is that the player at the center of the network will have a difficult time playing anyone against j's demands to the extent that everyone is strongly connected with j. The result is that constraint decreases as a network expands. Connections among contacts slow the decrease. The point is illustrated in the graph at the bottom of Figure 2.3. The dashed line shows continually decreasing constraint in a network of disconnected contacts. The decrease is marginal; additions to a large network decrease constraint less than additions to a small network. Constraint is higher in a completely interconnected network. This is the solid line in the graph. Expanding a one-contact network to include the first's close friend increases constraint, but all further additions decrease constraint. Size and density work together. Density increases constraint (the difference between the dashed and solid lines), less in large networks than in small networks. Size decreases constraint, more in dense networks than in sparse networks.[6]

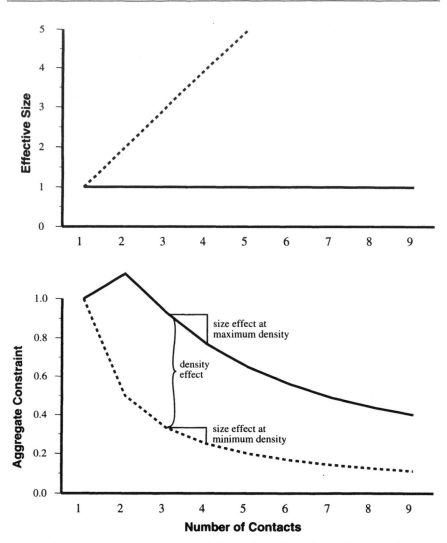

Figure 2.3   Comparisons across network size and density. (Each point on the horizontal axis refers to a different network. Solid lines describe maximum density networks. Dashed lines describe minimum density networks.)

Few networks reach the extremes of minimum and maximum density. The slices in the graph at the top of Figure 2.4 show how constraint varies with network size across levels of density. Each slice describes constraint at a different level of density.[7] The aggregate constraint in a network of given size and density is indicated by the height of the slice over the given size and density. The white slice at the front of the top graph

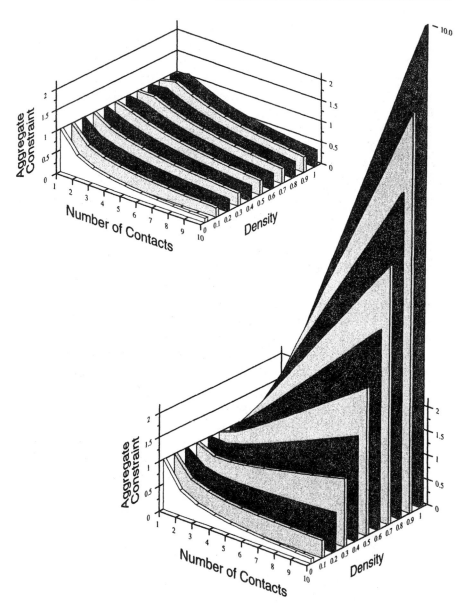

Figure 2.4   Alternative definitions of constraint across network size and density. (Proportional ties define constraint in the top graph, marginal ties in the bottom graph.)

describes constraint in zero density networks. This is the dashed line in the graph at the bottom of Figure 2.3. Constraint decreases from a value of 1.0 in a one-contact network to 0.1 in a 10-contact network. The dark slice at the back of the top graph describes constraint in maximum density networks. This is the solid line in the graph at the bottom of Figure 2.3.

The remaining slices describe constraint in networks between the extremes of density. Two points are illustrated. First, apart from the increase when the friend of an only contact enters the network, constraint decreases for all levels of density as network size increases. Second, the decrease is concentrated in sparse networks. Compare the ends of the slices over the networks containing ten contacts. The zero density slice is low. The 0.1 density slice is slightly higher. The 0.2 density is higher still, and so on. However the difference between adjacent slices is smaller as density increases. There is little difference in the height of the slices over 10-contact networks of 0.5, 0.6, 0.7, 0.8, 0.9 and 1.0 density. Density most increases constraint when connected contacts are first added to an otherwise sparse network.

The above remarks describe constraint under a presumption that exclusive relations between contacts close the structural holes between contacts. The implication is that it is difficult to exercise constraint in a large, dense network as illustrated in Figure 2.3 and in the graph at the top of Figure 2.4.

The presumption could be excessive. Perhaps all that is needed to span a structural hole is direct, personal access between contacts, as I presumed in measuring redundancy. Then the constraint measure has to be changed slightly. The extent to which j has an exclusive relationship from q, p_{qj}, should be replaced in Eq. (2.4) by the extent to which q's relation to j is among q's strongest relationships, m_{qj}:

$$(2.5) \qquad \left(p_{ij} + \sum_q p_{iq} m_{qj} \right)^2, \qquad i \neq q \neq j.$$

This slightly different constraint measure greatly changes the association with network size and density. The implication now is that it is easy for contacts to exercise constraint in a large, dense network. Additional contacts connected to existing contacts reinforce, rather than undermine, demands from any one contact. Two points are illustrated in the graph at the bottom of Figure 2.4.

First, the two constraint measures are identical in certain networks— networks containing one contact, and networks of all sizes with no connections between contacts. In both graphs in Figure 2.4, constraint equals 1.0 for networks containing one contact. Constraint in zero density networks is described by the white slice at the front of each Figure 2.4 graph. The two white slices are identical.

The difference between the measures lies in how they capture indirect constraint, which is the second point illustrated in Figure 2.4. Constraint based on proportional strength relations (top graph and Eq. 2.4) decreases as network size becomes large, regardless of density. Constraint based on marginal strength relations (bottom graph and Eq. 2.5) increases exponentially as network size and density increase together. At the extreme of a maximally dense network (at the back of the bottom graph in Figure 2.4), constraint increases linearly with the number of contacts—each additional contact adding another constraint on the person at the center of the network.

I have three reasons for discussing the alternative constraint measure. First, the dramatic differences between the two graphs in Figure 2.4 illustrate the magnitude of difference possible from a slight shift in the presumption about how indirect constraint operates. Second, playing contacts against one another is a triadic game of player versus two contacts. There is intuitive sense to the idea that the mere presence of relations between contacts makes it difficult to play them against one another, regardless of how exclusive their connections are with respect to the whole network. Third, existing evidence on constraint effects comes from a narrow range of network structures. Laboratory evidence for the importance of exclusive access is based on zero density networks (Cook and Emerson, 1978; Cook et al., 1983:fig. 1C; Marsden, 1983: 700; Markovsky, Willer, and Patton, 1988:222, 229). As illustrated by the two white slices in Figure 2.4, the two constraint measures are identical in such networks. Evidence outside the lab comes primarily from data on American markets defined by input-output tables (Burt, 1983, 1988a). The networks defining these markets are large and sparse. The 77 market networks described in the next chapter contain a mean of 59 supplier-customer contacts. The networks have a density of marginal strength relations near zero, 0.058. With respect to Figure 2.4, in other words, the available evidence of constraint effects comes from networks that lie in the graphs next to the white slice, at a distance on the "Number of Contacts" axis six times the length of the axis presented in Figure 2.4. It would be premature at this point to reject the alternative constraint measure without seeing how it performs in networks that more broadly represent variation in network size and density.

Nevertheless, I treat direct access as an aside in this argument because explicit tests between the two measures in the next chapters support the conclusion that exclusive access is the tie that spans a structural hole. The exclusive access measure in Eq. (2.4) is superior in the construct validity sense of providing stronger correlations with the conditions hypothesized to result from constraint. Results in the Appendix to Chapter 3 show that connected suppliers and customers are less detrimental to producer profits than are exclusive connections between suppliers and customers. Results in Appendix A to Chapter 4 show that connected contacts are less detrimental to early manager promotions than exclusive connections between contacts. Beyond the issue of measuring constraint, these results in two very different settings corroborate the small-group laboratory research that shows exchange benefits accumulating in people with exclusive exchange relations.

THE CONSTRAINT OF ABSENT PRIMARY AND SECONDARY HOLES

I have described contact j's constraint as the product of two terms: (a) the network time and energy you've invested to reach j, multiplied by (b) the lack of structural holes around j with which you could negotiate a favorable return on whatever was invested to reach j.

The second term is itself the product of two conditions: (a) the lack of primary structural holes between the contact and others in the player's network, and (b) the lack of secondary structural holes between the contact and others outside the network who could replace the contact. I've used the sum $(p_{ij} + \Sigma_q p_{iq} p_{qj})$ in Eq. (2.4) to measure the lack of primary structural holes around j. I need a measure of the extent to which players in the cluster around contact j are coordinated so as to eliminate the secondary structural holes necessary to negotiating advantage. The image I have in mind is oligopoly; in the extreme, monopoly. Let O_j be a measure of the organization of players within the cluster around contact j such that it would be difficult to replace j, or threaten him with being replaced, by some other player in the cluster. The lack of primary and secondary structural holes around j is the following product:

$$(2.6) \quad \text{lack of holes around } j = \left(p_{ij} + \sum_q p_{iq} p_{qj}\right) O_j, \quad i \neq q \neq j.$$

There are several ways of measuring O_j. With no loss in generality, I presume that the measure varies from a minimum of zero to an upper limit of one. The expression in Eq. (2.6) measuring the lack of structural holes around j then varies from a minimum of zero (numerous holes around j), up to a maximum of one (primary and secondary holes absent around j).

A variety of O measures exist. Picking one depends on available data and cluster boundaries in a study population. For the purposes here, three classes of measures can be distinguished to illustrate the measurement.

1. The most direct measure would be to have network data on players and relations within the cluster around contact j. To the extent that j is a central player connected with everyone else in the cluster, there are few structural holes to develop between him and the people with whom you could replace him. This centrality image was illustrated in Figure 1.8C (see Freeman, 1977; Burt, 1982:32–37, 61–63, for review) and most corresponds to the exclusive access ties that span structural holes between primary contacts. The central contacts in a cluster have exclusive relations with contacts on the periphery of the cluster.

2. Given data on the players in cluster j but not their relationships, Simmel's idea of completeness can be used to measure the lack of structural holes within the cluster (see Merton's, 1957:342ff., discussion of the role-set). The measure is the proportion of contacts in a cluster who are connected, for example, the proportion of workers in a plant who belong to the union. The concentration ratios used in market structure research are a popular example. Oligopoly is measured by the proportion of market output controlled by a small number (usually four) of the largest producers (for example, Shepherd, 1970:11–47; Caves, 1982:8–15; or the analysis in the next chapter). Here, too, there are elements of exclusive access. The union member is unlikely to belong to more than one union within the plant. Market establishments are typically owned by a single parent firm.

3. In the absence of any data on players or relations in the cluster, status-defining attributes provide crude measurement. People who share status-defining attributes such as sex, race, age, education, or income are in a crude sense substitutable for one another. For example, O_j for a cluster of elderly, black females could be set equal to one over the number of elderly, black females in the network. The more contacts available of any one kind, the more replaceable any single one of them is. This is a weak measure in two ways. First, it is likely to define cluster boundaries too broadly. Attributes are a weak definition of contact redundancy; for example, all elderly, black females don't provide the same network benefits. At the same time, it defines cluster boundaries too narrowly, because

it doesn't take into account the number of alternative contacts beyond the network (not all elderly, black females are in any one person's network).

With the lack of structural holes around *j* defined, constraint is defined. Constraint is your investment in reaching *j* multiplied by the lack of structural holes around *j* with which you could negotiate a favorable rate of return on the investment. The investment is the proportion of your network time and energy that leads to *j*, $(p_{ij} + \Sigma_q p_{iq} p_{qj})$ in Eq. (2.4), and the lack of holes around *j* is defined in Eq. (2.6). Their product defines *j*'s constraint on *i*:

(2.7) c_{ij} = (*i*'s investment in reaching *j*)(lack of holes around *j*)

$$= \left(p_{ij} + \sum_q p_{iq} p_{qj}\right)^2 O_j, \quad i \neq q \neq j,$$

and the aggregate constraint on *i* is the sum of constraint from *i*'s relationship with each of the *N* contacts: $C_i = \Sigma_j c_{ij}$. The contact-specific constraint in Eq. (2.7) varies from a minimum of zero up to a maximum of one. The maximum occurs if *j* is your only contact. The minimum occurs if *j* has no connection to the players with whom you could replace him.

Consider the network in Figure 2.5. This is the same network used in Figure 2.2 to illustrate constraint, except for two changes. First, relations between clusters are now presented with arrows to indicate source and target. Asymmetric relations in Figure 2.5 correspond to symmetric relations in Figure 2.2. The point is that the asymmetry doesn't matter. Constraint is based on the degree of exclusive connection, not the direction. The constraints in Figure 2.2 measure the lack of holes between clusters in Figure 2.5.

Second, the network in Figure 2.5 includes the data in Figure 1.9 on the number and organization of players within each cluster. Oligopoly in Figure 2.5 is the maximum proportion of contacts connected within a cluster. Many measures yield the same results in this example because there are only two values—high and low. Contacts in clusters A, D, and F are completely interconnected, so $1.0 = O_A = O_D = O_F$. Clusters B, C, and E each contain eight disconnected contacts, so O_j equals one over the number of cluster contacts: $0.125 = O_B = O_C = O_E$. If the players in a cluster are many and disorganized so there are numerous structural holes within the cluster, their potential constraint can be avoided by playing them against one another. Contact B in Figure 2.2 is the second most severe constraint. Figure 2.5 shows many disconnected alternative contacts within cluster B, so the effective constraint posed by a relationship with any one of them is lower than anticipated in Figure 2.2.[8]

Hole Signature

The investment and constraint characteristics of a player's relationships, compared across relationships, indicate where opportunities are abundant

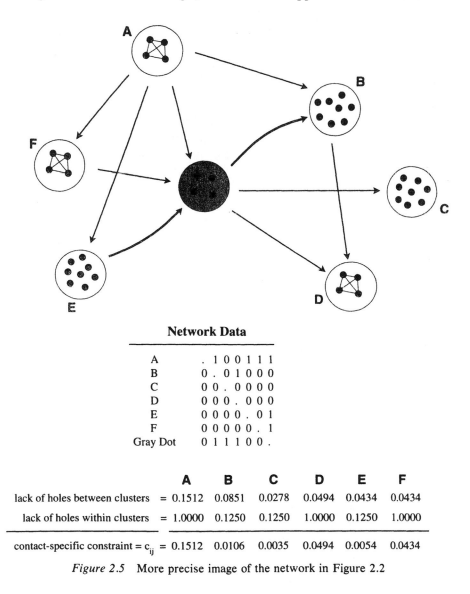

Network Data

A	. 1 0 0 1 1 1
B	0 . 0 1 0 0 0
C	0 0 . 0 0 0 0
D	0 0 0 . 0 0 0
E	0 0 0 0 . 0 1
F	0 0 0 0 0 . 1
Gray Dot	0 1 1 1 0 0 .

		A	B	C	D	E	F
lack of holes between clusters	=	0.1512	0.0851	0.0278	0.0494	0.0434	0.0434
lack of holes within clusters	=	1.0000	0.1250	0.1250	1.0000	0.1250	1.0000
contact-specific constraint = c_{ij}	=	0.1512	0.0106	0.0035	0.0494	0.0054	0.0434

Figure 2.5 More precise image of the network in Figure 2.2

and where they are rare for the player. The pattern of these characteristics across relationships is a signature with which players can be identified, studied, and compared for their entrepreneurial opportunities. In the language of structural holes, the pattern is a hole signature.

DEFINITION
Figure 2.6 is the hole signature for a hypothetical five-contact network. The bold line at the top of the shaded area describes the proportion, p_{ij}, of the player's network time and energy invested in each relationship. The thin line describes the extent to which each investment constrains the player's entrepreneurial opportunities, c_{ij}.[9] The thin line is close to the bold line when there are few structural holes for negotiating a relationship. Contacts are listed on the horizontal axis in descending order of investment, then constraint. In Figure 2.6, the player's strongest relationship is with contact D, listed first in the signature. The player has equal strength relations with contacts A and C, but the relation with contact C is more constrained, so C is listed before A. From left to right, relations are listed in order of their significance for the player's entrepreneurial opportunities.

The shaded area is the hole signature of the network, describing the distribution of opportunity and constraint across the individual relation-

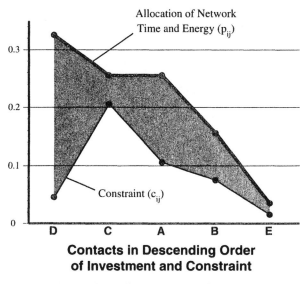

Figure 2.6   Illustrative hole signature

ships in a player's network.[10] The total volume of the player's network time and energy is the area beneath the bold line. The volume is standardized to 1.0 for comparisons across players. The p_{ij} define the bold line and sum to 1.0 across contacts. The thin line divides the player's total network time and energy in two: the empty area below the thin line is the constrained portion of the player's interaction ($\Sigma c_{ij} = C$). The shaded area above the thin line is the unconstrained portion ($\Sigma p_{ij} - \Sigma c_{ij} = 1 - C$). The hole signature provides a quick visual impression of the volume and locations of opportunity and constraint in a network. Two analytical uses follow.

KINDS OF RELATIONSHIPS

The jagged edges of a hole signature identify sites where the player has the most and the least opportunity for entrepreneurial behavior. Three kinds of relations are distinguished: opportunity, constraint, and sleeper.

A large band in the hole signature indicates an opportunity relationship. Such a band occurs when a relationship represents a large proportion of the player's network time and energy (high bold line at the top of the hole signature), and there are numerous structural holes around the contact reached with the relationship (low thin line at the bottom of the signature). Contacts D, and to a lesser extent contact A, are examples in Figure 2.6. These are the relationships in which the player has the greatest room to negotiate, and so control. The current terms of trade favor the player so he can be expected to protect the relation's form and interpretation against forces outside the network. For example, an organization doing business in markets D and A will oppose external regulation of the markets. The "free" market is regulating itself perfectly well.

A high, narrow band in the hole signature indicates a constraint relationship. Such a band occurs when a relationship represents a large proportion of player time and energy, but few structural holes surround the contact reached with the relationship (bold line at the top and thin line at the bottom of the signature are both high). Contact C is an example in Figure 2.6. The relationship with C is a large proportion of the player's network time and energy, but there are few structural holes around C with which the relationship can be negotiated. This is the relationship in which the player is most out of control. The player is at a disadvantage under the current terms of trade so he can be expected to do something about it. Strategies for doing something about it are the subject of Chapter 7. For example, if contact C is a truculent boss, the player could expand the network to include someone who could undermine the boss's control, perhaps a peer or superior to the boss who could be played against the truculent boss in a *tertius* strategy.

There are opportunities to protect, constraints to do something about, and then everything else. The third is a residual category of relations given little attention in the player's current activities. Contact E is an example in Figure 2.6. The relationship represents little time and energy, so there is little to protect and little to gain by alleviating constraint. The relationship is ignored. Yet it could be significant. Contact E could be rich in resources not essential to the player's current activities. If the player's activities change such that E's resources are valuable, time and energy will be allocated to reaching E, and the degree to which the relationship is negotiable determines whether the relationship is an opportunity or a constraint. The three categories of relationships refer to a player's network at a moment in time. The third category contains relations ignored for current purposes, not necessarily neglected for life. They are on hold, sleepers ready to wake.

KINDS OF ENVIRONMENTS

Looking across players, hole signatures distinguish kinds of opportunity and constraint environments in a study population. Two networks are the same kind of environment to the extent that they have identical hole signatures; the shaded area of a graph for one (such as Figure 2.6) is, point for point, identical to the shaded area of the graph for the other.

Distinctions among kinds are useful in two ways. They highlight conditions that most differ across kinds, and so identify opportunities and constraints most responsible for behavioral and outcome differences among players in the different environments. Second, they define the domain of environments in the population, and so identify limits to the mixtures of opportunity and constraint available to players. Both uses occur in the next two chapters. The market hole signatures in Chapter 3 are all hierarchical, which explains why hierarchy adds little to the explanatory power of aggregate constraint. The manager hole signatures in Chapter 4 vary between flat-structure and hierarchical forms, which leads to results that indicate the importance of sponsorship in the promotions of women and junior male managers.

Kinds of negotiating environments are illustrated in Figure 2.7. The networks at the left of the figure have the easily distinguished hole signatures to the right. Two extremes of undifferentiated contacts are illustrated in the top half of the figure. In the clique, every contact is strongly connected to every other. In the center-periphery network, the five con-

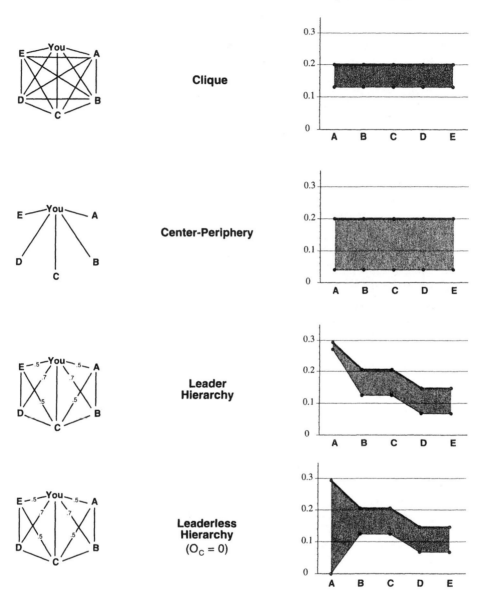

Figure 2.7   Hole signatures for illustrative networks. (Relations without assigned values have a value of 1.)

tacts are only connected through you. In both networks, the hole signature is a rectangle of shaded area, with the larger shaded area in the center-periphery signature indicating its abundance of structural holes. Recalling the discussion of exclusive access significant for exercising constraint, the difference between these two kinds of networks will disappear as the number of contacts gets large. The bold line of p_{ij} in the signature graph (equal to $1/N$ in these networks) will get closer and closer to the horizontal axis, blurring the difference between a large clique network and a large center-periphery network.

Two hierarchical networks are illustrated in the bottom half of the figure. In the hierarchy with a strong leader, your constraint relationship with the leader, contact C, most calls for strategic action. The relationship is a large proportion of your time and energy and is almost entirely constrained because of the leader's connections with all other contacts. In the last hierarchy, lieutenants B and D just below the leader are the prime target for strategic action. There is so much competition for the top position that the leader poses negligible constraint. Your relationship with her is primarily an opportunity to negotiate a favorable position for yourself. This is the situation, for example, of dealing with a politically appointed official at the top of a civil service hierarchy when the official will be replaced in the pending election. Senior civil service lieutenants most constrain the entrepreneurial activities of people below them, and special opportunities are available in negotiations with the lame duck leader before he or she leaves the organization. Context is critical. The incentive for strategic action to manage the lieutenants is constant in the sense that the time and energy spent reaching the lieutenants and the lack of structural holes around them are identical in the two hierarchical networks. In the leader hierarchy, they are clearly a secondary target for strategic action. In the leaderless hierarchy, they are just as clearly the primary target.

HIERARCHY

Hierarchy is a key part of the differences illustrated in Figure 2.7. It will be convenient to have a measure of the extent to which the aggregate constraint on a player is concentrated in the relationship with a single contact. I use the Coleman-Theil disorder index (see Coleman's, 1964:441–444, discussion of a "consequence-oriented" measure of hierarchy in sociometric choice data). The index has several desirable properties for network analysis (Burt, 1982:62–63, drawing on Allison's, 1978, discussion of the general problem of measuring inequality), and is provided in the STRUCTURE output for a structural autonomy analysis. The ratio of contact-specific constraint to the average in a relationship shows how much contact j is a more severe source of constraint than other contacts:

$$(2.8) \qquad \frac{c_{ij}}{C/N},$$

where c_{ij} from Eq. (2.7) measures the constraint posed by contact j, N is the number of contacts in the player's network, C is the sum of constraint across all N relationships, and C/N is the mean level of constraint per contact. The ratio is 1.0 for contact j posing an average level of constraint. The Coleman-Theil disorder index is the sum of this ratio multiplied by its natural logarithm, quantity divided by the maximum sum possible:

$$(2.9) \qquad \frac{\sum_{j}\left(\dfrac{c_{ij}}{C/N}\right)\ln\left(\dfrac{c_{ij}}{C/N}\right)}{N\ln(N)}.$$

This measure equals 0.0 when constraint (high or low) is the same for each of a player's relationships. It is zero, for example, for the two networks at the top of Figure 2.7. The measure equals 1.0 when all constraint is concentrated in a single relationship.

Structural Autonomy

The final step is to aggregate player opportunities and constraints in a summary measure of the player's advantage in the competitive arena. Players have structural autonomy to the extent that their relationships are free of structural holes at their own end and rich in structural holes at the other end. These are the players best positioned for the information and control benefits that a network can provide.

Figure 2.8 is a worst case. Four structural conditions limit your negotiation with contact j: (1) your investment to reach j consumes a large proportion of your network time and energy, (2) j has exclusive relations from your other contacts, (3) j is well organized with the people to whom you could turn in place of j, and (4) you are surrounded by people who could easily be used in place of yourself. The fourth condition brings in the secondary structural holes at your end of relationships. As the holes around contacts provide information and control benefits to the player, holes around the player can be developed by contacts for their benefit. The four substitutable players at the center of the network used to illustrate constraint in Figure 2.5 have no connections with one another. To manage the uncertainty of competitors, they could develop ties within the cluster so it would be difficult to play them against one another (an oligopoly strategy), or some might specialize in certain external relations in order to provide network benefits different from those the others provide (a differentiation strategy). Regardless, their negotiating position is weaker than expected from the distribution of structural holes around the contacts.

The extent to which a player is structurally autonomous increases with the extent to which his network differs from Figure 2.8. The level of a player's structural autonomy, A_i, increases with the lack of structural holes around the player (O_i), and decreases with the lack of structural holes around the player's contacts (C_i). Or, because the aggregate variables all describe player i: A increases with O and decreases with C as a function of the level and shape of constraint's distribution across the player's N contacts. The specific form of the function generating A is an empirical question to be resolved in specific study populations.

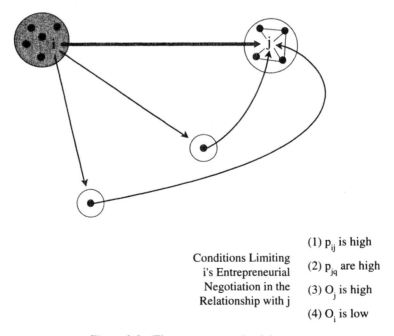

Conditions Limiting
i's Entrepreneurial
Negotiation in the
Relationship with j

(1) p_{ij} is high

(2) p_{jq} are high

(3) O_j is high

(4) O_i is low

Figure 2.8   The entrepreneur's nightmare

An answer to the empirical question is given in the next two chapters. In both chapters, structural holes are linked with competitive advantage and performance. In Chapter 3, structural holes are a competitive advantage for market producers negotiating transaction price, resulting in higher profit margins. In Chapter 4, structural holes are a competitive advantage for managers negotiating the terms of their jobs, resulting in early promotions. Beyond that, the analyses add two items of empirical information on constraint converted into structural autonomy. First, the conversion is nonlinear and multiplicative. Second, the pattern of constraint can have a positive effect that offsets the negative effect of high constraint.

FUNCTIONAL FORM

The most dramatic change in structural autonomy happens at low levels of constraint. At higher levels of constraint, autonomy declines linearly with decreasing structural holes. Where structural autonomy, A, is an expected rate of return defined by the extent to which entrepreneurial opportunities in a network are constrained, $(1 - O)$ measures the constraint of secondary structural holes around the person at the center of a network, and C measures the aggregate constraint of absent holes between and around the person's contacts, the functional form for structural autonomy is

(2.10) $A = \alpha(1 - O)^{\beta_o} C^{\cdot \beta_c}.$

Estimates of β_o and β_c are negative fractions, showing that structural holes have their greatest effect at low levels of constraint.

The nonlinear function is obvious in Chapter 3, where the function is introduced with market illustration (Figure 3.4). It is less apparent in Chapter 4. Evidence of hole effects on managers is presented in linear models.

The manager evidence of linear effects is consistent with, but more limited than, the market evidence of nonlinear effects. As in the markets, nonlinear effects for managers are negative fractions indicating marginally decreasing effects of constraint as constraint gets more intense (see Table 4.6). As in the markets, the nonlinear effect of constraint is only slightly stronger than the linear effect.

It is the nonlinear effect of market oligopoly that mandates the nonlinear function. There are no data on the secondary structural holes around each manager (nothing like the concentration ratios used to measure O in Chapter 3). The presumption, admittedly unlikely, is that each manager is similarly threatened by competitors. Further, there are no managers at the low level of constraint, where the market evidence of nonlinear effects is most apparent. The two populations operate at different levels of structural autonomy. The large networks of market suppliers and customers operate at the low-constraint end of structural autonomy. The smaller networks of manager work contacts operate at a higher level of constraint. At the levels of constraint observed among managers, market constraint too has a near linear effect on profit. In sum, the nonlinear function seems the best summary description across the two study populations.

POSITIVE CONSTRAINT

The market evidence on structural holes highlights the nonlinear nature of hole effects because there are markets operating at low levels of constraint, but the manager evidence, because the managers are differentiated on social and political dimensions, highlights another aspect of hole effects. To reach up through a political boundary, the *tertius* has to take on a strategic partner.

Hierarchy and Strategic Partners

The argument in this chapter describes a player in an imperfectly competitive, but open, arena. Complexity is such that you can't monitor, let alone control, opportunities. The information and control benefits of structural holes are a competitive advantage. But the arena has a frontier, a boundary between insiders and outsiders, defined by authority or social norms. Insiders negotiating relations are taken seriously. Outsiders negotiating relations are suspect. Hole effects are affected by how a player is positioned with respect to the boundary of the competitive arena.

In Chapter 4, women and entry-rank men must break through a political boundary separating them from the competitive arena of the corporate elite. The image of breaking through is appropriate here. Women and entry-rank men cannot make it alone. High-ranking men who are independent entrepreneurs, in the sense of having an opportunity-oriented network rich in structural holes, get promoted early. Women and entry-rank men who are independent entrepreneurs in the same sense end up with delayed promotions. Those promoted early have hierarchical networks built around one or two strategic partners. The network pattern is a strong relation with a strategic partner who is in turn strongly connected with otherwise disconnected contacts in the network. The earliest promotions for women and entry-rank men occur among those with a hierarchical network (Figure 4.9), built around a strategic partner other than the immediate supervisor (Figures 3.10 and 3.11), reinforced with extensive socializing within the immediate work group (Figure 4.12). These components are summarized in Figure 4.13. Hierarchical networks are rich in structural holes in the sense that density is lower in these networks than in any other kind of network.

But the holes in a hierarchical network are borrowed from the strategic partner, and that person's sponsorship determines the effectiveness of the network. Company leaders don't have time to check into the credibility of everyone making a bid for broader responsibilities. They are looking for quick, high-information cues about whether to treat a new person as a player like themselves or as a wage worker from the down side of the political boundary surrounding the elite. A manager's strategic partner provides the cues, sponsoring the manager as a legitimate player in the competitive arena of corporate elites.

The source of sponsorship is critical. This is illustrated by the results in Chapter 4, which indicate that a manager's immediate supervisor is a poor choice for strategic partner. Why this should be so involves a more general issue in identifying a strategic partner. First, the boss is too close. A more distant strategic partner lessens the risk that the relationship will go sour from the inevitable disagreements that arise between two people who work together. Second, the boss is too close. The manager gains more control over his or her own work, because the external sponsor can be leveraged against the boss for negotiating advantage when disagreements do arise. Third, the boss is too close. Even if negotiating is ignored and the manager has a good relation with the boss, there is the question of what constitutes the most legitimate, and most useful, sponsorship. Supervisors are expected to sponsor their subordinates. What they say about their subordinates reflects on their own work, so competent bosses usually say positive things about their subordinates. Having an external strategic partner means that there are two people in different places sponsoring the manager when new opportunities arise. This adds a corroborating external voice to the boss's sponsorship. The strategic partner has to be sufficiently close to sponsor the manager, but sufficiently distant to remain untarnished by day-to-day arguments and to speak with an authoritative voice of ostensible objectivity.

Analogies to the hierarchy effect of strategic partners among managers follow quickly. For example, a central result in Heinz and Laumann's (1982) analysis of stratification in the law profession is that lawyers distinguish one another primarily in terms of whom they service rather than what they do. Low-prestige lawyers are those who have low-prestige clients, in a context in which client prestige ranges from a high of large private corporations making financial decisions to a low of poor people resolving domestic squabbles. The implication is that having a track record with high-prestige clients is the key to being accepted by new clients.

This is not peculiar to the law profession. Service providers ranging from bankers to management consultants to general contractors to household maids cite prestigious clients as evidence of their suitability for work with a new client. The message to the targeted person is that you are in good company when you accept my services.

Nor is this peculiar to individuals. One way for a small firm to be accepted as a serious player in its market is to get a contract with a large prestigious firm. There is a big difference between the disk drive producer that supplies IBM and a firm the same size that supplies Atari. Similarly, companies that produce program compilers advertise by citing the prestigious companies that distribute popular software based on their compiler.

Strategic partners are a familiar aspect of academic life. It is one thing for a student to approach you at a conference and begin a long-winded description of his current work. It is another for a student to preface her remarks with the statement that she is an advanced student working with a professor whose work you esteem. The odds of getting your careful attention are better in the second case. More generally, strong relations with prestigious sponsors play a familiar, critical role in legitimating job applicants (for example, Murray, Rankin, and Magill, 1981, together with Granovetter's, 1983:211, interpretation of their results).

In short, an outsider working to be accepted as a legitimate member of a population has to develop a strong relation with a prestigious member of the population and develop a contact network in the population built around the person as a strategic partner. With respect to the structural hole argument, the strategic partner is your primary contact to the target population, which is the cluster surrounding the primary contact.

Adjusted Constraint

This adds a wrinkle to constraint. Aggregate constraint has to be adjusted for hierarchy in the distribution of constraint across contacts. For players who don't need a strategic partner, the adjustment is trivial. For players who do need a strategic partner, and build a network around the partner, the high constraint of a network built around a strategic partner needs to be adjusted downward. The constraint is only a by-product of getting the sponsorship initially essential to being accepted as a player. In the following equation, three coefficients measure the extent to which constraint is adjusted up or down for hierarchy:

$$(2.11) \quad C = \left(\sum_j c_{ij}\right) + (\lambda_1 + \lambda_2 L + \lambda_3 LS)(H - \bar{H}),$$

where C is aggregate constraint, the first term is the sum of contact-specific constraints proposed to measure aggregate constraint in Eq. (2.7), H is the measure of hierarchy in Eq. (2.9) that increases with the extent to which a single contact dominates the network, and $\bar{H}$ is the mean value of H in a study population (0.582 across the 77 markets, 0.060 across the 284 managers; see Figures 3.9 and 4.8 for data distributions).

The first lambda is an adjustment for the effect of hierarchy on players who don't need a strategic partner ($L = 0$). A positive value of λ_1 indicates that the concentration of constraint in a small number of individuals increases the aggregate constraint on the person at the center of the network. This adjustment is small to the extent that opportunities are determined by the level, rather than by the pattern, of constraint on a player.

The second adjustment measures the sponsorship advantages of hierarchy. As a crude measure, L is a dummy variable equal to 1 for individuals who would benefit from a legitimating strategic partner. There is no L adjustment in measuring market constraint. Among the managers, hierarchy can be an advantage for the 135 managers to the right of the vertical dividing line in Figure 4.14. These tend to be women and entry-rank men. A negative value of λ_2 indicates the extent to which the advantages of building a network around a strategic partner reduce the constraint of living in such a network.

The third adjustment is for the contact selected as a strategic partner. Again, this is not an issue in the market networks (though it could be if individual establishments were described rather than whole markets). In the manager population, hierarchical networks were most valuable when they were built around a strategic partner distant from the manager's immediate work group. The least effective were hierarchical networks built around the boss. The more distant the strategic partner, the more the partner's endorsement of the manager is independent of the sponsorship to be expected of a boss for subordinates. As a crude measure in the manager population of having an appropriate strategic partner, let S be a dummy variable equal to 1 if a manager's boss poses below-average constraint in his or her network. A negative value of λ_3 in the above definition of constraint indicates the extent to which the advantages of a hierarchical network are enhanced by building it around an appropriate strategic partner.

When I regress early promotion across these variables for the 284 managers studied in Chapter 4, I get the following results:[11]

$$\lambda_1 = 0.795 \qquad (1.7 \ t\text{-test})$$
$$\lambda_2 = -3.114 \qquad (-4.0 \ t\text{-test})$$
$$\lambda_3 = -0.303 \qquad (-0.3 \ t\text{-test})$$

and when I regress profit margins across the first two variables for the 77 production markets studied in Chapter 3—holding constant market differences in concentration and the significantly higher margins in non-manufacturing—I get the following results:

$$\lambda_1 = 0.805 \qquad (0.4 \ t\text{-test})$$

Three points are illustrated. First, λ_1 is positive but weak. Aggregate constraint increases if concentrated in the hands of a small number of contacts, but the increase is small relative to the sum of constraints across contacts. The information and control benefits of structural holes give producers and high-ranking men a competitive advantage in their arenas. Legitimacy and social acceptance are not an issue for them, so hierarchy is merely a negligible addition to constraint. The second and third points concern players in need of a strategic partner. The significantly negative estimate of λ_2 documents the advantage of a hierarchical network for a manager breaking upward through a political boundary. The implicit 1.0 effect of summed constraint is reduced by the -3.1 effect of hierarchy. The negligible negative estimate of λ_3 shows that having someone other than the boss as a strategic partner adds to the constraint reduction benefit of a hierarchical network, but is less important than having someone as a strategic partner.

SUMMARY EVIDENCE

To summarize the association between structural holes and performance, I have computed structural autonomy from the above equations for each market and each manager. The results are displayed in Figure 2.9. The horizontal axis of each graph is the natural log of structural autonomy.[12] The vertical axis is the natural log of a criterion rate of return variable.

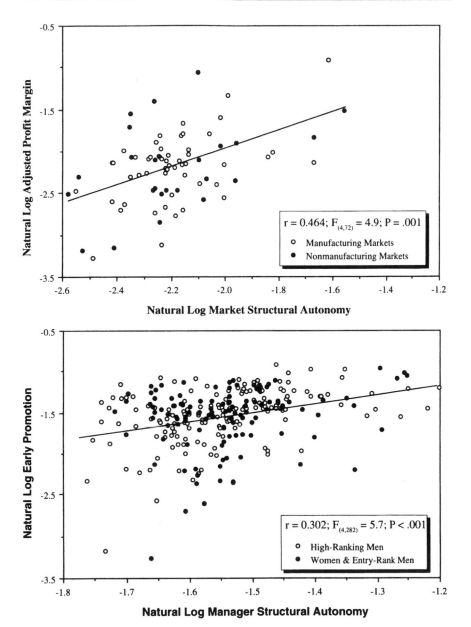

Figure 2.9 Performance improves with structural autonomy

Both graphs show the increasing rate of return expected from increasing access to structural holes.

In the graph at the top of Figure 2.9, the criterion variable on the vertical axis is market profit margin. Margins are adjusted for the higher profits in nonmanufacturing.[13] Profit margins are predicted across the 77 markets by structural autonomy defined as follows:

$$A = 0.049(1 - O)^{-.297}(C)^{-.220}.$$

The -3.4 t-test for the -0.297 effect of $(1 - O)$ shows profit margins eroded by structural holes within a market. The -3.7 t-test for the -0.220 effect of Eq. (2.11) constraint shows that profit margins are eroded by the lack of holes among suppliers and customers. The probability of either effect being zero is low ($P \approx .001$), with standardized effects of -0.357 and -0.392, respectively.[14] Autonomy here is the market profit margin expected from the distribution of structural holes around the transactions that define the market. The natural log of autonomy is the horizontal axis in the graph at the top of Figure 2.9. Hierarchy is ubiquitous in market structure and so adds little to explaining differences between markets. The above results with adjusted constraint are not much different from the results in Chapter 3 (compare Table 3.3).

In the graph at the bottom of Figure 2.9, the criterion variable is the length of time by which a manager was promoted to current rank earlier than peers. The variable is scaled to vary over the same range as the market profit margins so that the two graphs can be compared.[15] Early promotion differences at the bottom of Figure 2.9 are predicted across the 284 managers by structural autonomy defined as follows:

$$A = 0.142(C)^{-0.318}.$$

The -5.3 t-test for Eq. (2.11) constraint shows that promotions are delayed for managers with few holes between their work contacts, after constraint is adjusted for the advantages of hierarchy. The probability of this effect being zero is low ($P < .001$).[16] The standardized effect is the -0.302 correlation between constraint and early promotion. Autonomy here is the expected length of time by which a manager will be promoted earlier than peers, given the volume of structural holes between the manager's contacts. The natural log of autonomy is the horizontal axis in the graph at the bottom of Figure 2.9. The more significant effect obtained with adjusted constraint reflects the advantages of hierarchy for certain managers (-5.3 t-test here versus -2.5 for the linear effect in Table 4.2 and -2.6 for the nonlinear effect in Table 4.6). There are stronger effects reported in Chapter 4 for certain kinds of managers—for example, the near perfect correlation in Figure 4.6 between constraint and early promotion to the highest-rank positions, or the -6.0 t-test in Table 4.6 for the nonlinear effect among all 170 high-ranking men. Chapter 4 remains the best description of hole effects on the managers. The above results offer the better description across the two study populations.

Summary

The structural hole argument is here made ready for empirical research. I focus on the constraint of absent structural holes. In the course of creating a structural autonomy model, three points are demonstrated. First, the relations that span the control benefits of holes are ties of exclusive access. Second, structural autonomy is a nonlinear function of constraint, decreasing most sharply at low levels of constraint with the initial loss of structural holes. Third, the boundary around a competitive arena is an issue for players outside the arena. The information and control benefits of structural holes within the arena are not available to outsiders. To obtain the benefits, players outside the arena have to take on a strategic partner established in the arena. The partner's access to structural holes determines the outsider's entrepreneurial opportunities until the outsider is accepted as a legitimate player within the arena.

The action potential of a player's network is summarized in three ways. Effective size is the number of nonredundant contacts in the network. Structural autonomy is an interval scale measuring the extent to which the player, relative to others in a study population, has unconstrained access to structural holes. A hole signature summarizes the distribution of opportunity and constraint across each relationship in the network. The summary devices provide quantitative criteria with which players can be identified, studied, and compared with other players for their entrepreneurial opportunities.

The next two chapters are research applications of the measures. After this analysis of the empirical legitimacy of the argument, Chapter 5 will pick up the thread of the argument to illustrate its potential for other images of the competitive arena.

3

Turning a Profit

The most obvious place to test the argument is in economic transactions. Producers with networks rich in structural holes can negotiate favorable terms in their transactions with suppliers and customers, and so should enjoy higher rates of return on their investments. They do. The kind of analysis illustrated here is useful for the social science task of studying competition, as well as the more practical tasks of distinguishing customer segments for marketing strategies, understanding competitive pressures on potential buyers in each segment, and understanding the profit potential of a product.

Product Networks and Market Profit

A product brought to market has a predictable profit potential. Supply and demand tell you something about the potential. If there are customers for the product and the product isn't easily available, the product has profit potential.

This doesn't mean that the people and firms who produce the product will get rich. Characteristics of the producer's network of supplier and customer markets tell you how profit will be distributed among the players involved with it. Under available technology, the product is manufactured by producers buying certain kinds of supplies, processing the supplies through certain kinds of facilities, and selling the product to certain kinds of customers. There are sources for the raw materials, facilities, and people needed to make the product. There are places where the product can be sold for more than it costs to make it.

To the extent that the suppliers and customers are many and disorganized, the product network is rich in structural holes. The structurally autonomous producers in these networks have entrepreneurial opportunities to negotiate favorable prices, and so enjoy a comfortable profit margin as a high rate of return on investment. When you can negotiate a special deal with a supplier or shift to less expensive suppliers, you can increase profit. When you can negotiate a special deal with customers or shift to more lucrative customers, you can increase profit.

Other products put producers in a low-autonomy network of dominant suppliers or customers with whom there is little negotiating leverage. Even with massive demand for the product and massive supply of the product's components, low-autonomy producers will have a minority share in the profit. Strong suppliers will get a large share of whatever profits are obtained from customers. Strong customers will bid prices down to retain for themselves a large share of the product's profit potential.

In sum, supply and demand describe the profit possible with a product, not the producer's share in that profit. That share is determined by the structural autonomy allowed producers within the product network of suppliers and customers between whom producers turn their profit.

The elemental situation is a producer in market *i* negotiating a transaction with a supplier or customer in market *j*. Consider Figure 3.1. Producer *i* in the market at the left of Figure 3.1 is negotiating a transaction rich in structural holes. The producer at the right is negotiating a constrained transaction (compare the entrepreneur's nightmare in Figure 2.8, and the discussion of opportunity versus constraint relations in Figure 2.6).

On the producer's side, the lack of alternative producers in market *i* adds to producer control over the negotiation. For example, the four

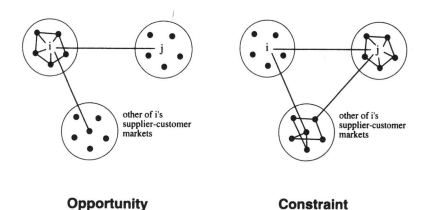

Opportunity   **Constraint**

Figure 3.1   Producer in market *i* negotiating market *j* transaction

product networks at the top of Figure 1.9 are competitors in the same market. The products are manufactured with the same kinds of supplies and sold to the same kinds of customers. Absent ties between the products at the bottom of Figure 1.9 means that their producers can be played against one another by entrepreneurial suppliers and customers. If the firms manufacturing the four products coordinate their activities, they gain control in their transactions with suppliers and customers. This is the familiar oligopoly effect, measured by O in the structural autonomy model. To the left of Figure 3.1, producer i is coordinated with other establishments in the market with which supplier-customer j could transact the business being negotiated. To the right, j can play i's price against prices offered by i's competitors. The more a market is dominated by a few large firms, then the more the firms can raise market price above production costs (Shepherd, 1970, and Caves, 1982, are often-cited texts). There is a healthy literature of empirical research on this theme in which the profit margin in a market—net market income divided by total income—is regressed over various measures of market oligopoly (for example, Burt, 1983:16–32, for review and illustrative results; *Industrial Organization Review* and *Review of Economics and Statistics,* for current research). When factors outside the market are included, they are introduced as empirical variables to consider or indicators of the abstract concept of countervailing power (Galbraith, 1952) in which a producer oligopoly is limited in its control of market price when dealing with a buyer oligopoly (for example, Brooks, 1973; Lustgarten, 1975; Clevenger and Campbell, 1977).

On the other side of the transaction, producer control is affected by the lack of structural holes beyond the market, measured by C in the structural autonomy model. To the left of Figure 3.1, supplier-customer j is disconnected from establishments in its own market and the other markets where producer i does business. To the right, j is coordinated with other establishments in its own market and i's other supplier-customer markets, in turn well organized.

The lack of structural holes among suppliers and customers affects the negotiation in two ways that mutually reinforce each other. First, the lack of structural holes between supplier and customer markets constrains producers. To the extent that market j is a large proportion of the producer's external transactions (p_{ij}), the negotiation becomes critical. Losses in this negotiation can't be balanced easily with gains elsewhere. To the extent that market j is itself dependent on transactions with the producer's other markets (p_{qj}), market j establishments are likely to be owned by the firms operating establishments in the other markets (the lesson of resource dependence, Pfeffer and Salancik, 1978), again constraining producer price negotiation. Market *j* establishments probably have good information on the costs and profits that the producer obtains in its other markets and can claim limits on their ability to accept the producer's suggested price because of preferential transfer pricing within firms spanning the markets. Second, the lack of structural holes within supplier-customer markets constrains producers. Market *j* establishments are more likely to have a standard market price enforced by the large firms that own them. The large firms can offer long-term stability in supplies or consumption and can maintain barriers to new entrants. This is a component in countervailing power. Moreover, the larger the firms in market *j*, the more likely it is that they are vertically integrated and so can exploit the lack of structural holes between markets as described in the first point.

Therefore, when the distribution of structural holes in a product network gives producers a negotiating advantage, producers can be expected to negotiate prices in their favor, visible as higher profit margins. The specific hypothesis is that profit margins increase with the lack of structural holes between producers, O, and decrease with the lack of holes between suppliers and customers, C.

The Study Population

Data to test the hypothesis are available on American markets from U.S. Department of Commerce publications. The analysis could be carried out with narrowly defined product categories or even with an individual brand. The structural equivalence criterion illustrated in Figure 1.9 for aggregating products into markets is easily determined with empirical data. Here I use data on the 77 broadly defined product markets distinguished in the 1963, 1967, 1972, and 1977 benchmark input-output tables published by the Department of Commerce. The multiple years of data enable me to average results over time to avoid short-term disturbances. The aggregate level of analysis simplifies data displays, facilitates comparisons over time (because market definitions are relatively stable over time at the aggregate level), and readily lends itself to a market framework for organization research (because the markets are sufficiently broad to allow whole firms to be assigned to individual markets).[1]

MARKET TOPOLOGY MAP

Figure 3.2 is a topology map of the markets (modified from Burt and Carlton, 1989:728). Product markets are identified by name. Two markets

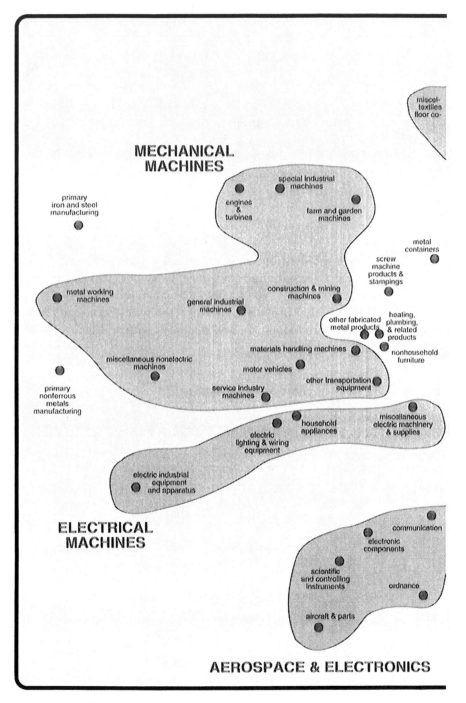

Figure 3.2   Market topology map of American economy

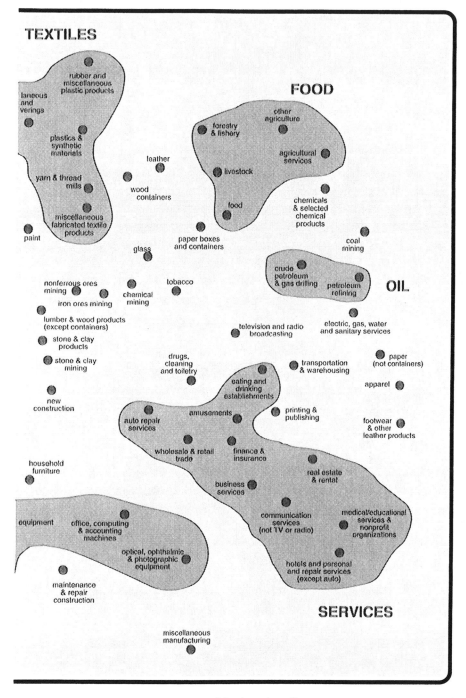

Figure 3.2 (continued)

are close together in the map to the extent that they are structurally equivalent, and so compete in the sense of depending on similar levels of purchases from the same supplier markets and similar levels of sales to the same customer markets. Relations are the buying and selling between markets. The relationship from i to j, z_{ij}, is the dollars of market i commodity purchased by establishments in market j. Dollar flow data are taken from input-output tables published in the *Survey of Current Business*.[2] These data define the network of intermarket transactions as a square table with 79 rows and columns. The first 77 rows and columns describe transactions between the product markets displayed in Figure 3.2. The data in row and column 78 describe transactions with people as individual customers (the household market). The data in row and column 79 describe transactions with government enterprises and agencies. They are included as potential sources of constraint in their role as supplier or customer markets for establishments in the 77 product markets.[3] Figure 3.2 is a multidimensional scaling of structural equivalencies defined by the marginal strength of a market's buying and selling with each of the other 78 markets. The map is stable from the early 1960s through the early 1980s, with a pocket of instability at the bottom of the map created by change over the two decades in transactions defining the ordnance, computers, and communication equipment markets (Burt, 1988a:362–368; Burt and Carlton, 1989:742–744). Details on the construction of the map are in Burt and Carlton (1989:749–752).

Shaded areas in the map connect contiguous markets often grouped together for their production activities. These areas are not proposed as structurally equivalent sets of markets, but as a heuristic for interpreting areas of the map. For example, there is obvious differentiation in mechanical machines between the internal combustion machines to the north of the area and the machines to the south that involve more electronic components. At the same time, related technologies are adjacent in the map. For example, the markets immediately next to the food area in the map—chemicals, containers, leather, and glass—are related to processing and distributing food. Oil and gas markets are next to the utilities and transportation markets. The markets just north of the aerospace markets are the related markets for electronic components and communication equipment. Primary metals manufacturing markets lie to the west of the markets for mechanical machines. Textile mills lie between agriculture and mechanical machines. Computers lie between professional services and electronics.

Standing back from the map, there are more abstract patterns to the distribution of markets. The east-west axis is a distinction between inorganic and organic products. To the east are the markets for food, fossil fuels, clothing, and services. To the west are the markets for machines. The north-south axis is a distinction between old and new technologies. To the north are the markets for mechanical machines, textile mills, and agriculture. To the south are the aerospace, computer, and professional services markets. There are also substantively interesting contrasts between the four corners. Plant and animal markets appear in the northeast, human services appear in the southeast, electric products appear in the southwest, and mechanical products appear in the northwest. Cutting the map in still another way, you can see the resource-grain contrast used in population ecology studies of organizations. Resources in the markets to the west of the map are coarse grained in the sense that their products are sold in large purchases scheduled long before delivery. One doesn't buy $500 worth of steel or $100 of space vehicle, and one typically contracts well in advance of delivery. Resources in the markets to the east of the map are fine grained in the sense that products are sold in small units and volume is volatile over time.

There are many contrasts in the map. The above merely highlight various interesting dimensions of substantive differentiation across the market topology. My specific concern in this chapter is to know how structural holes and profits are distributed across markets in the map.

MEASURING STRUCTURAL HOLES

The buying and selling between markets shows where transactions are strongest in the map, but to measure producer advantage in negotiating price in the transactions, the network data must be supplemented with data on the lack of structural holes within each market. I follow the usual practice of using concentration ratios. Varying from zero to one, the four-firm concentration ratio is the proportion of total market output produced by establishments owned by the four largest firms. A ratio of 0.5 means that 50% of market output is controlled by the four largest firms. A ratio close to one means there are few structural holes within the market. A ratio close to zero means there are many.

The concentration data are not published for input-output table markets and are not available from a single source. In manufacturing, four-firm concentration ratios are published by the Department of Commerce for Standard Industrial Classification (SIC) industries in the 1963, 1967, 1972, and 1977 *Census of Manufactures,* and a list of SIC industries within each input-output market is published by another branch of the Department of

Commerce with the benchmark input-output table data for the same years in the *Survey of Current Business*. I average concentration weighted by sales across SIC industries in the market: $O = w_1CR_1 + w_2CR_2 + \ldots$, where the weight w_k is the ratio of sales from four-digit SIC industry k divided by total sales summed across all four-digit SIC industries in the market, and CR_k is the four-firm concentration ratio in industry k.

Comparable concentration data are not available for nonmanufacturing markets. I approximate concentration ratios with sales data published in *News Front* compilations of the largest firms operating in four-digit SIC categories. With the *Survey of Current Business* maps of SIC categories to input-output sectors, the four largest firms in each sector are identified, their sales summed, and the sum divided by the total volume of sales for the sector reported in the input-output table. This measure exaggerates concentration because the four largest firms operate in multiple markets, but the data seem superior to approximations available from *Census* data on the size of firms within SIC categories (Burt 1983:291–292).[4] This procedure provides concentration data on nonmanufacturing markets in 1967, 1972, and 1977. Differences in concentration across nonmanufacturing markets are stable from one year to the next. The *News Front* listing for 1963 is less complete than listings in later years and seems inadequate for the purposes here. I complete the missing 1963 nonmanufacturing concentration data with the approximations for 1967.[5]

Table 3.1 contains the mean, minimum, and maximum scores across markets. Scores for each market are averaged across 1963, 1967, 1972, and 1977.[6] The results show that the markets are large, dense networks of weak relations.

Table 3.1   Market structure

	Mean	Minimum	Maximum
Supplier markets	46	19	62
Customer markets	45	1	78
Total contact markets	59	21	78
Proportional density	0.689	0.294	0.928
Density	0.044	0.031	0.062
Producer concentration (O)	0.352	0.004	0.900
Constrained supplier-customer transactions (C)	0.064	0.008	0.421

Note: Mean, minimum, and maximum are based on scores for each of the 77 production markets in Figure 3.2 averaged across 1963, 1967, 1972, and 1977. Numbers of contacts are rounded to the nearest integer.

The first five rows of the table describe the transaction data. The second row, for example, indicates that the average market sells its product to 45 different markets. There is at least one market that has only one customer market. At the other extreme, at least one market sells its product to every other sector in the economy. The average market transacts business with 59 other markets as suppliers or customers. In sum, the market networks are large. Further, they are dense. The fourth row of Table 3.1 describes proportional density. This is the proportion of nonzero relations between a producer's supplier and customer markets. A proportional density of 1.0 means that each supplier market sells to each customer market and that each customer market sells to each supplier market. The average proportional density is high: 0.689, varying across markets from 0.294 to 0.928, nearly reaching the maximum. However, the relations connecting suppliers and customers are typically weak. The fifth row of Table 3.1 describes density. This is the strength of the relationship between the average pair of suppliers and customers. Here, strength is the marginal volume of business between markets (the dollar flow from i to j, z_{ij}) divided by the maximum dollar flow from i to any one of its customer markets. A density of 1.0 means that each pair of supplier and customer sells to one another at a high volume. The low density in Table 3.1, 0.044 on average, shows that sales are concentrated in a small number of transactions. Producers typically sell a large proportion of their output to a small number of customer markets, with low volumes of sales to many other markets.

The bottom three rows of Table 3.1 describe the structural hole measures. Producer concentration, measuring the lack of structural holes between producers, varies from 0.004 to 0.900 with an average concentration of 0.352. Establishments owned by the four largest firms in the average market account for 35% of all market output. The transaction and concentration data define the constraint on producers in each of their transactions with other markets (Eq. 2.7), which sums across transactions to measure the aggregate constraint of organized suppliers and customers, C. This is low on average, reflecting the large, sparse networks characteristic among suppliers and customers. Aggregate constraint can vary from zero to one, but averages only 0.064 across the 77 markets.

Hole Effects

Table 3.2 contains estimates of the association between profit and structural holes. The graphs in Figure 3.3 display zero-order associations. Market profit is the price-cost margin proposed by Norman Collins and

Table 3.2   Hole effects across markets

Model	R^2	α	β_o	β_c	β_d
$[\alpha + \beta_o(1 - O) + \beta_c C] + \beta_d D$	0.438	0.228	$-.131$	$-.432$	0.171
			(-2.8)	(-2.6)	(7.4)
$[\alpha(1 - O)^{\beta_o} C^{\beta_c}] D^{\beta_d}$	0.528	0.050	$-.291$	$-.214$	0.767
			(-3.3)	(-3.6)	(7.9)

Note: Ordinary least-squares estimates of the coefficients are presented for predicting price-cost margins in the 77 production markets, where D is a dummy variable distinguishing nonmanufacturing markets. Routine t-tests are presented in parentheses. Profit and structural hole variables are averaged for each market over time before estimating effects.

Lee Preston (1968, 1969), a popular dependent variable in market structure research. The margin is a ratio of net income to total income. It is the dollars of value added in a market minus labor costs, quantity divided by total market sales. Price-cost margins for each market were computed for 1963, 1967, 1972, and 1977 from the input-output tables and averaged over time.[7] Solid dots in Figure 3.3 represent manufacturing markets. Hollow dots represent nonmanufacturing markets. Two points are illustrated in the table and graphs.

SIGNIFICANT EFFECTS
First, there is clear evidence of the hypothesized structural hole effects. The final autonomy model is displayed in the second row of Table 3.2, for which ordinary least-squares estimates were obtained with the natural log form of the model predicting price-cost margins:

$$\ln(P) = \ln(\alpha) + \beta_o[\ln(1 - O)] + \beta_c[\ln(C)] + \beta_d[\ln(D)] + \ln(p),$$

where $\ln(p)$ is the residual. The model describes 53% of the variation in profit margins with three predictors: a dummy variable identifying non-manufacturing markets (D, 7.9 t-test, $P < .001$), a measure of the extent to which producers are constrained by structural holes within their market $[(1 - O)$, -3.3 t-test, $P < .001]$, and a measure of the extent to which producers are constrained by absent structural holes among their suppliers and customers (C, -3.6 t-test, $P < .001$). The dummy variable adjusts for the significantly higher profit margins in nonmanufacturing. In

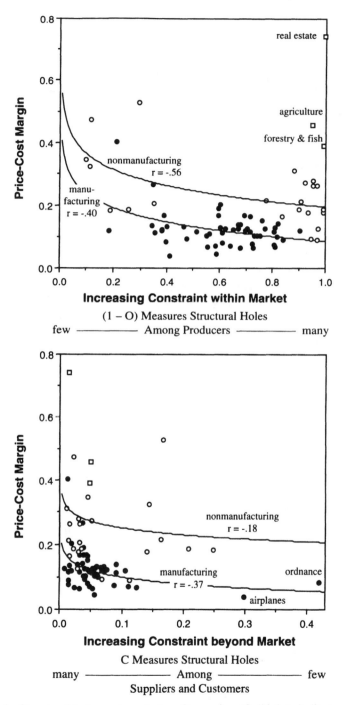

Figure 3.3   Structural holes and market profit margins. (Solid dots indicate manufacturing markets and hollow dots indicate nonmanufacturing markets.)

Figure 3.3 you can see that the hollow dots and the hole effects on profit margins are a level above the solid dots.[8]

NONLINEAR EFFECTS

The second point illustrated is that the hole effects are nonlinear. I tested linear, log, exponential, and polynomial functional forms. The strongest and simplest results were based on logarithms. I first used the natural log of concentration (O), but got stronger results with the natural log of the lack of concentration $(1 - O)$. I'll return to this point in a moment. The final model, Eq. (2.10) in Chapter 2, defines structural autonomy in terms of structural holes among producers $(1 - O)$ and the lack of structural holes between suppliers and customers (C):

$$A = \alpha(1 - O)^{\beta_o}C^{\beta_c},$$

which is the profit margin in a manufacturing market expected from the distribution of structural holes in the transaction network defining the market. The significantly negative estimate of β_o describes how autonomy decreases as the structural holes among producers increase. The significantly negative estimate of β_c describes how autonomy decreases as the structural holes among suppliers and customers decrease. An adjustment for the higher profit margins in nonmanufacturing is needed to define the expected profit margin for all markets:[9]

$$\hat{P} = AD^{\beta_d},$$

where the 0.767 estimate of β_d means that profit margins in nonmanufacturing are about twice the manufacturing margins ($e^{.767} = 2.15$).

The fractional metric estimates of β_o and β_c in Table 3.2 and the data distributions in Figure 3.3 show that structural holes have their greatest effect as unconstrained action begins to be constrained. Once action is constrained beyond a low level—market concentration lower than about 0.6 or supplier-customer constraint greater than about 0.05—further increases in constraint are almost superfluous.

The extreme cases are illustrated in Figure 3.4. The top line in Figure 3.4 describes what happens to the expected profit margin of an oligopolist with disorganized suppliers and customers as the market share of the largest firms declines (C is set to the minimum observed in any of the 77 product markets, 0.008). The line only extends over the observed range of concentration across the 77 product markets (0.9 down to 0.004, so

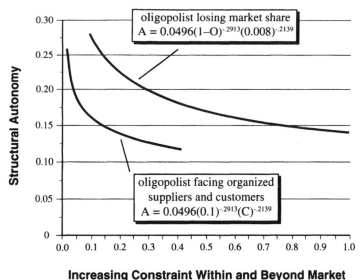

Figure 3.4   Structural autonomy profit with changing constraint

$1 - O$ varies from 0.1 up to 0.996 from left to right in Figure 3.4). At a market concentration of 0.9 (to the left in Figure 3.4), the oligopolist could expect a healthy profit of 27¢ on each dollar of sales (0.273 on the vertical axis in Figure 3.4). The expected margin drops sharply with small decreases in concentration: to 24¢ at 0.85 concentration and 21¢ at 0.75 concentration. In contrast, over the entire 50-point range of concentration from 0.50 to zero, the expected profit only drops three points, from 17¢ to 14¢ on a dollar of sales.

The effect of supplier-customer constraint is even more concentrated at low levels of constraint. Setting concentration to its highest level in any market (0.9; $1 - O = 0.1$), the bottom line in Figure 3.4 describes what happens to the oligopolist profit margin as structural holes disappear among suppliers and customers. The expected profit margin declines from an initial value of 26¢ for the most disorganized suppliers and customers ($C = 0.01$) to 18¢ around the average level of disorganization ($C = 0.05$). From there to an initial high level of constraint ($C = 0.1$; compare the graph at the bottom of Figure 3.3), the expected margin declines only another two points to 16¢, and from there over the 32-point range of constraint through the highest level at C equal to 0.42 it only declines another four points to 12¢. The hole effects are clearly concentrated at low levels of constraint—so much so that oligopolists are better off losing market share if it prevents increased organization of suppliers and customers (top line steeper than bottom line at low levels of constraint).

The nonlinear form is defined primarily by the effect of structural holes within markets, especially manufacturing markets. Supplier-customer constraint shows only slight nonlinearity. At the bottom of Figure 3.3, profits vary to disproportionately higher levels at low levels of constraint (left of the graph), but the association between profit margins and constraint is not much affected by taking the logarithm of constraint. The correlation between profit and constraint is $-.30$ across manufacturing markets and $-.15$ across nonmanufacturing markets. I get slightly higher correlations of $-.37$ and $-.18$, respectively, with the log of constraint.[10]

The association between profit margins and concentration is more sensitive to functional form. The correlation between concentration and profit is 0.34 across manufacturing markets and 0.18 across nonmanufacturing markets. The correlations with the natural log of concentration are lower, 0.27 and $-.05$, respectively. However, the log of concentration creates a variable that increases rapidly at low levels of concentration, then slows to smaller increases at high levels of concentration. In the graph at the top of Figure 3.3, just the opposite occurs between concentration and profit. Profit margins are relatively flat across concentration levels below 0.6 (putting to one side for the moment the three nonmanufacturing markets identified by hollow squares). There are relatively few low profit margins at higher levels of concentration (left of the graph). If I take the natural log of $(1 - O)$, the resulting variable increases rapidly as concentration declines from high levels, then slows to smaller increases at low levels of concentration. This generates stronger results than the linear form: correlations with profit of $-.40$ in manufacturing and $-.21$ in nonmanufacturing. If the three markets identified by hollow squares at the top of Figure 3.3 are excluded, the correlation in nonmanufacturing increases to $-.56$ as plotted in the graph. The three markets—real estate, agriculture, and forestry and fish products—contain many competitors yet return extremely high profit margins. They do not fit the prediction of market concentration. However, their suppliers and customers are numerous and disorganized according to the graph at the bottom of Figure 3.3. Their high profit margins do fit the constraint prediction. No special allowance is made for them in the estimation for Table 3.2.

The stronger results obtained with the log of $(1 - O)$ versus $\log(O)$ mean that the effect is better measured by the constraint of structural holes within a market $(1 - O)$ rather than measuring the advantage of having few holes within the market (O). This also means that the two structural hole variables measure structural autonomy effects in the same direction, $(1 - O)$ measuring the constraint of having structural holes among producers in a market and C measuring the constraint of having few structural holes among suppliers and customers. This gives a natural meaning to the implicit interaction between the two kinds of constraint in the final model.[11]

EFFECT STABILITY

The results in Table 3.3 extend the results in Table 3.2 to include variation over time. The observations increase from 77 in Table 3.2 to 306 in Table 3.3. The markets are so stable there are no surprises here (see Burt, 1988a, for a detailed discussion of autonomy effects over time). The estimates in the first row of Table 3.3 treat the 306 market observations as independent. The effects are similar to the results presented for the final model in the third row of Table 3.2, except the t-tests are stronger here because of the larger number of observations.

Observations exaggerate the degrees of freedom. The market conditions observed this year will be seen to some extent next year, or four years from now. The estimates in the second row of Table 3.3 are adjusted for autocorrelation over time within markets by adding 16 dummy variables to the model, each identifying a market that has a consistently high or low profit margin over time relative to the margin predicted by

Table 3.3   Hole effects over time and across markets

Model	R^2	α	β_o	β_c	β_d
Excluding market dummies	0.456	0.046	$-.266$	$-.234$	0.783
			(-5.7)	(-6.7)	(13.6)
Including market dummies	0.740	0.063	$-.172$	$-.161$	0.675
			(-4.7)	(-5.6)	(14.1)
Jackknife estimates		0.045	$-.267$	$-.237$	0.784
			(-3.6)	(-3.4)	(7.0)

Note: Metric regression coefficients are presented for the multiplicative model in Table 3.2 estimated across 306 observations: 76 markets observed in 1963, 76 observed in 1967, 77 observed in 1972, and 77 observed in 1977. The restaurant market is missing in the 1960s (see note 6). The first row contains ordinary least-squares estimates treating each observation as independent. These estimates have 302 degrees of freedom under routine statistical inference. The second row adds 16 dummy variables to the model to control for autocorrelation over time within markets (see note 12). These estimates have 286 degrees of freedom under routine statistical inference. The third row contains jackknife estimates for a robust test of effect stability over time and across markets (see note 13). These estimates have 76 degrees of freedom.

the structural hole variables. The adjustment is a severe control. Some cross-sectional structural effect is attributed to autocorrelation. I present the tests because they are a popular, practical method for controlling autocorrelation effects. The structural hole effects remain strong.[12]

Routine statistical inference is awkward here because the data are population data, not sample data. All markets in the economy are in the estimation. It is usual to treat such data as though they were sample data, but the practice is awkward. Therefore the third row of Table 3.3 presents jackknife estimates of the structural hole effects. In these estimates, the observed variation within the data is used to create confidence intervals around effects. The jackknife estimates in Table 3.3 are based on 77 estimates of each effect, the effect estimated when all four years on a market are deleted from the estimation. To the extent that an effect is influenced by a small number of markets over time, the effect will change when the markets are deleted from the estimation and this will increase the standard error of the jackknife estimate of the effect. Here again, there is strong evidence of stable structural hole effects. In the third row of Table 3.3, structural holes among producers within a market significantly decrease the market profit margin (-3.6 t-test for β_o), and a lack of structural holes among suppliers and customers significantly decreases the market profit margin (-3.4 t-test for β_c).[13]

The final point on stability concerns kinds of production activities. Figure 3.5 contains two maps corresponding to the market topology map in Figure 3.2. Each market in Figure 3.2 is a bubble in Figure 3.5. The size of a market's bubble in Figure 3.5 indicates the extent to which the market contributes to the evidence of hole effects. Large bubbles are markets that make a large contribution.[14] Some illustrative markets are identified in Figure 3.5. For example, the large bubbles for the tobacco market show that it fits the model well. It is profitable, highly concentrated, and unconstrained in its transactions with suppliers and customers. The real estate market is profitable and unconstrained but highly competitive, as noted in the discussion of Figure 3.3. In Figure 3.5, the real estate bubble in the top graph is small, indicating that the market does not conform to the predicted oligopoly effect β_o. The real estate bubble in the bottom graph is large, indicating that the market is an important part of the evidence for the predicted supplier-customer constraint effect, β_c.

The point illustrated is that the evidence of hole effects is homogeneous across the market topology. There are small and large bubbles in Figure

3.5, but there is no concentration of small bubbles next to one another or large bubbles next to one another. The bubbles are similar in size. Bubbles obviously large or small are surrounded by average-size bubbles. Formal tests for spatial concentrations of large or small bubbles fail to reject the null hypothesis (-0.9 t-test with 76 degrees of freedom for network autocorrelation in the top graph, and a 0.2 t-test for autocorrelation in the bottom graph).[15] In sum, the hypothesized structural hole

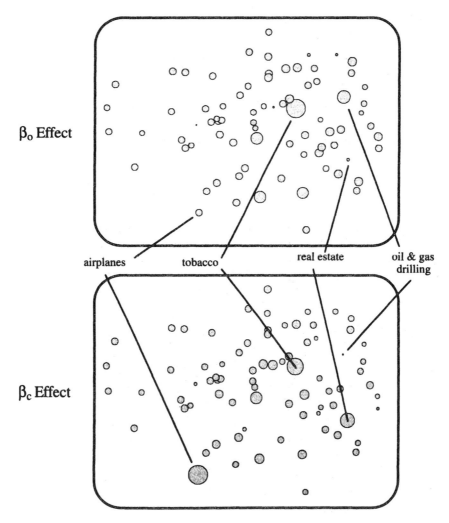

Figure 3.5   Effect variation across the market topology map

effects are strong and stable across the market topology map, which is to say, across kinds of production activities.

Market Hole Signatures

The level of constraint in transactions clearly reduces the profit margin of producers. The next step is to show how profit is affected, above and beyond the level of constraint, by its distribution across transactions.

Producers have a transaction with each of 78 other sectors of the economy. Some of these transactions involve a high proportion of producer buying and selling. Most involve little or none. There are 76 other product markets available as potential suppliers or customers, plus the household market as a potential customer and the government market as a potential supplier in some ways and customer in others. The dollars of business with each sector j represents some proportion, p_{ij}, of all producer transactions and involves some level of constraint, c_{ij}. To define a single hole signature for each market, I have averaged the p_{ij} and c_{ij} for each i-j transaction over time.[16] From the perspective of producers in any one market, their 78 supplier and customer transactions are rank ordered by p_{ij} and c_{ij} in the hole signature to represent the extent to which each transaction is a source of concern.

Markets can now be compared. Two markets are similar to the extent that they have identical distributions of p_{ij} and c_{ij} across the 78 rank-ordered transactions: identical proportions of business and constraint in their largest transaction, identical proportions of business and constraint in their second-largest transaction, and so on down to their smallest transaction.[17] The algebra of this comparison should not be confused with the structural equivalence comparison used to construct the market topology map in Figure 3.2. Two markets have substitutable production technologies, and so appear close together in the topology map, to the extent that they have similar input relations from the same supplier markets and similar sales relations to the same customer markets. The comparison with respect to hole signatures is quite different, more like a role equivalence analysis, because markets are not compared for the strength of their relations with specific other markets. They are compared for the similarity of their respective rank-order distributions of business and constraint across transactions, regardless of the specific markets with which business is transacted.

Figure 3.6 is a hierarchical cluster analysis of the markets. Each pair of markets can be connected through the lines in the cluster analysis.

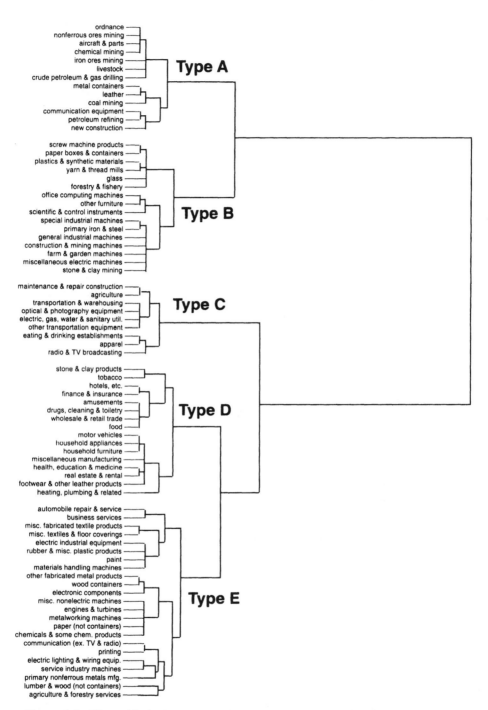

Figure 3.6 Hierarchical cluster analysis of market hole signatures. (Markets with very different signatures are connected by a line reaching to the far right of the diagram.)

Markets with different distributions of p_{ij} and c_{ij} are connected by a line that reaches to the far right of the diagram. For example, the markets for ordnance, nonferrous ore mining, and airplanes are similar. All three (located at the very top of the figure) are different from the lumber market (located at the very bottom of the figure). Five clusters are identified in Figure 3.6. Equivalence tests show homogeneity within clusters.[18]

WHAT DO THE KINDS OF DISTRIBUTIONS LOOK LIKE?
The substance of each hole signature is illustrated in Figure 3.7. The hole signature is presented for an example market within each of the five hole signature clusters. The selected markets have high reliability within each cluster (see note 18) and, to the extent possible, have levels of profit, concentration, and constraint characteristic of their cluster. Signatures are represented as a shaded area, bounded on top by the p_{ij} and below by the c_{ij}. In other words, each signature describes the distribution of unconstrained business ($p_{ij} - c_{ij}$) across transactions. Each signature contains 78 supplier-customer transactions, but the markets are so hierarchical—in the sense that business is concentrated in few transactions—that most of the variation among markets occurs in the largest of each market's supplier-customer transactions. In Figure 3.7, I characterize each hole signature by its ten largest supplier-customer transactions and sum the remaining 68 transactions in an eleventh category.

Figure 3.8 shows the location of each kind of signature in the market topology map. Based on an inspection of individual and average signatures in the clusters, I have characterized the five kinds of signatures in terms of hierarchy and constraint. The symbols in Figure 3.8 indicate these qualities—large dark triangles for the high constraint hierarchy in Type A, large hollow triangles for the equally hierarchical low constraint Type D, and smaller squares for the three less hierarchical Types B, C, and E, with squares shaded to indicate their high (Type B) to low (Type E) aggregate constraint.

Type A Signature: Constrained Mono-Market Producers
The Type A signature is characterized by a critical supplier or customer transaction. For iron ores mining, displayed at the top of Figure 3.7, the critical transaction is sales to firms that produce iron and steel products. Of all the business transacted with other markets by iron ore firms, 70.9% is conducted with steel plants. The steel industry is moderately concentrated (.448), so there is a substantial level of constraint on the iron ore firms negotiating the transaction. Other transactions are minor in

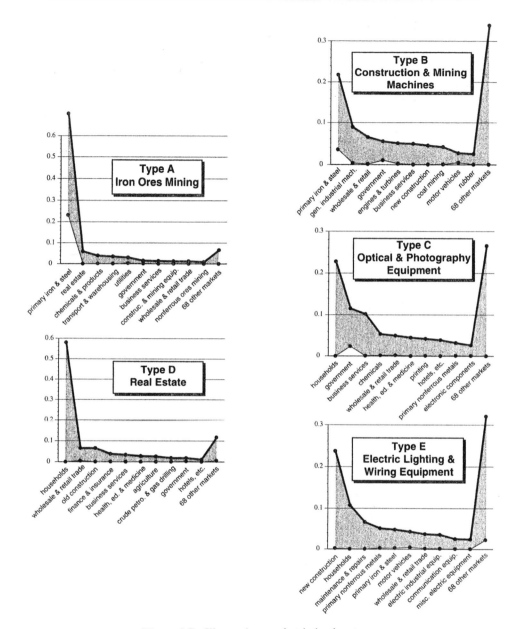

Figure 3.7   Illustrative market hole signatures

comparison. In Figure 3.7, one can see that small proportions of iron ore business are transacted with other markets and that they involve little or no constraint.

In Figure 3.8, the Type A signature is concentrated in the northeast quadrant of the market topology map (containing 8 of the 13 Type A markets, indicated by large dark triangles). It is completely absent in the southeast quadrant, which contains services, and there is only one in the northwest quadrant, which contains the markets for mechanical machines. In the northeast, the Type A signature appears in markets involved in the business of extracting a product from the earth and selling

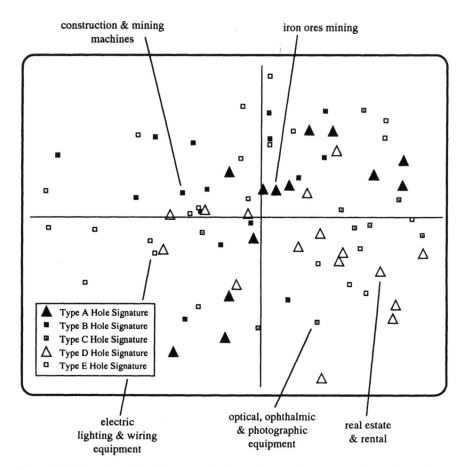

Figure 3.8   Locating hole signatures in the market topology map. (Example markets are named and displayed in Figure 3.7. Lines in the map distinguish negative from nonzero points on the axes of the multidimensional scaling used to create the map for Figure 3.2.)

it to a single market: livestock firms selling to the food industry, chemical mining firms selling to chemical manufacturing, crude petroleum and gas drilling firms selling to the petroleum refining industry, and so on. In the southwest quadrant of Figure 3.8, the airplane and ordnance markets depend heavily on purchases by government agencies (49% and 59%, respectively, of their supplier-customer business). There are also Type A signatures in markets with critical supplier transactions, such as the dependence of petroleum refining firms on petroleum drilling firms, but the bulk of the Type A signatures involve a critical sales relationship to a customer market. Of the total business in the leading transaction of each Type A signature, 89% on average is sales to a critical customer market.

As a group, the 13 Type A markets yield a below-average profit, but not significantly so (17¢ on a dollar of sales). They have the highest average concentration (mean O of 0.477, 1.9 t-test relative to other markets), and their dependence on a single transaction exposes them to the highest level of external constraint (mean C of 0.176, 10.2 t-test relative to other markets). The overall impression is that a firm will grow large if it can secure a revenue stream in the market's one critical transaction, or else it will die. These are not markets conducive to small, entrepreneurial firms.

Type D Signature: Unconstrained Mono-Market Producers

The Type D signature is similar to the Type A signature. The two are displayed next to one another at the top of Figure 3.7 and look nearly identical. Both are characterized by a single dominant supplier or customer transaction. The difference is that the Type D signature involves little or no constraint in the critical transaction. Further, the critical transaction in Type D signatures consists entirely of sales to a customer market. The second-largest transaction is typically with a supplier. The critical transaction in Type A signatures tends to be with a customer and the second-largest transaction is as much with a customer as with a supplier.

The signature is well illustrated by the real estate market in Figure 3.7. Real estate firms are virtually unconstrained in their transactions with suppliers and customers. The bulk of their business involves sales to the household sector. Other transactions are minor in comparison. This is typical of the signature. For 14 of the 16 markets—hotels, miscellaneous manufacturing such as jewelry and toys, finance and insurance, education and medicine, amusements, and so on—the critical customer transaction is with the household sector. These markets are concentrated in the southeast quadrant of the market topology map in Figure 3.8 (containing 9 of the 16 Type D markets, indicated by large hollow triangles). For the other two Type D markets—stone and clay products, and heating and plumbing products—the critical customer transaction is with the highly competitive market for new construction.

As a group, the 16 Type D markets yield the highest average profit (21¢ on a dollar of sales), have the lowest average concentration (mean O of 0.287), and are exposed to the lowest level of supplier-customer constraint (mean C of 0.020), though only the last of these is significantly different from other markets on average (-3.2 t-test, $P = .002$). The overall impression is that, in contrast to the Type A markets in which a firm will be large if it survives, the high competition within the Type D markets and the lucrative customer transaction concentrated in a single critical market make these markets conducive to small, entrepreneurial firms.

Type B, C, and E Signatures: Lesser Hierarchies
The Type B, C, and E signatures are similarly different from those of Types A and D in the direction of being lesser hierarchies. The bold lines describing volumes of business are similar for these three kinds of markets in Figure 3.7. The largest transaction accounts for a smaller proportion of total producer business (note that the vertical axes in the Type B, C, and E graphs are only half as large as the vertical axes describing Types A and D). The second and third transactions account for larger proportions of total producer business. A large proportion of business is conducted in many low-volume transactions with different supplier and customer markets.

These characteristics are illustrated in Figure 3.7 by the construction and mining machines market (Type B signature), the market for optical and photographic equipment (Type C signature), and the electric light and wiring market (Type E signature). The largest transaction in Figure 3.7 for construction and mining equipment firms is their supplier relationship with the steel industry (22% of all supplier-customer business). The corresponding transaction for optical firms is their sales relationship to the household sector (23%). The corresponding transaction for electric lighting and wiring firms is their sales relationship to the new construction sector (24%). These primary transactions are down from an average of 48% in the Type A signatures and 52% in the Type D signatures. At the other extreme, the bold lines over "68 other markets" in the signatures for the Type B, C, and E markets show that producers respectively transact 34%, 27%, and 32% of their buying and selling in transactions that individually account for less than 2% of their total business with suppliers and customers. The comparable figures for the Type A and D markets are lower, at 12% and 15%, respectively.

What makes the Type B, C, and E signatures different from one another are the conditions under which transactions are negotiated. Across the 48 markets with Type B, C, or E signatures, the largest transaction is larger than the second largest (24% versus 14%). Type B signature markets are most constrained in the largest transaction (7.3 *t*-test, *P* < .001). Markets with a Type C signature are the most constrained in the second-largest transaction (6.5 *t*-test, *P* < .001), a transaction accounting for a smaller proportion of market business. Markets with a Type E signature are the most constrained in the low-volume transactions combined in the "68 other markets" category in Figure 3.7 (2.6 *t*-test, *P* = .01). Because the decreasing volumes of business in these transactions lower the aggregate constraint they pose for producers, signature B markets operate under the highest aggregate levels of constraint (2.7 *t*-test, *P* = .01) and yield the lowest average profit margins of all five market clusters (14¢ on a dollar of sales).[19]

In Figure 3.8, the higher-constraint Type B signature is concentrated in the north central and northwest areas of the market topology. These are the areas of mechanical machine manufacturers, negotiating their highest-volume transaction in relatively high concentration supplier and customer markets. There is only one in the southeast quadrant of the map. With the exact opposite distribution, the lower-constraint Type C signature markets are completely absent in the northwest quadrant and are concentrated in the southeast of the map, where there are highly competitive and lucrative customer markets. The Type E signature is distributed throughout the map with no concentration in any one area.

SIGNATURES, PROFIT, AND CONSTRAINT

The variation among hole signatures suggests that profitability lies in having the bulk of a business in a single, competitive market—a Type D instead of a Type B signature. Sales strategies directed at the one critical market can inform one another, and customers in the market are too disorganized to pose an effective countervailing power in price negotiation.

Evidence can be found to support such an argument. For example, profit margins are strongly correlated with having a large volume of unconstrained business in the largest of a market's transactions. This is the shaded area—the difference between p_{ij} and c_{ij}—over the leading market in the Figure 3.7 hole signatures. There is a 0.37 correlation between this area and profit margins across the 77 markets (3.4 t-test, 75 d.f., $P <$ .001). In the same vein, the negative correlation between profit margins and aggregate constraint in manufacturing is not lower if constraint is measured just in the largest of a market's transactions ($r = -.30$ for C and $-.26$ for c_{ij} in producer i's maximum p_{ij} transaction).

However, this line of reasoning adds nothing to the evidence of hole effects already presented. Constraint's distribution across transactions is so hierarchical for each of the markets that distribution measures add little to measures of aggregate constraint alone, and constraint in the largest of a market's transactions indicates total constraint on the market. There is a near perfect 0.98 correlation across the 77 markets between aggregate constraint, C, and constraint in the largest transaction (c_{ij} in producer i's maximum p_{ij} transaction).

Consider Figure 3.9. I have plotted the aggregate constraint on producers against the extent to which constraint's distribution across transactions is hierarchical in the sense of being concentrated in the transaction with a single supplier or customer market (Eq. 2.9). A market constrained by a single supplier or customer would have a score of one on the vertical axis. A market equally constrained by all 78 other markets would have a score of zero.

Two points are illustrated in Figure 3.9. First, the markets do not vary between being hierarchical and not hierarchical so much as they vary in the degree to which they are completely hierarchical. As illustrated by the hole signatures in Figure 3.7, producers in almost all markets transact the bulk of their business with suppliers and customers in a few markets and make small sales and purchases in many markets. This point was also made in the discussion of Table 3.1. Suppliers and customers are typically connected to one another (0.70 mean proportional density), but the average strength of relationship between them is extremely low (0.04 mean density of marginal strength transactions). In Figure 3.9, the markets are distributed high on the vertical axis measuring hierarchy, varying around a mean of 0.582, from a minimum of 0.326 to a maximum of 0.940, near the upper limit of one. In contrast, the manager networks analyzed in the next chapter vary around a mean of 0.060, from a minimum of 0.000 to a maximum of 0.259, and hierarchy has effects distinct from constraint (Figure 4.8).

The second point illustrated is the connection between hierarchy, the five kinds of hole signatures, and the aggregate level of constraint. The five kinds of markets distinguished by hole signature are similarly distinguished by aggregate constraint. The severely constrained markets to the right in Figure 3.9 all have Type A hole signatures. Almost all the unconstrained markets to the left in Figure 3.9 have Type D signatures. Between these extremes are clusters of markets for each of the other three kinds of hole signatures. Although aggregate constraint is held constant in the cluster analysis (c^* in note 17), it is closely associated with the distribution across transactions. Aggregate constraint is strongly correlated with hierarchy in the distribution of constraint across transactions (0.75), and differs significantly among the five clusters distinguished in terms of hole signatures (28.8 *F*-test with 4,72 d.f., $P < .001$).

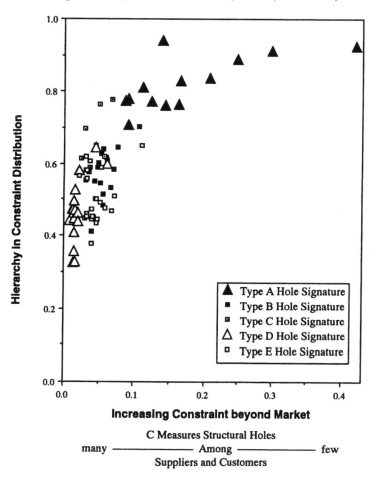

Figure 3.9 Aggregate constraint, hierarchy, and types of hole signatures are closely related

The result is that distribution doesn't improve upon aggregate constraint. Adding the level of constraint c_{ij} in each market's largest transaction to the final autonomy model in the second row of Table 3.2 is a trivial extension to the model (R^2 increases from 0.528 to 0.534, 72 d.f., P = .35 for no difference). Little is added by a measure of the unconstrained business in the market's largest transaction, $p_{ij} - c_{ij}$, though this has a strong 0.37 zero-order correlation with profit margins (R^2 increases to 0.535; P = .30 for no difference). Summary measures of the shape of constraint's distribution across transactions fare no better. The measure of constraint hierarchy in Figure 3.9 is a trivial extension to the model (R^2 increases to 0.529, P = .53), and dummy variables distinguishing the five clusters of market hole signatures adds no prediction (R^2 increases to 0.566 with four additional predictors; 1.53 F-test with 4,69 d.f., P = .20). The dummy variables have a stronger effect with a pooled estimation over time (second row of Table 3.3), but it disappears with robust jack-knife estimation (third row of Table 3.3).

Summary

When the distribution of structural holes gives producers an advantage in negotiating transactions with suppliers and customers, they are expected to negotiate prices in their favor. The ratio of net income to total sales should increase across product markets with the structural autonomy of producers. This is true of the 77 American product markets over the twenty-year interval studied here. Three points have been established.

First, as general support for the structural hole argument, profit margins are eroded by structural holes among producers and are enhanced by structural holes among suppliers and customers. Margins increase with O and decrease with C.

Second, more specifically, hole effects are nonlinear and multiplicative in the final structural autonomy model predicting profit margins. Structural holes have their greatest effect as completely unconstrained action begins to be constrained. Once action is constrained beyond a low level—concentration less than about 0.6 or supplier-customer constraint greater than about 0.05—further increase in constraint is almost superfluous.

Third, the bulk of business for most producers is concentrated in no more than a handful of critical transactions. Constraint's distribution across transactions is so hierarchical for each market that: (a) distribution measures add little to the prediction of profit beyond the prediction by aggregate constraint alone, and (b) the level of constraint in the largest of a market's transactions by and large indicates the aggregate constraint on the market. There is a near perfect 0.98 correlation between the constraint on producers in their largest transaction and the aggregate constraint they face across all their transactions. The third point should not be overgeneralized. When hierarchy is less connected with aggregate constraint, the two can have independent effects. This is the case for managers at the top of one of America's leading high-technology firms, as I will show in the next chapter.

Appendix: Weighing Alternatives

The results in Table 3.4 show how the hole effects change across alternative measures of constraint. To make comparisons easier, the results in Table 3.2 are the first two rows of Table 3.4. Two questions are answered with these results. Both concern the role of exclusive access in constraint.

The first question is the importance of exclusive access between contacts (see the discussion of Figure 2.4). Based on results in laboratory exchange networks and prior studies of market structure, the proposed constraint measure is based on an assumption that exclusive access spans the hole between two contacts (Eqs. 2.4, 2.7). The alternative is that any strong, direct connection can span the hole (Eq. 2.5). The operational choice is between defining indirect constraint in terms of the proportional, p_{qj}, or marginal, m_{qj}, strength of ties between contacts as illustrated in Figure 2.4.

The results in Table 3.4 show weaker effects when constraint is measured in terms of the latter. Across a variety of models, two of which are presented in the third and fourth rows of Table 3.4, estimates of β_c are consistently weaker when the alternative constraint measure is used in place of the measure based on proportional strength relations. Reading from the fourth row of Table 3.4, the alternative constraint measure generates a negligible constraint effect in the final model (-1.3 t-test versus -3.6 for constraint based on proportional relations). The graph for the alternative constraint measure in Figure 3.10 is analogous to the constraint graph at the bottom of Figure 3.3. The results in Figure 3.10 are different in three ways from those in Figure 3.3. Most obviously, the alternative constraint measure reports higher levels of constraint, because it registers so much indirect constraint between supplier and customer markets. Second, the alternative constraint measure spreads the markets out more evenly. At the bottom of Figure 3.3, markets are compressed to the left of the graph with a handful of outliers in the middle and right of the graph. But third, and most important, the alternative constraint measure has a weaker association with profit margins. Profit margins are correlated $-.13$ with constraint in manufacturing and $-.16$ in nonmanufacturing. Correlations with the natural log of constraint are no better ($-.07$ and $-.18$, respectively, as plotted in Figure 3.10). I tried alternative functional forms and tried re-estimating effects with possible outlier markets deleted. I found no evidence to revise the conclusion

Table 3.4   Hole effects with alternative constraint measures

Model	R^2	α	β_o	β_c	β_d
Access in and beyond Product Network					
Exclusive access (Table 3.2)					
Linear	0.438	0.228	$-.131$	$-.432$	0.171
			(-2.8)	(-2.6)	(7.4)
Nonlinear	0.528	0.050	$-.291$	$-.214$	0.767
			(-3.3)	(-3.6)	(7.9)
Marginal access					
Linear	0.409	0.227	$-.109$	$-.128$	0.155
			(-2.3)	(-1.6)	(6.4)
Nonlinear	0.458	0.082	$-.250$	$-.139$	0.730
			(-2.6)	(-1.3)	(6.8)
Access within Product Network					
Exclusive access					
Linear	0.441	0.231	$-.134$	$-.433$	0.173
			(-2.8)	(-2.7)	(7.4)
Nonlinear	0.532	0.049	$-.297$	$-.220$	0.770
			(-3.3)	(-3.7)	(8.0)
Marginal access					
Linear	0.445	0.258	$-.144$	$-.143$	0.167
			(-3.0)	(-2.8)	(7.3)
Nonlinear	0.491	0.072	$-.293$	$-.229$	0.734
			(-3.1)	(-2.6)	(7.2)

Note: Ordinary least-squares estimates of the coefficients are presented for predicting price-cost margins in the 77 production markets, where D is a dummy variable distinguishing nonmanufacturing markets. Routine *t*-tests are presented in parentheses. Profit and structural hole variables are averaged for each market over time before estimating effects. The linear and nonlinear models are given in the two rows of Table 3.2.

that the alternative constraint measure is inferior for describing market constraint.

The second question answered in Table 3.4 concerns the frame of reference for exclusive access. Is there any difference between using the entire economy or the product network as a frame of reference? The results in Table 3.2, Figure 3.3, and the top half of Table 3.4 are based on the entire economy as a frame of reference. The proportional trade relation from market q to market j is the sum of buying and selling between the markets divided by the total volume of market q buying and selling with all other markets in the economy [in other words, $p_{qj} = (z_{qj} + z_{jq})/\Sigma_j(z_{qj} + z_{jq})$, $j \neq q$]. This calculation is only possible when complete data are available on each contact's network. This is not always the case. In survey network data, illustrated by the manager network data in the next chapter, data are usually available only on that portion of each contact's network that involves the other contacts in the focal person's network. It is significant to know, therefore, if the results in Table 3.2 depend on defining proportional relations with respect to the whole economy. The bottom half in Table 3.4 present results with constraint computed from proportional

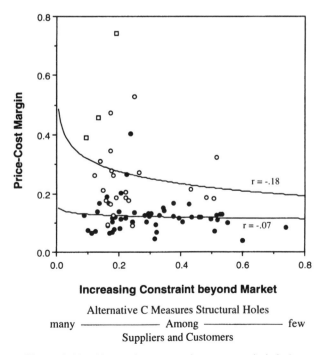

Increasing Constraint beyond Market

Alternative C Measures Structural Holes

many —————————— Among —————————— few

Suppliers and Customers

Figure 3.10 Alternative constraint measure is inferior

relations defined within product networks (in other words, p_{qj} in producer i's network equals the above calculation, where j and q are included only if both do business with producer i).

There is no evidence of a problem in limiting proportional strength relations to the product network. Compare the fifth and sixth rows of Table 3.4 with the first two rows. The results are stronger in the third decimal place using the product network as a frame of reference, but this is to say that the results are virtually identical. Constraint computed from proportions defined with respect to the entire economy is correlated 0.998 with constraint computed from proportions defined within product networks. Constraint in this study population can be estimated accurately from the limited information typically provided by survey network data.

4

Getting Ahead

In this chapter the main conclusion from Chapter 1 is tested with data on the networks and achievements of senior managers in one of America's leading high-technology firms. Managers with networks rich in structural holes get promoted faster and at a younger age than do their peers. The analysis here is more complex than the analysis of economic transactions. The network generating constraint involves more kinds of relationships. The criterion rate of return affected by constraint has more dimensions. The kind of analysis that follows is useful for the social science task of studying competition and occupational achievement, as well as the more practical tasks of understanding how specific kinds of individuals rise in a firm, detecting barriers to achievement for kinds of individuals within the firm, assessing the leadership abilities of individuals or groups, and developing programs to enhance leadership abilities in target individuals or groups.

Contact Networks and Manager Achievement

Jeffrey Pfeffer, of the Stanford Business School, once explained to a group of executives in a leadership seminar that one of a manager's most important and difficult tasks is to forget what he or she learned in school—not the substance, but the practice. Education is a matter of individual achievement. You study, take tests, write papers, state opinions in class, and are graded as an individual. Continue that practice in corporate life and you have the career potential of live bait. Coordination with others is now the *modus operandi*. You are recruited, reviewed, and rewarded for what you can accomplish with other people.

The structural hole argument has something to say about who succeeds within the corporation. If connections with other players matter, the manner in which you are connected matters. Managers with contact networks rich in structural holes—with networks providing the manager structural autonomy—are the players who know about, have a hand in, and exercise control over more rewarding opportunities. They have broader access to information because of their diverse contacts (the information access benefit of holes). That means they are more often aware of new opportunities and aware earlier than their peers (information timing benefits). They are also more likely to be the people discussed as suitable candidates for inclusion in new opportunities (referral benefits). They are also more likely to have sharpened and displayed their capabilities, because they have more control over the substance of their work, defined by relationships with subordinates, superiors, and colleagues (control benefits). These benefits reinforce one another at any moment in time, and cumulate on one another over time.

The rewards to the firm are considerable. The *tertius* monitors information about activities in the firm more effectively than bureaucratic control can. Gossip moves faster and to more people than memos. The *tertius* knows the parameters of organization problems early. The *tertius*, easily shifting network time and energy from one solution to another, is highly mobile relative to the bureaucracy. The *tertius* tailors solutions to the specific players being coordinated, thus replacing the boilerplate solutions of formal bureaucracy. To these benefits of faster, better solutions, add cost; the *tertius* is low cost relative to the bureaucracy that would otherwise monitor personnel. In short, operating somewhere between the force of corporate authority and the dexterity of markets, the *tertius* is a critical player in the corporate response to disorder and demoralization, rushing coordination to structural holes that could be usefully closed.

The rewards to the *tertius* are also many. I will discuss specific rewards after introducing the study population, but I first want to clarify the association between structural holes and rewards generally.

Given two otherwise similar people, the one richer in structural holes will reach higher levels of achievement. Consider a concrete example. You have human capital in the form of a level of educational achievement, E, and you have a job from which you obtain an annual income, I. Investment in your human capital yields a return; E and I are correlated across people. The slope coefficient b in the following regression equation should be significantly positive:

$$I = a + bE + i,$$

where b is the rate of income returns to education and i is the residual of unpredicted income. Over the full range of values this is generally true, with well-educated people earning higher incomes than uneducated people.

The more interesting point lies in explaining how the rate of return varies between groups: men versus women, or blacks versus whites, or managers versus workers. For example, Erik Wright, infusing a Marxist meaning into varying rates of return, cites higher income returns to education for managers than for workers (Wright, 1978; Wright and Perrone, 1977). In one sample of data, workers received average additional $851 in annual income for every increment of their education while managers received an average additional $1,689 (Wright, 1978:1376). Managers are distinguished from workers by the former's control over the labor power of others ("Do you supervise the work of others, or tell other employees what work to do?" and "Do you have any say in the pay and promotions of your subordinates?" Wright, 1978:1370). The greater rate at which managers are rewarded for their job performances is explained by the "link between the legitimation function of education within hierarchies and the use of income as a control mechanism within authority hierarchies" (Wright, 1978:1372). Different levels of educational achievement are used to legitimate inequalities of control (higher education associated with wider spheres of control), and income is used to encourage managers to exercise their greater control in ways serving the interests of their corporate employer. The measurement is expanded in a later study to distinguish five employee categories on the manager-worker continuum. Categories are defined by multiple criteria: participation in decision making, manager-supervisor-nonmanagement job titles, authority over others, and six categories of job autonomy based on an open-ended question soliciting a concrete example of the respondent's job autonomy (Wright et al., 1982, esp. pp. 712–717).

This is a crude illustration of hole effects. It seems safe to presume from available research that a worker's network contains fewer structural holes than does a manager's network. The worker's contacts are more likely to be closely connected with one another, and his or her immediate supervisor is more likely to dictate how the worker's job should be performed. Managers have more structural autonomy, so the value of b in the returns to education equation is higher for managers than for workers.

Beyond this crude illustration, the structural hole argument makes a more precise empirical statement. The slope coefficient b in the above equation measures the aggregate rate of return to education. Let R be an individual's rate of return measured as income divided by expected income,

$$R = \frac{I}{\hat{I}},$$

where the income an individual can expect from his or her education is given by the earlier equation $\hat{I} = a + bE$. The average value of R is 1, but some individuals have values greater than 1, indicating that their income is higher than expected from their education and others have values less than 1, indicating that their income is lower than expected from their education. From Wright's evidence, workers have values of R less than 1 and managers have values greater than 1. The structural hole argument predicts that the value of R for each individual increases with structural autonomy:

$$R = \alpha + \beta A + r,$$

where r is again a residual term and β is expected to be positive. More specifically, R should decrease with the extent to which a person is only one of many substitutable competitors $(1 - O)$ and decrease with the extent to which the person's work relations are dominated by the people at the other end of them (C). This hypothesis cuts past the aggregate categories of individuals distinguished as workers versus managers, or broad categories on a continuum of worker versus manager, to define rates of return expected from the specific social structural circumstances of each individual.

The Study Population

The data to test the hypothesis come from personnel records and a mail survey of top managers in one of America's largest high-technology firms. The firm is one in which supervision flows through a matrix instead of down lines of bureaucratic authority. Employees here, as in other matrix firms, distinguish two kinds of supervisory relations. Solid lines connect supervisors and subordinates. The supervisor is responsible for salary recommendations and periodic reviews of the subordinate's work. Lines of informal supervision, "dotted line" relations in the firm, connect managers with people useful in the completion of a project. The dotted lines are defined in various ways, in part by the history of managers doing the same work and in large part by the tastes of the individual manager. Davis and Lawrence (1977) describe the history and operation of matrix firms. Rosabeth Kanter (1983) provides a rich annotation of the entrepreneurial process in which managers are expected to find for themselves the supervisory dotted line relations necessary to launch and complete a project.

In the fall of 1989, the firm employed well over 100,000 people, of whom 3,303 occupied the four managerial ranks below the rank of vice-president. The 3,303 managers are the study population. They are nicely suited to studying structural holes. They work in a dynamic political environment, at the top of one of America's largest firms, in one of the most volatile industries in the American economy (see Burt and Carlton, 1989:744, on the concentrated instability in this area of the economy). Theirs is a world of constant change, frequent reorganization, and short-lived entrepreneurial opportunities. It is an environment in which the information access, timing, referral, and control benefits of structural holes should be especially valuable.

SAMPLING MANAGERS

With the aid of the firm's personnel files, a sampling frame was designed with strata defined by geographic location, sex, functional division, rank, and seniority. The sampling strata are displayed in Figure 4.1. Bars show the population, sample, and respondent managers in each stratum. The firm's plants are concentrated in one geographic area, termed "core locations" in Figure 4.1; 72% of the study population managers work in core locations. The great majority of the managers are men (87%). The firm is differentiated into field (sales and service), production (engineering, manufacturing, and marketing), and corporate divisions (operations, finance, and human resources). Field managers and production managers are each about 40% of the study population. For sampling, managers in the top two ranks of the study population are distinguished from the lower two ranks. The top two ranks contain 28% of the study population. These sampling strata of geographic location, sex, division, and rank define a four-variable profile characterizing each manager as a kind of manager. For each unique profile, the average years of employment were computed and managers who had served longer with the firm were distinguished from their more recently hired peers. Managers tend to be equally distributed above and below the averages, so half of the population in Figure 4.1 is in the category of "managers long with the firm."

The five sampling variables jointly define 48 categories of managers. The striped bars in Figure 4.1 describe managers sampled at random from the categories. Managers were drawn from as necessary to make the proportion of the sample managers in the category equal to the proportion of the study population in the category. A minimum of 5 were drawn from each of the 48 sampling categories. The sample includes slightly more managers from rare categories than would occur in a simple random sample (for example, higher percentages of women and noncore managers).

RESPONDENT MANAGERS

The sampled managers were sent a sociometric booklet asking about their contacts in and beyond the firm. Managers in the firm are often asked to participate in surveys. My contact in the firm said that 10% is an accepted response rate. This survey, however, had a 52% response rate. Of the 547 sample managers, 284 completed the sociometric booklet (7 had left the firm or were no longer managers at the time of the study).[1]

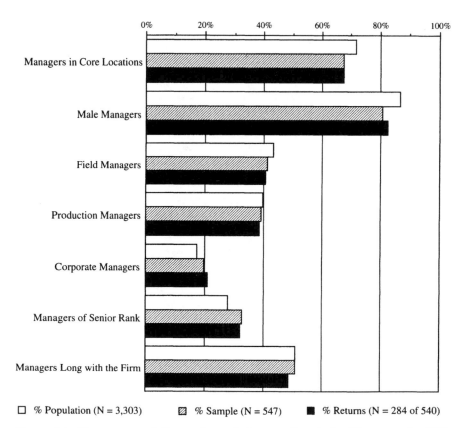

□ % Population (N = 3,303)   ▨ % Sample (N = 547)   ■ % Returns (N = 284 of 540)

Figure 4.1 Manager population and sample by sampling strata. (For example, 72% of the managers in the study population work at the firm's core locations.)

This response rate is excellent relative to the firm's standard established by less difficult surveys, but it still leaves many sample managers not responding. I used data from the personnel files to test for nonresponse bias. The shaded bars in Figure 4.1 show the respondents from each sampling strata. If a certain kind of manager did not respond to the questionnaire, the shaded bar would be different from its adjacent striped bar. There is no evidence of such a difference in the graph. I used loglinear models to test for significant differences between the nonrespondents and the managers who returned a completed questionnaire. Differences are negligible on each sampling variable.

The data quality is further indicated by the fact that 94% of the respondents took the option of asking for analyses of their networks, which gave them an extra incentive to provide accurate information. The data are limited to a single firm, but the firm is large and diversified, so the sample is heterogeneous. The managers come from diverse geographic regions, both sexes, and vary in age from the late twenties to the mid-sixties with the average age in the early forties. The managers represent diverse activities—ranging from sales and service to engineering and production to finance and personnel. They represent varying spans of control below the rank of vice-president (some mangers have no subordinate managers, others have many), and they are distributed across several decades of employment with the firm.

SAMPLING NETWORK CONTACTS

There was a page at the end of the sociometric booklet for comments. Incomplete was the most common comment (7% of the respondents). The gist of this comment was that manager networks involved more people than the ones discussed in the booklet and that any good manager adjusted the composition of his or her network to the needs of immediate projects. This is to be expected. The specific people included in a network change. The network is a dynamic social construction between the manager and the environment, and so changes with the manager's activities. Change is within the limits of the manager's abilities and preferences. Different people maintain different kinds of networks. Some prefer the trust and commitment of a few interconnected contacts. Others prefer the flexibility of many disconnected contacts.

Survey network methods presume those stable abilities and preferences. There is no practical method for conducting a census of a survey respondent's contact network. Even highly inferential methods require a long time; a good study yields an average of a few hundred contacts in eight hours (Killworth and Bernard, 1978). The most widely used alternative is to identify core contacts in a person's network and, from the structure of relations with and among the core contacts, to make inferences about the kind of network that the person maintains. A respondent is presented with one or more name-generator items, such as "Who are your closest friends?" "Who is most important to your success at work?" These sociometric questions generate a list of names, core contacts in the respondent's network. One or more name-interpreter items are then presented. These ask the respondent to characterize the relationship with each listed person and the relationships among the listed people.

Following some introductory opinion and background questions, the sociometric booklet for this study presented nine name-generator items concerning the manager's social and work relations. The items were drawn from previous work relevant to this study population. Name-generator items were followed by name-interpreter items. For each cited contact, managers were asked about the contact's relations with the other cited contacts, contact age, sex, authority relation with the respondent (solid line, dotted line), outside relation with the respondent (co-member of an organization, friend, family), years known to the respondent, frequency of speaking with the contact, emotional closeness, and, for contacts in the firm, their division and years with the firm.

The name-generator items are listed in Figure 4.2 in the order they appear in the sociometric booklet. The relations concern socializing, personal and professional advice, and getting along at work. Listed at the end of each question is the minimum, mean, and maximum number of names that the question generated per respondent.

THE RESULTING NETWORKS

Figure 4.3 is a quick synopsis of the resulting contact networks. The composition of the average network is illustrated by the pie chart at the top of the figure. I began with 27 kinds of relations (the nine sociometric name-generators in Figure 4.2; the four work role relations in Figure 4.3; the outside roles of friend, family, and co-member of an organization; and categories of how frequently the manager met each contact, how close he or she felt to the contact, and how long the manager had known each contact). The 27 kinds of relations sort into four kinds within the firm and two kinds beyond the firm as distinguished in the Figure 4.3 pie chart.

Of the 12.6 contacts in the average-size network, two are outside the firm. Family contacts are 6% of all people cited and friends outside the

Now to your network. The first step is to identify core relationships in it. The next few questions ask for the names of people with whom you have specific kinds of relations. People with whom you have more than one kind of relation can be listed more than once. To make later questions easier to answer, just list the first names or initials of the people with whom you are most strongly connected by each kind of relation.

1. We'll start with a general question. From time to time, most people discuss important matters with other people, people they trust. The range of important matters varies from person to person across work, leisure, family, politics, whatever. The range of relations varies across work, family, friends, and advisors. **If you look back over the last six months, who are the four or five people with whom you discussed matters important to you?** Remember, just list their first names or initials. [2 - 4.9 - 11 names]

2. Consider the people with whom you like to spend your free time. **Over the last six months, who are the three people you have been with most often for informal social activities such as going out to lunch, dinner, drinks, films, visiting one another's homes, and so on?** [0 - 2.9 - 4 names]

3. Do your job responsibilities include assigning work to direct report managers? If YES: **In your opinion, who among them is the most likely to be successful at [THE FIRM]?** [0 - 0.7 - 4 names]

4. **Who would be considered to be your immediate supervisor?** [0 - 1.0 - 2 names]

5. **Of all the people working for [THE FIRM], who are the four or five people who have contributed most to your professional growth within [THE FIRM] — your most valued work contacts?** [0 - 4.2 - 6 names]

6. Making things happen at [THE FIRM], as in many high technology firms, requires buy-in from people working in other groups within the firm. Suppose you were moving to a new job and wanted to leave behind the best network advice you could for the person moving into your current job. **Who are the three or four people you would name to your replacement as essential sources of buy-in for initiatives coming out of your office?** [1 - 3.6 - 6 names]

7. **Of all the people you know at [THE FIRM], whom do you see as your single most important contact for your continued success within the firm?** [0 - 1.0 - 3 names]

8. **At the other extreme, who among the people working for [THE FIRM] has made it the most difficult for you to carry out your job responsibilities?** Again, just list the person's first name or initials (and remember that these data will not be released from the Research Program at Columbia except as aggregate statistics on groups of managers). [0 - 0.9 - 2 names]

9. **If you decided to find a job with another firm doing the kind of work you do at [THE FIRM], who are the two or three people with whom you would most likely discuss and evaluate your job options?** These could be people who work at [THE FIRM], or people outside the firm such as friends, family, or people who work at other firms. [0 - 2.8 - 5 names]

Figure 4.2   Name-generator items. (The numbers at the end of each question give the minimum-mean-maximum number of names generated per respondent.)

firm are another 10%. This is usually the spouse and one close friend beyond the manager's family.

This chapter is about the four kinds of work contacts: two kinds of "solid line" relations of direct supervision, "dotted line" relations of informal supervision and "thin line" relations of personal relevance to the manager citing them. The solid line contacts divide into relations with the manager's immediate supervisor versus all others. The others are typically two subordinates, but several managers included their boss's boss as a direct solid line contact. Beyond the immediate work group,

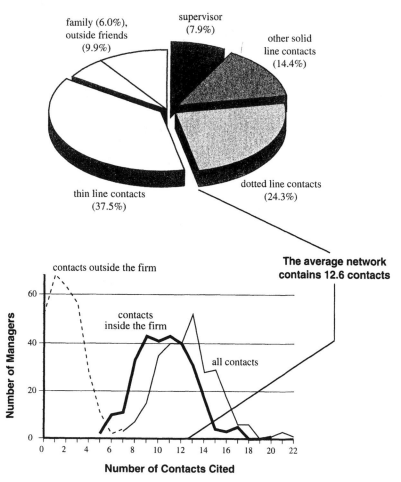

Figure 4.3 Network size and typical composition. (The graph shows numbers of contacts cited and the pie shows the average proportions of each kind of contact cited.)

about three dotted line contacts appear in the average network (24% of all cited contacts). These are lateral or upward lines of informal supervision from other managers. Any contact within the firm who is neither a solid line nor a dotted line is put in the thin line category. The thin line relations survive for diverse reasons for individual managers and for different reasons for different managers: friendship, past association on projects, information exchange, and so on. Bypassing lines of direct and informal supervision, there are about four thin line contacts in the average network (38% of all cited contacts).

The composition characterized in the pie chart is stable across kinds of managers. I estimated regression models predicting the number of each kind of contact from network size, followed by the manager's location, sex, division, rank, and years with the firm. The same models were estimated (excluding network size) to predict proportions of each kind of contact. There are no significant associations in these models except with manager rank—an association more noteworthy for its complexity than for its magnitude. Network size increases with rank, primarily for women with respect to social contacts within and beyond the firm.

Variation in network size is displayed at the bottom of Figure 4.3. The bold line describes the number of work contacts cited. These are the solid, dotted, and thin line contacts in the pie chart. The number of cited work contacts ranges from a minimum of 5 up to a maximum of 20, with an average of 10. Most managers cite between 8 and 13. The dashed line in the Figure 4.3 graph shows that the managers are more homogeneous in citing between 1 and 3 people outside the firm. These are the family and outside friends in the pie chart. Together, the cited work and outside contacts vary from a total of 7 up to 22, with an average of 12.6 contacts.

MEASURING STRUCTURAL HOLES

Respondents were asked to describe the strength of relationships. The manager's relation with each contact was sorted into one of four categories: especially close ("in the sense that this is one of your closest personal contacts"), close ("in the sense that you enjoy the person, but don't count him or her among your closest personal contacts"), less close ("in the sense that you don't mind working with the person, but you have no desire to develop a friendship"), or distant ("in the sense that you really don't enjoy spending time with the person unless it is necessary"). In a matrix of relations between each pair of contacts, respondents were asked to indicate which pairs of contacts were especially close (as above) or distant ("in the sense that they are total strangers or do not enjoy one another's company"). Respondents were to leave blank the cells of the matrix for any pair of contacts whose relationship was somewhere between especially close and distant. From these data, I estimated z_{ij}, the strength of the relation between i and j, for each pair of people in a manager's network, including the manager. The z_{ij} are symmetric ($z_{ij} = z_{ji}$) and vary from a minimum of 0, indicating a distant or nonexistent relation, up to a maximum of 1, indicating an especially close relationship.[2]

These data are sufficient to measure structural holes between primary contacts, but I have no data on secondary structural holes around each contact. I assume that managers and contacts view one another as unique sources of interaction ($O = 1$), so constraint defined by Eq. (2.7) can be measured as defined in Eq. (2.4). Measured constraint from contact j, c_{ij}, is high to the extent that manager i's relationship with contact j is especially close and the contact has exclusive relations with each other contact in the manager's network. Aggregate constraint, C, is the sum of the c_{ij} for all work contacts in the manager's network. I tried other ways of using the raw network data to define constraint, but the above generates the strongest results. As a guide for future work, I have summarized the results obtained with alternatives in Appendix A to this chapter.

The important point here is that my estimates of hole effects are conservative. The analogous situation would be running the analysis in the preceding chapter without data on coordination within markets. In the graphs to be presented, some managers achieve levels higher than expected from constraint and others achieve below expected levels. The over-achievers could either have few people who could do their job (O_i higher than for other managers) or have contacts who could be easily replaced (O_j lower than for other managers). For example, oil and gas drilling is a market discussed in the preceding chapter that doesn't fit the supplier-customer constraint prediction (small β_c bubble at the bottom of Figure 3.5). Profits in the market are higher than expected from the organization of their suppliers and customers. The profits are better predicted when coordination among drilling firms is included in the prediction (large β_o bubble at the top of Figure 3.5).

MEASURING ACHIEVEMENT

There are many kinds of achievement in the study population. My sense from working with managers like these is that the most significant achievement is to participate in an innovative, high-visibility project with broad implications for the firm. Successful participation in such a project is personally rewarding, opens doors for advancement, and, more important, keeps the person in play for participation in future such projects. It is difficult to get systematic data to measure this kind of achievement. Supervisor evaluations of the managers could have been a useful source, but I did not have access to evaluation reports. Similarly, I did not have salary data, although income is closely tied to rank and does not seem to have the visceral meaning to managers that project-based achievement does. I did have data on rank and promotion—visible correlates of project-based achievement. Managers who are quickly promoted from job to job, making it to a high-rank position at a young age, are commonly the subject of career gossip among managers. Conversely, being passed over for promotion again and again is a signal of low achievement, akin to the academic who spends an unusually long time waiting for promotion to full professor.

From personnel files, I knew when managers had entered the firm (year, month, day) and when they had been promoted to their current rank. From the entry date, I could calculate their years with the firm (study date minus entry date). The most recently hired manager had been with the firm for 163 days and the most senior had been with the firm for 28 years. From the promotion date, I knew how long a manager had been in his or her current rank. The newest manager was also the most recently promoted (163 days) and there was one manager who had been in the same rank for more than 10 years. On average, managers had been at their current rank for 2.8 years. Managers were asked in the questionnaire for the year in which they graduated from college. With this I could calculate the time between college graduation and promotion to current rank. I added 21 years to to define the manager's probable age at promotion to current rank.[3]

The meaning of time in rank varies with position in the firm, personal background, reason for departure, and when the time occurs in a person's career. Conceptual frames in which occupational achievement depends on organization and career context (for example, Doeringer and Piore, 1971; Stinchcombe, 1979; Baron and Bielby, 1980; Granovetter, 1981; Rosenbaum, 1984; Spilerman, 1977, 1986) and statistical techniques for disaggregating time-dependent variation (for example, Tuma, 1985; Carroll and Mayer, 1986) have opened this topic to careful study. Peterson, Spilerman, and Dahl (1989) and Spilerman and Lunde (1991), for example, describe time in rank for the roughly 16,000 employees in a large insurance firm. They develop models predicting the time an employee can expect to spend in the same rank before being promoted to the next rank. Expected time is predicted by demographic, human capital, and organizational context variables. Spilerman and Lunde (1991), for example, describe expected time in rank contingent on educational background.

Crudely analogous findings are presented in Table 4.1 to describe the time in rank and promotion age expected for specific kinds of managers

Table 4.1   Promotion timing for kinds of managers

	Mean age at promotion to current rank	Mean years in current rank
All managers	39.31	2.81
Plant location		
Core	39.73	2.91
Remote	38.32	2.60
	$(F_{(1,245)} = 3.31, \; P = .07)$	$(F_{(1,282)} = 1.67, \; P = .20)$
Sex		
Male	39.98	2.93
Female	36.59	2.25
	$(F_{(1,245)} = 15.20, \; P < .001)$	$(F_{(1,282)} = 5.35, \; P = .02)$
Division		
Sales	37.71	2.55
Service	38.62	2.73
Manufacturing	39.78	3.32
Engineering	39.65	3.04
Marketing	41.26	2.58
MIS	41.31	2.61
Finance	38.95	2.55
Personnel	39.41	2.67
	$(F_{(7,239)} = 1.23, \; P = .29)$	$(F_{(7,276)} = 0.81, \; P = .58)$
Rank		
Entry	38.24	2.38
Higher	38.78	2.69
Next	39.58	3.10
Highest	41.61	3.78
	$(F_{(3,243)} = 2.77, \; P = .04)$	$(F_{(3,280)} = 5.14, \; P = .002)$
Seniority		
Recent	38.52	1.38
Long with the firm	40.51	2.34
	$(F_{(1,245)} = 3.86, \; P = .05)$	$(F_{(1,282)} = 19.44, \; P < .001)$

Note: Criterion variables are described in the text and kinds of managers are distinguished on the dimensions of the sampling strata in Figure 4.1. The F-tests for division increase to 2.57 ($P = .08$) and 1.65 ($P = 19$) if the eight division categories are replaced with the three categories in Figure 4.1 of field, production, and corporate.

in the study firm. From the averages in the first column, women were younger than men when they reached their current rank (37 years old versus 40). Sales managers were younger than management information systems (MIS) managers. The people promoted to the entry rank in the study population were younger than people promoted to the highest rank (38 years old versus 42). From the averages in the second column, women were promoted to their current rank more recently than men (2.3 years versus almost 3 years for men). Sales managers were more recently promoted than manufacturing managers (2.6 years versus 3.3). Entry-rank managers were more recently promoted than the highest-level managers (2.4 years versus 3.8).

In contrast to the analyses exemplified by the above-cited articles, I am only interested in the determinants of promotion timing so that I can eliminate them. My primary interest is identifying managers who move ahead of their expected promotion dates and those who fall behind. It is variable rates of return that are predicted by structural holes. Demographic, human capital, and organizational variables that predict promotion dates are *ceteris paribus* conditions for the hypothesis under study.

The matter can be stated succinctly with Merton's (1984) concept of a socially expected duration (SED)—a socially prescribed or collectively patterned expectation about temporal duration embedded in social structure of various kinds (compare Merton, 1984:265–266). The SED for your position in a firm is how long people like you can expect to spend in the position (not how long you actually stay, but rather how long you are expected to stay). The SEDs in an organization can be studied in two ways. They can be studied as a description of the organization or as a baseline from which individuals deviate. The mean times in Table 4.1 are SEDs to the extent that managers know about them. In a more thorough way, the above-cited articles on time in rank decompose SEDs into demographic, human capital, and organizational components. People with certain demographic and human capital backgrounds can expect to spend specific lengths of time in specific positions in their firm, in their industry, in their economy. I am interested in the other aspect of SEDs. I want to identify the manager about whom her peers say, "My, she was certainly young to get that promotion!" or, "Yes, John has been waiting a long time for his promotion." These are statements about differences between observed and expected time. They describe how a person stands relative to the SED for his or her position in the firm. I expect persons ahead of their SED to have networks rich in structural holes. I expect persons behind their SED to have high-constraint networks.

I computed each manager's expected promotion age and expected time in rank from the categories in Table 4.1 and the manager's years with the firm.[4] For example, a female sales manager in an entry rank at a remote plant can expect promotion to her current rank at a younger age than can a male MIS manager at a higher rank at a core plant. When I compare expected age to observed age,

$$[E(\text{age}) - \text{age}]/E(\text{age}),$$

I have a measure of (a) the extent to which the manager was promoted to his or her current rank at a younger age than would be expected for similar managers in the same line of work, and (b) the extent to which the manager has been at his or her current rank for less time than would be expected for similar managers in the same line of work.[5]

The first measure is early promotion and the second is fast promotion. Negative values indicate managers promoted later than expected. These are the managers who should have few structural holes in their contact networks. The lack of entrepreneurial opportunities in their networks leaves them in the same rank for longer periods of time and older than average when promoted. Zero indicates a manager promoted at the expected time. Positive values indicate managers moving ahead of their peers. These are the managers who should have contact networks rich in structural holes, funneling to them disproportionate information and control benefits relevant to moving ahead in the firm.

Both measures warrant cautious interpretation as criterion variables. First, early promotion might be defined by biological age instead of years after college graduation. Biological age is not available for this analysis, but I am not certain that it would be better in as much as college graduation more accurately measures labor force entry.[6] Second, spending a long time in the same rank is a signal of low achievement, but someone who has just been promoted might or might not end up spending a long time in the same rank. Negative values on the fast promotion measure indicate spending a long time in the same rank, but high positive values merely indicate recent promotion. Ideally, fast promotion would be measured by the length of time spent in the prior rank, but those data were not available. I will show that stronger effects are obtained when recent promotion is distinguished from fast promotion. Third, early, fast promotion might be the cause, not the result, of a manager's network. I cannot prove causal order with the available data. I will return to the causal order question in Appendix B at the end of the chapter to argue, from the pattern of documented hole effects, for the causal priority of the structural holes and to suggest more precise data for future research. What I have is a theoretical argument explaining how structural holes are a competitive advantage, and evidence on markets that supports the argument. The argument in Chapter 1 predicts an association between structural holes and manager promotions. The task at hand is to establish whether the association actually exists.

Hole Effects

Estimates of the association between promotion and constraint are presented in Table 4.2. The results illustrate two points. First, there is significant evidence of hole effects. The associations are negative, showing that a lack of structural holes delays promotion, and the associations are significant. Constrained managers are older when promoted (-2.5 t-test for early promotion, $P = .01$) and stay in the same rank for a long time (-2.8 t-test for fast promotion, $P = .003$), especially if recent promotions are excluded from the estimated hole effect on fast promotion (-3.7 t-test, $P < .001$). However, and this is the second point, the correlations are disappointingly small.

I searched through data graphs for variation between kinds of managers. Is the association between promotion and constraint consistent across all managers or are there some for whom it is stronger? Jackknife pseudovalues quickly reveal that the latter is true. In contrast to the results in the preceding chapter—which show that the hole effects in markets are stable across kinds of production activities (Figure 3.5)—

Table 4.2   Aggregate evidence of hole effects

	Intercept	Slope	Correlation	t-test
Early promotion	0.088	$-.349$	$-.149$	-2.54
Fast promotion	0.481	-1.674	$-.164$	-2.79
Fast promotion (excluding recent promotions)	0.509	-2.211	$-.235$	-3.73

Note: Ordinary least-squares estimates of the coefficients are presented predicting promotions for the 284 respondents from the aggregate level of constraint in their contact networks. The routine degrees of freedom for testing the prediction would be 282. However, 14 degrees of freedom are lost in computing expected age from the categories in Table 4.1 and years with the firm, which lowers the degrees of freedom to 268. Further, 37 of the promotion ages are imputed, so the hole effect on early promotion has 231 degrees of freedom. The hole effect on fast promotion in the second row has 268 degrees of freedom, which drops to 224 in the third row because 44 managers are excluded who have been in their current rank for less than a year.

hole effects vary dramatically between kinds of managers, and in an interesting way.

Hole effects are most evident for managers operating on a social frontier. A social frontier is anyplace where two social worlds meet, where people of one kind meet people of a different kind. Individuals who live on a social frontier are more likely to live by their entrepreneurial wits than are individuals in socially homogeneous environments. At the frontier, a manager maintains relations with other kinds of people—the people across the frontier. Relations that cross the frontier involve continual negotiation between the expectations of the manager and the expectations in the world across the frontier. Away from the frontier, where people are more homogeneous, contradictory expectations of relations are less frequent and thus less entrepreneurial skill is required for survival. With these familiar sociological thoughts in mind, it is not surprising to see that managers on social frontiers show stronger network effects.

The point is illustrated in Figure 4.4 with correlations between promotion and constraint for different kinds of managers. The vertical axis in Figure 4.4 is the correlation between promotion and constraint. For example, there is a $-.75$ correlation between constraint and early promotion for men in the highest-ranking positions. The gray area covers two standard errors around the aggregate correlation between constraint and promotion in Table 4.2.[7] Lines outside the gray area indicate managers for whom hole effects are especially pronounced.

STRUCTURAL HOLES AND FAST PROMOTION

Consider the hole effects on fast promotion—the dashed lines in Figure 4.4. A negative correlation indicates faster promotions for managers with networks rich in structural holes. The point illustrated is that hole effects are stronger for managers on a social frontier. Reading from left to right in Figure 4.4, it is slightly stronger for managers in remote plants than managers in core plants (the dashed line is lower for remote plants than for core plants). The effect is stronger for women than for men. It is stronger for field managers than for other managers. It is stronger for recently hired managers than for managers long with the firm. Each of these differences illustrates the greater importance of structural holes for managers on a social frontier.

The hole effect is slightly stronger for managers in remote plant locations. The firm operates an enormous cluster of establishments in its core location, with frequent contact among establishments. Managers working in core locations are typically surrounded by other employees of the firm.

Managers working in remote plant locations are on a social frontier of the firm in the sense of being more isolated from the society of other company employees and more exposed to employees of other firms.

The hole effect is stronger for women. Women are a conspicuous minority at this level of management. There are 446 women in the study population of 3,303 managers (14%). High-level women in this firm (and most other large firms) operate on a sexual frontier. They continually negotiate relations across a sexual frontier demarking people like themselves from the surrounding male environment.

The hole effect is stronger for field managers than other managers. This contrast is similar to the contrast between managers in remote versus core plants. Production and corporate managers live more in a world

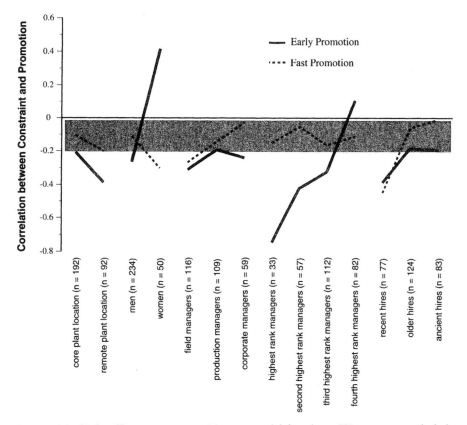

Figure 4.4 Hole effects are most evident on social frontiers. (Women are excluded from the correlations with early promotion except in the fourth column, and the gray area covers two standard errors around the jackknife estimate of the effect for all managers.)

of other company employees. Their responsibilities for designing and assembling products, keeping information flowing smoothly through the firm, keeping budgets under control, and monitoring personnel do not require negotiations with people outside the firm. Responsible managers have contact with some mix of customers, suppliers, and colleagues in other firms, but these contacts are not the substance of work as they are for field managers. Field managers define the social frontier of the firm between insiders and outsiders. Their responsibilities in sales and service require good relations with customers outside the firm. At the same time, the field managers maintain good relations with production and corporate employees deeper in the firm. This is good for career advancement within and beyond the field, and ensures timely delivery of products to important customers.

The hole effect is stronger for recently hired managers. The longer a manager works for the firm, the more relations develop within the firm, and the more life revolves around activities in the firm. This is a natural by-product for anyone spending time in the same place with the same kinds of people for a long time. Managers were asked how long their contacts had been employed by the firm. From these data, and data supplied by the firm on the respondent's own years with the firm, relations between employees by years of seniority were constructed to detect age statuses in the study population. Five age statuses can be distinguished, and the managers in them have the following relative tendencies to cite contacts outside the firm:

$$3.80 \quad \text{Age Status I (most recent hires, } n = 40)$$
$$-1.03 \quad \text{Age Status II } (n = 37)$$
$$-1.66 \quad \text{Age Status III } (n = 124)$$
$$0.30 \quad \text{Age Status IV } (n = 47)$$
$$-1.49 \quad \text{Age Status V (the firm's first employees, } n = 36)$$

where the tendencies are measured by z-score coefficients in a loglinear model of the frequency with which managers in each age status cite contacts outside the firm. The years defining each age status are not reported, because they provide a hiring pattern from which the firm can be identified. The tendency to cite outsiders declines from a strong tendency among recent hires (3.80 z-score, $P < .001$) to negligible tendencies among managers longer with the firm.[8] After only four years with the firm (the time covered by the first age status), managers have been absorbed into the firm. They are no longer likely to cite outsiders. In Figure 4.4, the recent hires are managers in the two youngest age statuses, the older hires are managers in a large wave of hiring about a decade ago, and the ancient hires are managers hired before the wave. The correlation between constraint and fast promotion is strong for the recent hires, and weakens with the time spent in the firm. In other words, the hole effect on fast promotion is strongest for managers on the social frontier of entering the firm from the outside world. The further he or she gets from that frontier of maintaining relations inside and outside the firm, the less promotion is affected by network structure.

With so many social frontiers in the firm, it is easier to compare managers with respect to those who are on none of the frontiers. I'll call such a manager an insider. Defined by the sampling strata in Figure 4.4, an insider is a man who is a production or corporate manager at a core plant and has worked for the firm for a long time (older or ancient hire). By this reckoning, the 284 sample managers divide into 88 who are insiders versus 196 whose networks span one or more social frontiers in the firm (31% versus 69%).

The insider distinction greatly clarifies the evidence of hole effects. Figure 4.5 is a graph of fast promotion against aggregate constraint, excluding the insider managers. Table 4.3 contains estimates of the hole effect on fast promotion, with adjustments for recent and insider promotions. Three points are illustrated in the table and graph.

First, there is clear evidence of the hole effect on fast promotion. The effect in Table 4.3 estimated in a model of all managers has t-tests of -4.7 and -4.4 ($P \ll .001$). Excluding recent promotions and insider managers, the effect across the remaining 161 managers in Figure 4.5 has a t-test of -4.9 ($P \ll .001$). The strong effects are not due to outliers. The distribution of hollow dots in Figure 4.5 shows the negative effect of constraint, moving from the upper left of the graph (low constraint, fast promotion) to the lower right (high constraint, delayed promotion).

Second, the insider managers are distinguished by the relevance of their networks to promotion, not by their tendency to be promoted. There is no significant tendency for insiders to be promoted more quickly or more slowly than other managers (0.7 t-test in Table 4.3). They are different in that the volume of structural holes in their networks has no effect on their chances for fast promotion. The significant slope adjustment for insider managers in Table 4.3 completely erases the advantages of structural holes for other managers (insider hole effect is $0.186 = 2.749 - 2.563$).[9]

Third, Figure 4.5 illustrates the distinction between recent and fast promotion. The band of solid dots across the top of the graph represents managers who have been in their current rank for less than a year. They vary from some whose networks are rich in structural holes (at the left of the graph) to others whose networks contain few holes (at the right of the graph). Judging from the achievements of the other managers in the graph, the recently promoted managers at the left of the graph can expect quick promotions to the next higher rank. The recently promoted managers to the right of the graph can expect to continue in their current rank for a long time.[10]

STRUCTURAL HOLES AND EARLY PROMOTION
Fast promotions cumulate over time to determine early promotion. Managers quickly promoted through the lower ranks of the study population are comparatively young when they reach the top. Accordingly, it is not surprising to see stronger hole effects on early promotion for the managers on social frontiers. Hole effects on early promotion are the solid lines in Figure 4.4. Negative correlation indicates earlier promotions for managers with networks rich in structural holes. Three points are illustrated.

Table 4.3   Hole effects on fast promotion

Multiple correlation	0.594	0.588
Level effects		
Intercept	0.706	0.617
Adjustment for recent promotion	0.790	0.790
	(11.0)	(11.0)
Adjustment for insider managers	0.042	
	(0.7)	
Hole effect		
Effect of increasing constraint	−2.922	−2.563
	[−.286]	[−.251]
	(−4.7)	(−4.4)
Adjustment for recent promotion	2.034	
	(1.6)	
Adjustment for insider managers	2.769	2.749
	(2.5)	(2.5)

Note: Ordinary least-squares estimates of the coefficients are presented predicting fast promotion for the 284 respondents. Standardized estimates are presented in brackets and routine *t*-tests are presented in parentheses. There are 264 degrees of freedom for the *t*-tests in the first column and 266 for the tests in the second column.

First, the hole effects on early promotion, as for fast promotion, are stronger for managers whose networks span a social frontier: managers at remote plants, women, field managers, and recently hired managers.

Second, women are an obvious special case. The correlation between constraint and early promotion is stronger for women, but it is reversed. Constraint has a strong positive correlation with early promotion for women (0.42 versus the − .27 correlation for men). This positive correlation is created by the importance of sponsorship for women. I will return to this issue for detailed analysis, but let me put women to one side for

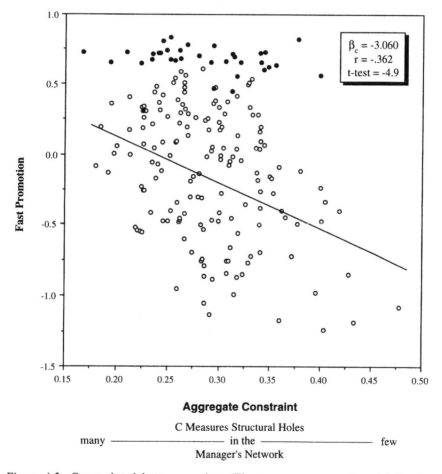

Aggregate Constraint

C Measures Structural Holes
many ————————————— in the ————————————— few
Manager's Network

Figure 4.5 Constraint delays promotion. (These are managers at social frontiers within the firm; managers at remote plants, women, field managers and recent hires. Solid dots are managers promoted to their current rank within the last year.)

the moment. The solid lines in Figure 4.4 are based only on male managers (except in the fourth column) in order to assess the direct effect of aggregate constraint more clearly.

Third, the most striking contrast in Figure 4.4 is between men at different ranks in the study population. The correlation between constraint and early promotion varies from a negligible positive value among entry level managers to an extremely strong negative correlation of −.75 among the highest-rank managers. The data are plotted in Figure 4.6. Table 4.4 contains estimates of hole effects with adjustments for insider managers

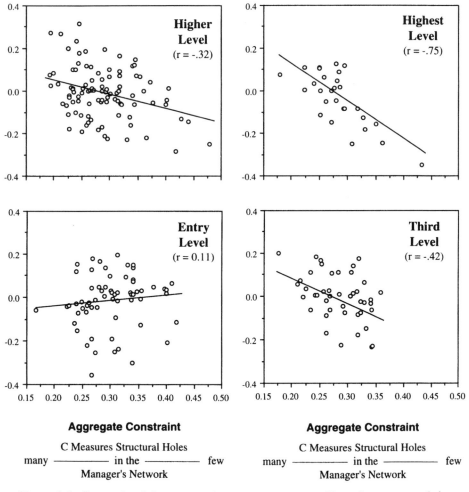

Figure 4.6 Constraint delays promotion so managers are older when promoted, increasingly so for the highest promotions. (Vertical axis is early promotion for men and horizontal is level of constraint.)

and manager rank. Combining the top two ranks, there is a $-.65$ correlation in Table 4.4 between constraint and early promotion, for a t-test of -4.9 ($P \ll .001$). It is half as strong for managers in the second rank (.762 versus the 1.432 effect in the highest ranks), and disappears for entry-rank managers ($1.655 - 1.432 = .223$ hole effect for entry rank, 0.8 t-test). The graphs in Figure 4.6 display the data distributions behind these effects. As a manager moves up the ranks, early promotion is increasingly connected with constraint. At the highest rank, the data are distributed in an almost perfectly linear negative association between early promotion and constraint. The insider distinction is irrelevant with rank held constant. The level and slope adjustments for insider managers in Table 4.4 are both negligible. Structural holes improve the chances of early promotion to the highest ranks for all men in the study population. This is different from the results on fast promotion. Level and slope adjustments for rank in the Table 4.3 regression models are all negligible (aggregate F-test of 1.53 with 4,262 d.f., $P = 0.19$), as might be

Table 4.4   Hole effects on early promotion

Multiple correlation	0.377	0.371
Level effects		
Intercept	0.406	0.397
Adjustment for insider managers	0.002 (0.1)	
Adjustment for entry rank	0.001 (0.1)	
Adjustment for next higher rank	0.012 (0.7)	
Hole effect		
Effect of increasing constraint in two highest ranks	-1.486 [$-.661$] (-5.0)	-1.432 [$-.637$] (-4.9)
Adjustment for insider managers	0.225 (0.7)	
Adjustment for entry rank	1.660 (4.1)	1.655 (4.2)
Adjustment for next higher rank	0.735 (2.1)	0.762 (2.2)

Note: Ordinary least-squares estimates of the coefficients are presented predicting early promotion for the 234 respondents. Standardized estimates are presented in brackets and routine t-tests are presented in parentheses. There are 176 degrees of freedom for the t-tests in the first column and 180 for the tests in the second column.

expected from the dashed line over rank consistently in the gray area of Figure 4.4.

My conclusion is that constraint delays promotion at all ranks, but its effects cumulate across the history of a manager's promotions to make constrained managers older when and if they move up the corporate hierarchy, and increasingly older with each higher rank they reach. The evidence of hole effects on delayed promotions is consistent with the hole effects on fast promotions among managers operating across social frontiers, but the frontier here is different. It is a frontier constructed by the manager. It seemed from the comments in the questionnaires that many of the managers in the lower ranks focused only on their immediate job, concentrating on completing assigned tasks on time in a satisfying way. To move up the corporate hierarchy, into the higher ranks of this study population, a manager has to change that frame of reference to one that extends well beyond immediate tasks to include initiatives by competitors in other firms and external factors that shape the firm's global markets. I will present evidence that perspective shifts with rank in the discussion below of institutional holes in the contact networks. Higher up the corporate hierarchy, work is increasingly political as well as technical. High-rank managers have to think and behave more like equity players in the firm rather than getting along as employees working for a wage. The frontier is the boundary between being an employee protected by the firm and being a leader responsible for the firm. This is the kind of environment in which the information and control benefits of structural holes serve to distinguish leaders from the led, a point to which Figure 4.6 attests.

Hierarchy

The aggregate lack of structural holes in a manager's contact network is associated with promotion. The next step is to show how promotion is affected, above and beyond the level of constraint, by the distribution of constraint across contacts. Comparing the hole signatures of the manager networks shows, as in the analysis of markets, how constraint and opportunity distributions vary among managers and how that variation is linked to promotion.

KINDS OF HOLE SIGNATURES

Four kinds of signatures can be distinguished from a cluster analysis of the 284 manager hole signatures. Illustrative managers of each kind are displayed in Figure 4.7. The illustrative managers were selected for their high reliability as indicators of each kind of signature and the level of constraint and hierarchy that characterizes each kind of signature. Each hole signature is defined by the distribution of p_{ij} and c_{ij} across contacts, rank ordered with respect to the strength of the manager's relation with each and the constraint each poses (compare Figure 2.6). I have named contacts in Figure 4.7 by the kind of relation they have with the respondent manager: the manager's immediate supervisor, solid line (other di-

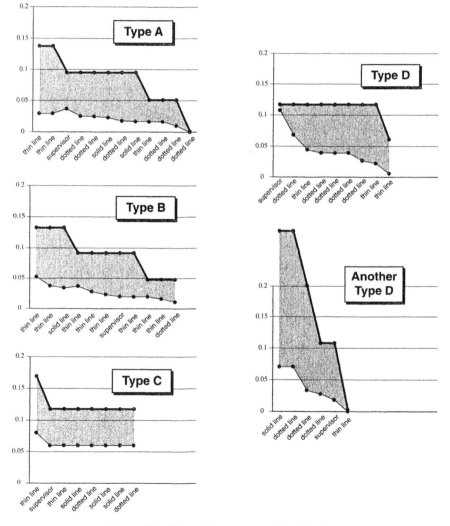

Figure 4.7 Illustrative manager hole signatures

rect supervision above or below the manager), dotted line (informal supervision), or thin line (nonsupervisory relation).[11]

Figure 4.7 is a census of kinds of networks in the study population. A discriminant function analysis shows that the four kinds of hole signatures are not associated with any particular kind of manager (identified by core plant location, sex, division, rank, or seniority). The simplest and strongest prediction of a manager's hole signature involves two variables, the aggregate level of constraint in the manager's network and the extent to which constraint is concentrated in a single contact. The point is illustrated in Figure 4.8. From Eq. (2.9), hierarchy is the extent to which the constraint on a manager is concentrated in a single relationship.

Types A and B: Entrepreneurial Signature
The first two kinds of hole signatures describe entrepreneurial networks. The networks contain many contacts, no one contact poses dramatically more constraint than all other contacts, and all pose low constraint. These are hollow circles and squares in Figure 4.8, concentrated in the lower left corner of the graph (low constraint, low hierarchy).

The illustrative Type A signature in Figure 4.7 is for a high-ranking manager in engineering. He is younger than the average person promoted to his rank in engineering and has been at his current rank for about half the time that a person like himself can expect to stay at his rank. He cites twelve contacts in the firm. He is especially close to two, neither of whom is connected to him by a formal or informal line of supervision. Both are thin line contacts in his network. His immediate supervisor is next in the signature, along with several solid and dotted line contacts. He has developed a dislike for one of his dotted line contacts, listed at the end of the signature. The bottom of the shaded area defining the hole signature of his network is close to zero and declines slowly from his closest to his most distant contact, a pattern indicating numerous structural holes in his network.

The illustrative Type B signature in Figure 4.7 is different in scale rather than in substance. It is one contact smaller and contains a third especially close relationship. The thin line contact listed first is better connected with other contacts than is true of the first contact in the Type A signature, which results in a higher level of constraint. In Figure 4.8, the Type B signatures are similar to Type A signatures in being nonhierarchical, but different in containing a higher level of constraint. The illustrative Type B signature in Figure 4.7 is for a high-ranking manager in finance. He is younger than the average person promoted to his rank in finance and has been at his current rank for the average time that a person like himself can expect to stay at his rank.

Type C: Clique Signature

The third kind of hole signature describes clique networks. The clique networks are smaller on average than the entrepreneurial networks (9 versus 13 contacts) and are characterized by strong relations between contacts. They are no more likely to have connected contacts—86% of the relations in clique networks are nonzero and 85% of the relations in entrepreneurial networks are nonzero—but the relations that exist are

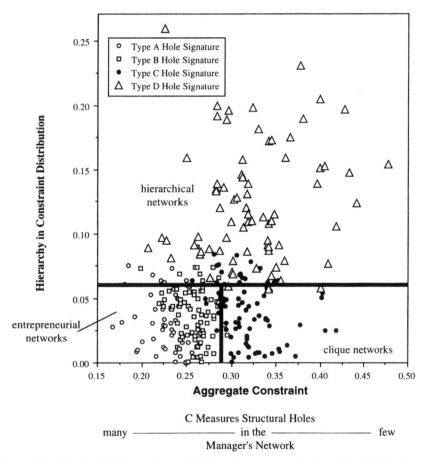

Figure 4.8   Constraint, hierarchy, and kinds of manager networks. (The bold horizontal line marks the mean of hierarchy and the bold vertical line marks the mean of aggregate constraint.)

more likely to be strong. Density is 0.50 in the average clique network, the highest of all four types, and 0.44 in the average entrepreneurial network (where density is the mean relation between any two contacts). The clique networks appear as small dark circles in Figure 4.8, concentrated in the lower right of the graph (high constraint, low hierarchy).

The illustrative Type C signature in Figure 4.7 is for an entry-rank manager in sales. He has been with the firm for a long time and was nearly twice as old as the average person promoted to his rank. Of the eight contacts he cited in the firm, he feels especially close to one person, a thin line contact beyond his immediate work group, and close to everyone else. The characteristic that makes this a clique network is the fact that everyone in his network is close or especially close to everyone else.

Type D: Hierarchical Signature

The fourth kind of hole signature describes hierarchical networks. These networks are the same size as the clique networks on average (9 contacts), and so smaller than the entrepreneurial networks. They are distinct from the clique networks in the low density of relations within them. One out of every two pairs of contacts is disconnected (0.67 proportional density), and the average relationship is "less close" (0.43 density). The hierarchical networks are distinct from both the entrepreneurial and the clique networks in that whatever constraint they contain is concentrated in the hands of a small minority of the contacts. The hierarchical networks appear as triangles in Figure 4.8, distributed at the top of the graph across levels of constraint.

Two Type D signatures are presented in Figure 4.7 to illustrate different ways in which the hierarchical networks are structured. The Type D signature to the right is a middle-rank MIS manager. He joined the firm within the last five years, and when he was promoted to his current rank he was younger than the average person promoted to the same position. He cited nine contacts in the firm and feels especially close to all but the ninth person, to whom he feels close. This would suggest that he had a clique structure, but the relations between his contacts are unequal. His immediate supervisor has an especially close relationship with most of his contacts, and there are few strong relations between any of the other contacts. Accordingly, his supervisor poses a high level of constraint and the other contacts pose lower levels. Constraint is concentrated in the relation with his immediate supervisor. This manager has borrowed his supervisor's network. He is in serious trouble if the relationship with his supervisor turns sour.

The other Type D signature in Figure 4.7 is more obviously hierarchical. This is a middle-rank manager in manufacturing. He has been with the firm for a little less than a decade and was promoted to his current rank at an age typical of managers like himself. He cited six contacts and feels especially close to two of them, his boss's boss and a dotted line contact. Note the supervisor near the end of the signature. This is a network anchored outside the manager's immediate work group.

IMPLICATIONS FOR PROMOTION

The hole signatures show that the managers differ from one another not only in their aggregate level of constraint but also in the shape of constraint's distribution across contacts. In contrast, the market networks in the preceding chapter all have a hierarchical structure, so much so that constraint in the largest transaction is strongly correlated with aggregate constraint. The correlation between constraint and hierarchy is 0.36 across the managers, versus the 0.75 correlation for markets (compare Figure 4.8 with Figure 3.9).

Hierarchy is a significant piece to the puzzle of why some managers get promoted before others. Hierarchy has no association with fast promotion from a position, but it is associated with the cumulative promotions that determine early or late arrival at a manager's current rank.[12] Recall from Figure 4.4 that there are two kinds of managers for whom constraint leads to early promotion rather than delaying it: women, and men in entry-rank positions. For others, constraint significantly delays promotion. Hierarchy explains the deviations.

The promotions of the deviant managers are keyed to the extent to which they have built their networks around one or two strategic partners. Across all managers, hierarchy is a negligible consideration. The results in the first row of Table 4.5 show that managers with low-constraint networks get promoted early. This effect is slightly stronger than the effect without holding hierarchy constant (-2.9 t-test in Table 4.5 versus the -2.5 t-test in Table 4.2), but the direct effect of hierarchy is negligible.

The aggregate effects mask two opposite patterns of effects. For high-ranking men, displayed in the second row of Table 4.5, early promotion is dramatically determined by constraint. Hierarchy is negligible. In contrast, hierarchy determines early promotion for women and entry-rank men. The results in the third row of Table 4.5 show that the previously positive correlation with constraint is negligible when hierarchy is held constant and the direct effect of hierarchy is significant (2.6 t-test, P $<$

.01). The data underlying this association are displayed in Figure 4.9 to show that the association holds for entry-rank men ($r = 0.25$, $n = 64$), entry-rank women ($r = 0.27$, $n = 32$), and women in higher-rank positions ($r = 0.48$, $n = 18$). The association is not as strong as observed for aggregate constraint, but there is a general flow of data from the lower left of the graph (low hierarchy, delayed promotion) to the upper right of the graph (high hierarchy, early promotion).[13]

In sum, two kinds of managers benefit from structural holes in different ways. The results in Table 4.5 do not suggest that each manager's promotions are affected by constraint and a little less by hierarchy. They suggest that a manager's promotion is affected by constraint, or hierarchy, but not both. There are some managers who build their networks to have direct contact with the entrepreneurial opportunities of structural holes. There are other managers who build hierarchical networks around one or two strategic partners, and have extensive holes between the contacts they reach through their strategic partners. Both kinds of networks can be rich in structural holes, as illustrated by the gray areas in Figure 4.7. The difference is that managers in the hierarchical networks are more at risk if something goes sour in the relationship with the strategic partner around whom their network is built.

All of which begs the political question of why certain managers are obliged to rely on strategic partners. Thinking in terms of personality and socialization, one might attribute the importance of strategic partners for women to their having been socialized to rely on a strong partner. But this explanation doesn't account for the men who also rely on strategic

Table 4.5 Constraint and hierarchy effects on early promotion

	R	Intercept	Constraint	Hierarchy
All managers ($n = 284$)	0.175	0.097	−.431	0.247
			[−.185]	[0.097]
			(−2.9)	(1.5)
High-ranking men ($n = 170$)	0.405	0.250	−.927	0.059
			[−.414]	[0.026]
			(−5.4)	(0.3)
Women and entry-rank men ($n = 114$)	0.323	−.154	0.328	0.748
			[0.132]	[0.251]
			(1.3)	(2.6)

Note: Ordinary least-squares estimates of the coefficients are presented, with standardized estimates in brackets, routine *t*-tests in parentheses, and the multiple correlation in the first column.

partners. In this study population these are the men at the bottom of the hierarchy. The entry-rank managers—men and women—are the least established managers in this study population, and their early promotions are predicted more by hierarchy than by constraint. The unpleasant implication of this reasoning is that women don't escape the weak position of entry-rank managers after they are promoted to higher ranks. The early promotions of women at all ranks are predicted more by hierarchy than by constraint. Entry-rank men, and women at all ranks, tend to get promoted late unless they have a contact network built around one or two strategic partners.

There is a difference between being in a weak position and feeling weak. As persons just entering this population of high-level managers, entry-rank men might feel uncertain about how to go about their business and therefore prefer to make contacts through a strategic partner. As a conspicuous minority, women might feel that they are in a weaker position than their male colleagues even if there is no justification for such a feeling from an analysis of promotions. Recall from Table 4.1 that women

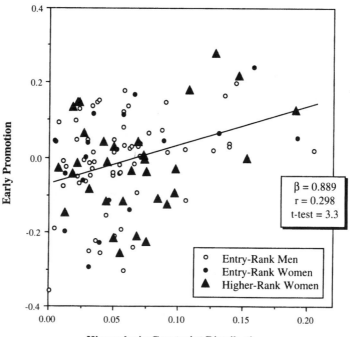

$\beta = 0.889$
$r = 0.298$
t-test = 3.3

○ Entry-Rank Men
● Entry-Rank Women
▲ Higher-Rank Women

Hierarchy in Constraint Distribution

Figure 4.9 Hierarchy and early promotion

are more likely than men to be promoted early to their current rank. But if the stronger effect of hierarchy for women and entry-rank men merely reflects psychosomatic feelings of uncertainty, then any manager who has just been promoted can be expected to feel nervous about how to proceed in the new position and therefore to have a hierarchical network. Consider the following results:

0 years ($n = 44$)	32%	0.066	0.36
1 year ($n = 69$)	30%	0.062	0.25
2 years ($n = 74$)	27%	0.058	0.38
3 years ($n = 38$)	26%	0.052	0.17
4+ years ($n = 59$)	18%	0.060	0.09

Rows indicate the number of years that a manager has been at his or her current rank. On average, managers have been in their current rank for 2.8 years. The first column is the percentage of managers who have Type D, or hierarchical, networks. The tendency for a manager to have a hierarchical network decreases with the years he or she has spent at the same rank, a pattern suggesting that managers new to their position are more likely than experienced managers to build their network around strategic partners. Similarly, the mean hierarchy scores in the second column show hierarchy decreasing through the third year in rank. Although suggestive, these differences are negligible. Type D signature networks are independent of years in rank (3.2 chi-square, 4 d.f., $P = .53$) and hierarchy scores vary as much between managers with the same years in rank as between managers with different years in rank (0.33 F-test with 3,280 d.f., $P = .81$). Moreover, the correlation between early promotion and hierarchy for women and entry-level men—the third column in the above results—is positive up through the average length of time a manager can expect to spend in the same rank.

My conclusion is that the importance of strategic partners to women and entry-rank men should not be attributed to background socialization or to psychosomatic feelings of uncertainty about how to do their work. It more likely reflects these managers' weaker positions in the study population. This interpretation is further supported by the institutional holes spanned by their networks.

Institutional Holes

I have measured structural holes between a manager's contacts. But the manager's network is a social construction laid on top of the firm's bureaucratic structure, and there are holes in the bureaucratic structure that can be advantageous. For example, a manager with two contacts who are strongly tied to one another has no hole between the contacts according to the analysis up to this point. But if the first contact is head of engineering and the second is head of sales, the contacts take on a new light. The manager is in a good position to negotiate the natural tension between the first manager's interest in developing a state-of-the-art product regardless of sales potential and the second manager's interest in selling the product regardless of its technological features.

There is already evidence that institutional holes are important. The managers on social frontiers in the firm are presumed to have networks that span institutional holes. Managers in remote plants, field managers, and newly hired managers are more likely to have networks that span the boundary around the firm between insiders and outsiders. These are presumptions. I have no measures of the extent to which one field manager's network spans the insider-outsider boundary more than another field manager's network.

For data on institutional holes, I asked respondents to name the division of the firm in which each of their cited contacts worked. However, the question was poorly designed for this study population. Functional divisions are clearer on paper than in practice. Respondents interpreted division boundaries in so many ways that the data are useless. Divisions should have been precoded in the questionnaire.

Nevertheless, data were obtained that reveal the importance of building contacts across structural holes within the organization. In an intriguing search through the data, it became apparent that promotions were affected by the way that a manager maintained contacts across the boundary around his or her immediate work group. Some managers built their networks to reach beyond their immediate work group, and so benefited from the access to institutional structural holes between their work group and other groups in the firm. Without data on the divisions in which contacts were made, I do not know the volume of holes provided by the networks that reached beyond the immediate work group. But I do know that a network that reached beyond the work group contained more institutional structural holes than a network concentrated in the work group, and that the difference is linked with promotions.

PICKING THE STRATEGIC PARTNER

The person at the top of the hierarchical network is distinct from other contacts in the network. He or she is the principal source of constraint.

Across the 106 managers with above-average hierarchy scores (managers above the bold horizontal line in Figure 4.8), the person at the top of the hierarchy poses an average constraint of 0.071 (versus 0.046 in low-hierarchy networks), which drops to 0.054 for the second person, and 0.046 for the third (versus 0.040 and 0.036, respectively, for low-hierarchy networks).

Managers have a choice in picking the top person. The most obvious choice is their immediate supervisor. The supervisor is the closest person of higher authority, is familiar with the manager's work, and is responsible for evaluation reports and salary recommendations. The MIS manager whose network hole signature is displayed as "Type D" in Figure 4.7 built his network around his boss as a strategic partner. But a manager can always make other people aware of his or her work. The manufacturing manager whose network hole signature is displayed as "Another Type D" in Figure 4.7 built his network around the boss's boss as a strategic partner. More generally, the 106 managers with above-average hierarchy scores prefer dotted and thin line contacts as strategic partners. A third of them (35 of the 106) built their network around a thin line contact and the same number built around a dotted line contact. The networks built around the boss are slightly more hierarchical, but not significantly (0.7 t-test). High-ranking men with a hierarchical network have a preference for building around a solid line contact other than the boss (2.3 z-score, two-tail P of .02), while women and entry-rank men have a slight preference for thin line contacts (-1.9 z-score, $P = .06$).

As noted in Chapter 2, there are at least three benefits to selecting someone other than one's boss as a strategic partner. First, the critical relation with the strategic partner is less at risk of going sour from the inevitable disagreements that occur between people who work together. Second, given that there is always a boss, a manager gains more control over his or her own work with an external sponsor, because this person can be leveraged against the boss for negotiating advantage when disagreements do arise. Third, even if negotiating is ignored and the manager has a terrific relationship with the boss, the issue of how to generate the most convincing sponsorship arises. Supervisors are expected to sponsor their subordinates. What they say about their subordinates reflects on their own work, so bosses usually say positive things about subordinates. Having an external strategic partner means that there are two people in different places who sponsor the manager when new opportunities arise. This adds a corroborating external voice to the boss's sponsorship.

The graph in Figure 4.10 shows that these benefits are significant. The vertical axis is the correlation between hierarchy and early promotion for women and entry-rank men. The horizontal axis is the relative constraint posed by the manager's boss (c_{ij} for the boss divided by C/N, where N is the number of contacts in the network; see Eq. 2.8). At the far right of the graph, all women and entry-rank men are included in the correlation. Hierarchy is correlated 0.30 with early promotion, as illustrated in Figure 4.9. Next, managers are excluded from the correlation if their boss poses as much as twice the average constraint per contact. The correlation is about the same as for all managers. The correlation increases slightly to 0.33 if managers are excluded when the boss poses as much as one and a half times the average constraint. The correlation increases to 0.39 if the boss poses less than the average constraint, and increases to 0.58 if the boss poses less than half the average constraint. Looking at the specific person at the top of the hierarchy, there is little difference between building around a dotted line contact or around a solid line contact other than the boss. Hierarchy and early promotion are weakly, but positively, correlated ($r = 0.15$ across the 40 managers). However, the correlation is 0.43 if the network is built around a thin line contact and disappears at 0.03 if the network is built around the immediate supervisor.

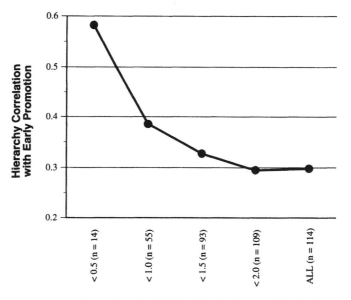

Boss Constraint Relative to Average Contact

Figure 4.10   Hierarchical networks are most effective when the boss is not a dominant contact. (Correlations are computed for the women and entry-rank men displayed in Figure 4.9.)

Moreover, there are implications for what happens after the manager is promoted. Women and entry-rank men who build hierarchical networks around their immediate supervisor not only lose the hierarchy effect on early promotion but end up staying in the same rank for a longer period of time. Figure 4.11 shows how early promotion is associated with fast promotion for women and entry-rank men who have built their network around their boss (lower graph, boss poses average or higher constraint) versus someone else (upper graph, boss poses below-average constraint).

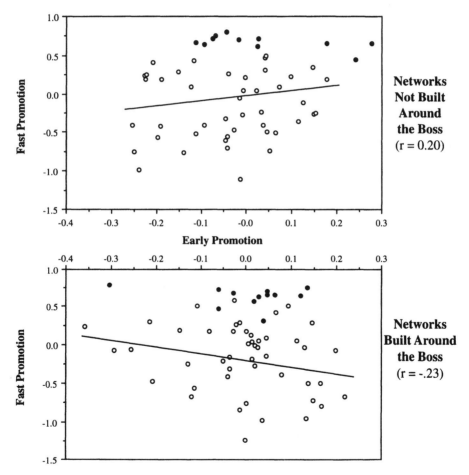

Figure 4.11   Again, hierarchical networks are most effective when the boss is not a dominant contact. (These are women and entry-rank men. Managers in the top graph have networks in which the boss poses less constraint than the average per contact. Solid dots mark managers promoted less than a year ago and excluded from the correlations.)

The slopes are small, with few observations, so I do not want to make too much of their magnitude. However, the difference between the slopes is significant (1.9 t-test, 75 d.f., P = .03), and consistent with the effect of building a network around the immediate supervisor. When the boss is a dominant contact (bottom graph), managers promoted early to their current rank tend to be left in the rank for a long time. The managers quickly promoted are those who came to the rank late. The tendency is just the opposite for managers with networks in which the boss is not one of the critical contacts (top graph). Managers promoted early to their current rank tend to be promoted quickly to the next rank. Managers promoted late tend to stay in the same rank for a long time.

In sum, the benefits of building a hierarchical network depend on the contact around whom it is built. Building around the immediate supervisor is unproductive. The early promotion advantage of hierarchy is lost, and subsequent promotion is delayed to the extent that the promotion to the current rank was early. The greatest benefit is from building around a person completely removed from the immediate work group—a thin line contact, a person who has neither formal nor informal lines of supervision to the manager. These networks most clearly span institutional structural holes in the organization and are associated with early, fast promotion.

BUILDING BRIDGES BEYOND THE IMMEDIATE WORK GROUP

There is also more general evidence of institutional structural holes. Where the immediate work group is defined by solid line contacts, and dotted lines of informal supervision constitute a buffer zone between the work group and the rest of the firm, relations with thin line contacts reach across structural holes in the organization.

Consider the table at the top of Figure 4.12. Columns distinguish managers by the extent to which their contacts involve the immediate job. Core work contacts are the people with whom the manager has lines of supervision regarding the immediate job, from the formal extreme of the boss to the informal extreme of thin line contacts whose endorsement is cited as important to have for projects coming out of the manager's office. These are distinct from thin line contacts who have no immediate relevance to the immediate job. These relations involve neither formal nor informal lines of supervision. Judging from the comments in the sociometric booklet, thin line relations beyond the immediate work group are maintained for instrumental reasons of exposure to other parts of the company and personal reasons of friendship and pleasant time together on early projects. Although all managers have relations within their immediate work group, they differ in contacts beyond the work group. Some have few. Core work contacts compose 75% to 100% of the networks for a third of the managers (third column of the table; average is 84%). At the other extreme, slightly more than a quarter of the managers draw at least half of their network from thin line relations beyond their core work activities (first column of the table; average is 44% core work contacts).

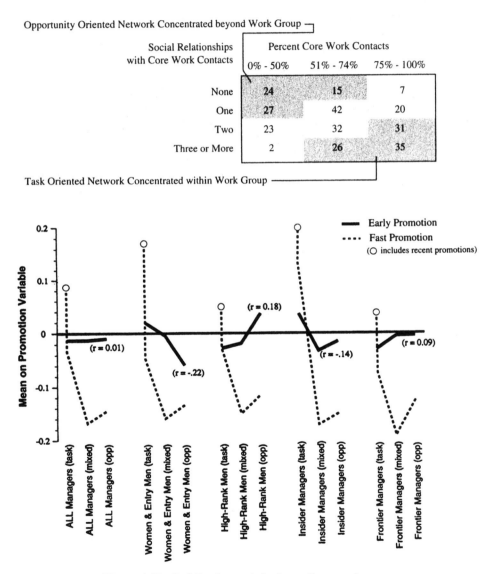

Figure 4.12   Building beyond the immediate work group

The rows of the table distinguish managers by the extent to which they socialize with core work contacts. Socializing refers to Question 9 in Figure 4.2, about discussing the pros and cons of taking a job in another firm, and Question 2, about going out for lunch or drinks, visiting one another's homes, and so on. These questions typically elicited the names of the manager's spouse and an outside friend, but contacts at work were also named. Rows in the Figure 4.12 table indicate how often core work contacts were named. Sixteen percent of the managers do not socialize with their core work contacts (first row of the table). The majority, 62%, socialize with one or two core work contacts.

Three kinds of networks are distinguished in the table. The managers in the lower right corner have task-oriented networks in the sense that most of their contacts are related to their current work and they socialize extensively within their work group. The managers in the upper left corner have opportunity-oriented networks in the sense that the majority of their contacts are thin line contacts beyond the immediate work group and little or none of their socializing is with other people in their work group. Managers in the unshaded middle of the table mix qualities of task- and opportunity-oriented networks.

The graph in Figure 4.12 illustrates the connection with promotions. Solid lines indicate mean scores on the early promotion variable. Dashed lines indicate mean scores on the fast promotion variable. The graph illustrates two points.

First, there is a connection with the time managers have spent at their current rank. Managers who have been at their current rank for less than a year are excluded from the fast promotion averages, but the white dots show the averages when they are included among managers with task-oriented networks (the group most affected by their deletion). The dashed line is higher over task-oriented networks for every kind of manager. The white dots show how much higher the task-oriented averages would be if recently promoted managers were included. This makes sense. The first people you meet after promotion are the people in your immediate work group. It is natural to expect that there is a period of integration during which socializing is more intense within the group.

The more important observation is the consistent lack of a significant difference in fast promotion between mixed and opportunity-oriented networks. Managers might have task-oriented networks just after promotion, then expand beyond the immediate work group, but they have no systematic tendency to shift to opportunity networks. Across all 284 managers, task-oriented networks are significantly associated with short times in rank, but opportunity-oriented networks have no association with time in rank (2.1 versus 0.6 *t*-tests respectively, relative to the mixed networks). There isn't even a zero-order association with opportunity-oriented networks (-1.1 *t*-test, 231 d.f., two-tail $P = .29$).

This is important because constraint is only associated with opportunity-oriented networks. If constraint is predicted from the three kinds of networks, task-oriented networks have no association with constraint and opportunity-oriented networks have a strong negative association (-0.7 versus -3.8 *t*-tests, respectively, again relative to the mixed networks).

In other words, time in rank is associated with expanding beyond the work group, but not in a way that creates entrepreneurial opportunities. Recently promoted managers begin with networks concentrated in the work group, then expand beyond the group. However, they do not acquire additional structural holes between their contacts when they expand across the boundary of the immediate work group. Friends of other group members are added to the network. The expansion to distant, disconnected contacts in the firm is only significant for the managers who have opportunity-oriented networks, and having that kind of network is independent of time in rank.

Further, that kind of network is significantly linked with early promotion in a way that complements the results on hierarchy's effect. This is the second point illustrated in Figure 4.12. From the solid line over the three kinds of networks for all 284 managers, you can see that there is no difference in early promotion among the networks (0.02 *F*-test with 2,230 d.f., $P = .98$). The results are stronger, but still negligible, for insider managers and managers whose networks span one or more social frontiers (2.1 and 1.0 *F*-tests). The significant effects occur among the managers distinguished by hierarchy's effect—high-ranking men versus women and entry-rank men. The bold line in Figure 4.12 over women and entry-rank men declines from task-oriented to opportunity-oriented networks. The delay is significant (-2.4 *t*-test). The bold line over high-ranking men is exactly the opposite, increasing from task-oriented networks to opportunity-oriented networks. The improved chances of early promotion are significant (2.3 *t*-test), primarily due to the earlier promotions of men with opportunity-oriented networks (2.3 *t*-test for opportunity-oriented networks versus a -0.4 *t*-test for task-oriented networks).

The same factors that make it important for women and entry-rank men to build a hierarchical network around a strategic partner make it advantageous for them to build strong relations within their immediate work group. The strategic partner can act as their sponsor to the rest of the firm, and the strong base of support within the work group can be cited as evidence. The fact that both factors are important to the early promotion of women and entry-rank men—and that building their own contacts to distant parts of firm significantly delays promotion—speaks to their more defensive positions in the firm. In moving from entry-rank to higher-rank positions, a man has to change his strategy. To be promoted as an independent leader, the high-ranking man has to build a broad base of independent contacts beyond the immediate work group.

Selecting a Network

To set the stage for my final result in this analysis, let me pose a practical question from a manager reading through the above discussion: What kind of network should I develop? The answer is in two parts, the first distinguishing the manager's choices and the second recommending a choice.

WHAT ARE THE CHOICES?

Figure 4.13 summarizes distinctions between kinds of manager networks that emerged in the analysis.[14] The most basic choice is between a flat network in which no single contact is dramatically more central than others versus a hierarchical network built around one or two strategic partners. There is a preference for the flat structure networks in this study population. Dividing the managers at the mean value of the hierarchy measure (indicated by the bold horizontal line in Figure 4.8), slightly less than two thirds of them have nonhierarchical networks (178, or 63%).

If a flat structure network is selected, there is a choice about how contacts are to be connected within the network. Some managers prefer to have everyone connected in a dense, typically small, network of colleagues. These are the managers with clique networks. Other managers prefer a large network of disconnected contacts. These are the managers with entrepreneurial networks.

If a hierarchical network is selected, there is the question of whom to select as the strategic partner at the top of the network. The critical choice is between the boss and someone else, especially someone outside the manager's immediate work group. Managers are about evenly split between the boss and someone else.

Regardless of the aggregate network structure selected, there is a choice between concentrating the network in the immediate work group or concentrating on distant contacts beyond the work group. In Figure 4.13 I have distinguished the managers with opportunity-oriented networks from the managers with task-oriented or mixed networks. It is the step to an opportunity network that is most advantageous for early promotions among high-ranking men and most detrimental for women and entry-rank men. There is no significant tendency for managers with

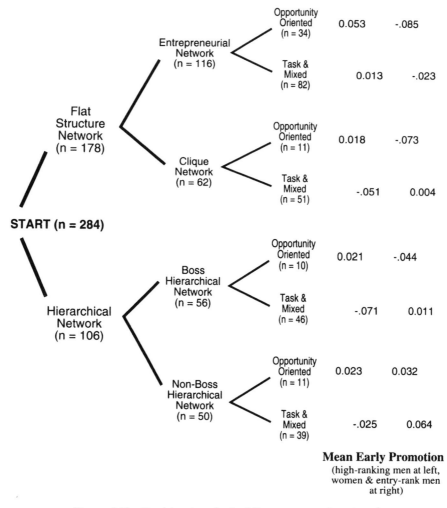

Figure 4.13   Decision tree for building a manager's network

any one of the four broadly defined structures to prefer an opportunity-oriented network (4.4 chi-square, 3 d.f., $P = .22$).

WHICH SHOULD I CHOOSE?

Figure 4.13 contains mean early promotion scores for managers in each kind of network. Reading down the first column, the best network for a high-ranking man is across the top of the decision tree—a flat-structure, entrepreneurial, opportunity-oriented network. High-ranking men with this network were promoted significantly early to their current rank (2.3 t-test). The worst situation is to be a high-ranking man with a hierarchical network built around the boss and concentrated in the immediate work group (-2.6 t-test). Between these extremes, promotions are early (positive means) for all high-ranking men with opportunity-oriented networks.

Reading down the second column, the best network for a women or an entry-rank man is across the bottom of the decision tree—a hierarchical, task-oriented network built around a strategic partner other than the boss. This preserves the essential strategic partner, develops the opportunity-oriented contacts so important for men getting promoted early to high-rank positions, and avoids the detrimental effects of building an opportunity-oriented network without a strategic partner. The worst network for women and entry-rank men is the one best for high-ranking men. Women and entry-rank men with entrepreneurial, opportunity-oriented networks were promoted late to their current rank (-2.6 t-test).

The differences between the networks in Figure 4.13 have clear implications for manager promotions, but there are no differences between managers in their tendencies to have one network rather than another. Tests for interaction effects between the eight kinds of networks in Figure 4.13 and the kinds of managers sampled for this study (Figure 4.1) show no significant results. This is especially striking with respect to the sex and rank differences so significant in distinguishing network effects— women are no different from men in the kind of network they have (8.2 chi-square, 7 d.f., $P = .32$), and there are no differences in the kinds of networks observed at the four ranks in the study population (15.5 chi-square, 21 d.f., $P = .80$). In other words, a person's position in the firm is less a cause or consequence of the person's network than it is a context defining the manner in which the network contributes to promotion. Every kind of network can be found among any group of managers.

However, certain kinds of networks contribute to early promotion for certain kinds of managers. The essential message for managers is to build the network that works best for their current position in the firm. The results suggest that either they cannot change their personal preferences and skills to build networks suited to the demands of their jobs, or they are not conscious of what works best for their position in the firm. Otherwise, hierarchical networks built around a strategic partner other than the boss would be more often observed among women and entry-rank men and entrepreneurial, opportunity-oriented networks would be more often observed among high-ranking men.

This shouldn't be taken too far. These are statistical tendencies, not absolutes. A hierarchical network built around a strategic partner offers a particular kind of advantage, and that advantage tends to be one from which women and entry-rank men most often benefit in this study population. However, high-ranking men working to break through a political boundary would also benefit from a hierarchical network. Women or entry-rank men not faced with a political boundary would benefit from an entrepreneurial network.

The point is illustrated in Figure 4.14. Managers appear on the horizontal axis in rank order of their contribution to the evidence that constraint delays promotion. A manager contributes to the evidence if she has a low-constraint network and has been promoted early, or if he has a high-constraint network and has been promoted late.[15] The bold line that snakes through the graph from the lower left to the upper right plots the correlation between constraint and early promotion for a subsample of managers. The subsample at each point on the horizontal axis is the manager at that point plus the ten managers to the left and the ten to the right. Let me describe the two extremes of the graph.

The 21 managers in the subsample at the extreme left of the graph are the people who most conform to the predicted effect of structural holes on promotion. The correlations with early promotion for these managers are $-.83$ for constraint and $-.26$ for hierarchy. For these managers, in other words, hierarchy is just another form of constraint associated with late promotion. As would be expected from the results already presented, these managers are all men. However, there are as many entry-rank men as there are men at the highest rank.

At the extreme right of the graph is the subsample of 21 managers who least conform to the predicted hole effect on promotion. There is a 0.73 correlation between constraint and early promotion for them and a 0.60 correlation between hierarchy and early promotion. For these managers, a hierarchical network around a strategic partner triggers early promotion. Again, as would be expected from the preceding results, these man-

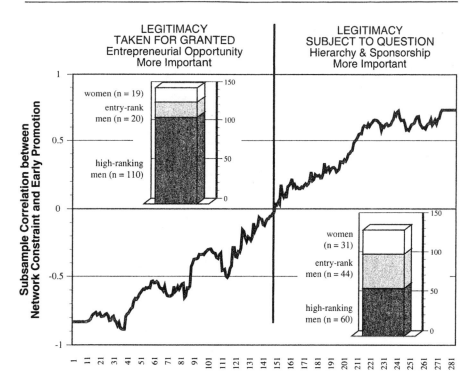

Managers in Rank Order of Their Contributions
to Negative Correlation between Constraint and Early Promotion

Figure 4.14   Identifying managers for whom hierarchy can be an advantage. (Correlations are computed for each subsample of a manager plus 10 managers to the left and 10 to the right of the manager's position in the rank order on the horizontal axis. Bar graphs show the kinds of managers on either side of the vertical line.)

agers are disproportionately women and entry-rank men. Ten of the 21 are women (47%, versus 18% women in the sample of all 284 managers). Another six are entry-rank men. Even at this extreme, however, there are men from higher ranks. The remaining five managers occupy the second and third ranks in the study population.

Between the extreme ends of the graph, managers are ordered by the extent to which they resemble one extreme or the other. For illustration, I have divided managers at the point where the bold line crosses the zero point in the graph. The 149 managers to the left of this point benefit from having an entrepreneurial network—or are disadvantaged by their lack of such a network—as characterized by the above-described men at the extreme left of the graph. The 135 managers to the right of this point benefit from having a hierarchical network—or are disadvantaged by their lack of such a network—as characterized by the above-described men and women at the extreme right of the graph. The contrast between these categories could be discussed as a difference between high- and low-legitimacy managers, but that wording is slightly off target. The legitimacy of the managers at the left of Figure 4.14 is not so much high as it is taken for granted. These managers are accepted as members of the company's top leadership unless there is evidence to the contrary. The reverse characterizes managers on the other side of the graph. They are presumed not to be members of the company's top leadership, unless there is evidence to the contrary. Without evidence, such as an appropriate sponsor's endorsement, their legitimacy as a player suitable for top leadership is open to question.

The bar graphs in Figure 4.14 describe the managers in the two categories. Women are significantly more likely to be in the "legitimacy subject to question" category (2.7 z-score, $P = .004$).[16] Men in the top two ranks of the study population are significantly more likely to be in the "legitimacy taken for granted" category (3.5 z-score, $P < .001$). The more important point is that hierarchy benefits, or the need for hierarchy benefits, are not determined by sex and rank. Sixty men over the entry rank are in the "legitimacy subject to question" category on the right side of Figure 4.14. They are not breaking up through the political boundary around the firm's top leadership, but there are other ways in which their legitimacy could be subject to question. One of them has a background in marketing, for example, but his current position is in engineering. His legitimacy as an manager of engineers is subject to question by the surrounding leadership in engineering. Similarly, not all women or entry-rank men are subject to the legitimacy questions confronting the average woman or entry-rank man. There are 20 entry-rank men and 19 women in the "legitimacy taken for granted" category on the left side of Figure 4.14. On average, women are more likely to be in the category of managers whose legitimacy is subject to question, but 38% of them are in the "legitimacy taken for granted" category. There is no significant tendency for women in either category to be in any particular division of the firm (5.5 chi-square, 6 d.f., $P = .48$), to have been with the firm for a long time (0.4 chi-square, 1 d.f., $P = .51$), to work in a core plant (0.02 chi-square, 1 d.f., $P = .90$), or to have a professional degree (1.5 chi-square, 1 d.f., $P = .23$). Manager attributes are correlated with the manner in which structural holes have their effect. They don't determine the effects. The message is that a network should be selected for its particular advantage—entrepreneurial opportunity or breaking through a political boundary—not for the kind of manager who has in the past most often benefited from its advantage.

Summary

The information and control benefits of structural holes are an advantage to managers, and the managers who develop those benefits are an asset to the firm employing them. The managers described in this chapter operate at the top of one of America's leading high-technology firms. Guided by the argument in Chapter 1, I have traced the speed with which a manager gets promoted to the network structure of the manager's contacts. Five points have been established.

First, managers with networks rich in structural holes tend to be promoted faster, and they tend to reach their current rank earlier (Table 4.2). Distinct processes are confounded in the aggregate evidence. In contrast to the markets in the preceding chapter, in which hole effects are stable over time and across kinds of production activities, structural holes are not equally advantageous to all managers in the same way.

Second, hole effects are most evident for managers operating on a social frontier. A social frontier is any place where two social worlds meet, where people of one kind meet people of another kind. Individuals who live on a social frontier are more likely to live by their entrepreneurial wits than are individuals in socially homogeneous environments. At the frontier, a manager maintains relations with other kinds of people—the people across the frontier. Relations that cross the frontier involve continual negotiation between the expectations of the manager and the expectations in the world across the frontier. Away from the frontier, where people are more homogeneous, contradictory expectations of relations are less frequent. Less entrepreneurial skill is required to survive.

It is not surprising to find that managers on social frontiers show stronger network effects. Hole effects are stronger for managers in remote plant locations than in core locations. The former are more on the periphery of the firm, relatively isolated from the center of social ties in the core locations. Hole effects are stronger for women than for men. Women are a conspicuous minority in this study population, and are therefore conscious of the need to negotiate across the sexual boundary between themselves and the majority population in the firm. Hole effects are stronger for field managers than for production and corporate managers. The former operate on the frontier between customer and producer, between outsider and insider. Hole effects are stronger for recently hired managers. This effect disappears after three or four years with the firm, after the manager has become integrated as a member of the firm. Hole effects are increasingly strong as managers move up the corporate hierarchy, pushing through the political frontier separating top management from lower-level employees who carry out assigned tasks for a wage.

Third, the most serious frontier is the political boundary between top leadership and the rest of the firm. Structural holes affect the early promotions of high-ranking men in a way different from their effect on the early promotions of women and entry-rank men. Men above entry rank in the study population—where "entry" means entry into the firm's top leadership—are best described by the structural hole argument in Chapter 1. It seemed from the comments in the questionnaires that many of the managers in the lower ranks focused only on their immediate job, concentrating on completing assigned tasks on time in a satisfying way. To move up the corporate hierarchy, into the higher ranks of this study population, a manager has to change to a frame of reference that extends well beyond immediate tasks to include initiatives by competitors in other firms and external factors that shape the firm's global markets. Promotions are delayed for managers whose networks remain concentrated in their immediate work group. Higher up the corporate hierarchy, work is increasingly political as well as technical. The high-rank managers have to think and behave more like equity players in the firm rather than getting along as employees working for a wage. Their frontier, in other words, is the boundary between being an employee protected by the firm and a leader responsible for the firm. This is exactly the kind of environment in which the information and control benefits available from structural holes serve to distinguish the leaders from the led. Figure 4.6 shows the increasing extent to which early promotion is associated with structural holes and Figure 4.13 shows that early promotions are most likely for high-ranking men with entrepreneurial, opportunity-oriented networks.

Fourth, on the other side of the political frontier, competition has a more personal flavor. Women and entry-rank men must break into the leadership environment in which the men already described are scrambling for the highest-rank positions. I use the phrase "break into" because women and entry-rank men cannot make it alone. Those who built opportunity-oriented networks rich in structural holes have delayed promotions. This is the single worst network they can have, as illustrated in Figure 4.13. The women and entry-rank men promoted early are those who have a hierarchical network around a strategic partner. The pattern is a strong relation with a strategic partner who is in turn strongly connected with otherwise disconnected contacts in the network. The earliest promotions for women and entry-rank men occur among those with a hierarchical network, built around a strategic partner other than the immediate supervisor, reinforced with extensive socializing within the immediate work group. Components in this sentence are summarized in Figure 4.13. In their own way, hierarchical networks are rich in structural holes. Density is the lowest in these networks. However, the structural holes in these networks are borrowed from the strategic partner. That person's sponsorship determines the effectiveness of the network.

The frontier being crossed by the higher-rank man is his own prior frame of reference. The frontier being crossed by women and entry-rank men, by contrast, is that plus the opinions of the higher-rank men. The company's top leaders do not have time to check into the credibility of everyone making a bid for broader leadership responsibilities. They are looking for quick, high-information cues about whether to treat a new person as a player like themselves or as a wage worker from the other side of the political boundary surrounding top leadership. The strategic partner at the top of a hierarchical network provides the cues, sponsoring the manager as a legitimate player for top leadership.

For the critical sponsorship role of the top contact in a hierarchical network, there are at least three benefits to selecting someone other than the boss as a strategic partner. First, the critical relation with the strategic partner is less at risk of going sour from the inevitable disagreements that arise between people working together. Second, because there is always a boss, the manager gains more control over his or her work; the external sponsor can be leveraged against the boss for negotiating advantage when disagreements do arise. Third, even if negotiating is ignored and the manager has an excellent relationship with the boss, the boss may not be the most convincing sponsor. Supervisors are expected to sponsor their subordinates. Having an external strategic partner means that there are two people in different places who are in a position to sponsor the manager when new opportunities arise.

Fifth, although the reported differences between the manager networks have clear implications for promotions, there are no differences among managers in their tendencies to have one network rather than another. This is especially striking with respect to the sex and rank differences that are observed to be so significant in distinguishing network effects. Nevertheless, women are no different from men in the kinds of networks they have, and there are no differences in the kinds of networks observed at the four ranks in the study population. In other words, a manager's physical or functional position in the firm is less a cause or consequence of the manager's network than it is a context defining the manner in which the network contributes to promotion. Every kind of network can be found among any group of managers, but only certain kinds of networks contribute to early promotion for certain kinds of managers. The frustration for women is that on average they cannot escape the need for a strategic partner—at least within the scope of recent promotions in this firm. Early promotion for women at all ranks is associated with the task-oriented, hierarchical networks needed by entry-rank men to break into top leadership. Entry-rank men must pass through a less frustrating, if more difficult, process. Their promotion to the next higher rank means that they have to shift strategy and build an entrepreneurial network clearly independent of their former strategic partner's network. The task-oriented, hierarchical networks associated with early promotion for entry-rank men are associated with late promotion for higher-rank men.

The message for managers is to build the network that works best for their current position in the firm. The results suggest, however, that in practice either they cannot change their personal preferences and skills to build networks suited to the demands of their jobs or they are not conscious of what works best for their position in the firm. Otherwise, hierarchical networks built around a strategic partner other than the boss would be more often observed among women and entry-rank men, and entrepreneurial, opportunity-oriented networks would be more often observed among high-ranking men. At the same time, a hierarchical network can benefit high-ranking men in this study population and an entrepreneurial network can benefit women or entry-rank men. A network should be selected for its particular advantage—breaking through a political boundary or entrepreneurial opportunity—not for the kind of manager who has in the past most often benefited from its advantage.

Appendix A: Weighing Alternatives

To guide future work, and as an indicator of the stability of the results reported here, it is valuable to know how much is lost with alternative measures of constraint.

EFFECTIVE SIZE, EFFICIENCY, AND CONSTRAINT

The flip side of constraint is effective size. Managers with many nonredundant contacts are rich in structural holes. Across the 284 managers, constraint is correlated − .75 with the number of nonredundant contacts in a network (Eq. 2.2). The intuitive metric of effective network size makes it an attractive alternative for expressing hole effects.

Figure 4.15 shows how effective size increases with cited work contacts (compare Figure 1.5). The manager networks are well below complete efficiency and vary between managers; however, effective size increases with size. The data fall away from the bold line as size increases. The largest networks contain more redundant contacts, more friends of friends, than do small networks. Managers with networks of 15 to 20 people do not have many more nonredundant contacts than do managers with networks of 12 to 14 people (averages of 8 and 7 nonredundant contacts, respectively).

The graphs in Figure 4.16 show how managers with large effective networks get promoted faster and so reach their current rank at younger ages. The managers in the top graph are the same people displayed in Figure 4.5. The managers in the bottom graph are the men displayed in the graphs for the three top-rank positions in Figure 4.6.

Effective network size has positive effects in Figure 4.16, but the effects are weaker than the corresponding negative effects of constraint. The effective-size effect on fast promotion across the managers who have

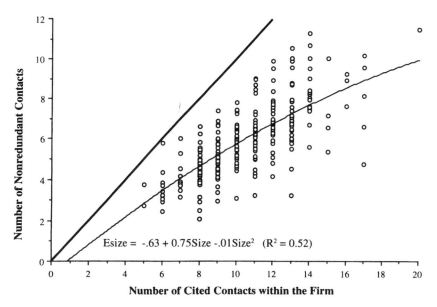

Figure 4.15 Network size, effective size, and efficiency

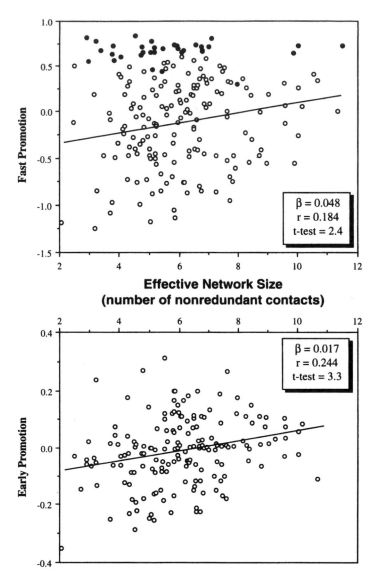

Figure 4.16   Managers with more nonredundant contacts get promoted faster and younger. (The managers in the top graph are the 196 social frontier managers displayed in Figure 4.5, and the bottom graph contains the 170 males over the entry rank, see Figure 4.6.)

been in their current rank for a year or more has a *t*-test of 2.2, which increases slightly to 2.4 for the social frontier managers at the top of Figure 4.16. The corresponding *t*-tests for constraint's effect are -3.7 in Table 4.2 and -4.9 in Figure 4.5. The effective size effect on early promotion across all 284 managers has a negligible 0.8 *t*-test, which increases to the significant 3.3 *t*-test for the men in high-ranking positions at the bottom of Figure 4.16. The corresponding *t*-tests for constraint's effect are -2.5 in Table 4.2 and -5.7 for the men in the top three graphs in Figure 4.6. The stronger evidence of hole effects with constraint means that exclusive access is a quality of relations that spans structural holes between contacts, as discussed in Chapter 2.

CONSTRAINT AND EXCLUSIVE ACCESS

With these results in mind, it is not surprising to see that the alternative constraint measure based on any direct connection between contacts, rather than exclusive access, provides weaker evidence of hole effects. Drawing on laboratory exchange networks and prior studies of the connection between market structure and profit, the proposed constraint measure is based on an assumption that exclusive access to other contacts is necessary for a contact to constrain the central person in a network. The alternative is for constraint to be possible if a contact is merely connected to other contacts.

The choice is between defining constraint in terms of the proportional, p_{qj} in Eqs. (2.4) and (2.7), or marginal, m_{qj} in Eq. (2.5), strength of ties between contacts, as discussed with respect to Figure 2.4. There is no association between the alternative constraint measure and fast promotion (0.6 *t*-test, excluding recent promotions), or early promotion (0.7 *t*-test). These results correspond, respectively, to the -3.7 *t*-test in the third row of Table 4.2 and the -2.5 *t*-test in the first row of the table. Even among frontier and high-rank managers, the evidence of hole effects with the alternative constraint measure is negligible (1.2 *t*-test for fast promotion, 0.9 *t*-test for early promotion).

NONLINEAR HOLE EFFECTS

Table 4.6 contains estimates for the nonlinear effects useful in Chapter 3. To compute natural logs of the promotion variables, I scaled them to vary from 1.0 for the fastest, youngest promotion, down to 0.01 for the slowest, oldest promotion. This scaling has no effect on the correlations presented in the text between promotion and constraint.

The nonlinear effects in Table 4.6 are similar to the linear effects presented in the text. The linear effect on fast promotion is slightly stronger in Table 4.2, but the linear and nonlinear effects on fast promotion among social frontier managers are the same (t-tests of -4.9 and -5.0). The linear and nonlinear effects on early promotion are similar (t-tests of -2.6 for both across all managers, and -5.7 versus -6.0 for men in the highest ranks). Since the nonlinear effects are no stronger than linear effects, I have only discussed the linear effects in the text.

These results do not contradict the results obtained in the markets in Chapter 3. As in the markets, the nonlinear effects in Table 4.6 are negative fractions indicating marginally decreasing effects of constraint as constraint gets more intense. As in the markets, the nonlinear effect of constraint is only slightly stronger than the linear effect. It was the strongly nonlinear effect of market oligopoly that required a nonlinear model to describe the markets. Here I have no data on the secondary structural holes around each manager. Further, the levels of constraint being considered here are higher than the levels observed in the markets. Few managers have an aggregate level of constraint below 0.2, but there are only four markets beyond a 0.2 level of constraint, and the nonlinear effect of constraint in the markets occurs at levels below 0.1 (compare Figure 4.8 with Figure 3.9). At the higher levels of constraint observed among managers, market constraint too has a near-linear effect on profit. My summary conclusion is that the nonlinearity of hole effects is probably as true of the managers as it is of the markets, but the kinds of

Table 4.6 Evidence of nonlinear hole effects

	Intercept	Slope	Correlation	t-test
Fast promotion (excluding recent promotions)				
All managers ($n = 240$)	0.286	$-.523$	$-.164$	-2.56
Social frontier managers ($n = 161$)	0.217	$-.761$	$-.369$	-5.01
Early promotion				
All managers ($n = 284$)	0.332	$-.338$	$-.153$	-2.61
High-ranking men ($n = 170$)	0.173	$-.860$	$-.422$	-6.03

Note: Ordinary least-squares estimates of the coefficients are presented predicting promotions for the 284 respondents from the aggregate level of constraint in their contact networks. The functional form of the model is $P = \alpha C^{\beta}$, which has been estimated as $\log(P) = \log(\alpha) + \beta[\log(C)]$, where P is a promotion variable scaled to vary from .01 to 1 as discussed in the text. The results in the first row correspond to the third row of Table 4.2. The second row corresponds to the results in Figure 4.5. The third row corresponds to the first row of Table 4.2. The fourth row contains the pooled sample of men displayed in the top three graphs in Figure 4.6.

networks in which contraint's effect is nonlinear do not exist among the managers, so I can use the simpler linear functional form to describe effects.

HOW MUCH IS LOST WITH LESS DETAILED NETWORK DATA?
I used network questions similar to the one used in the General Social Survey. I considered simpifying the instrument in three ways. In the absence of evidence on the cost of the simplifications, I adopted none of them. I can now assess that decision.

Table 4.7 contains hole effect t-tests for constraint computed without certain kinds of network data. The strongest effects are obtained when constraint is measured in terms of all available data (first row). However, the consequences of ignoring specific aspects of the data vary, and in a way consistent with the structural hole argument.

Table 4.7   Hole effect evidence with certain network data ignored

	Fast promotion (excluding recent promotions)		Early promotion	
	All managers (n = 240)	Social frontier managers (n = 161)	All managers (n = 284)	High-ranking men (n = 170)
Using all available data	−3.73	−4.90	−2.54	−5.73
Ignoring outsiders	−3.36	−4.28	−2.06	−5.38
Ignoring the strength of the relation to each contact	−3.63	−4.45	−1.98	−5.01
Ignoring the strength of the relation between contacts	−3.19	−4.80	−2.04	−4.65
Ignoring less than especially close relations between contacts	−2.20	−1.41	−0.93	−3.81

Note: Routine t-tests for ordinary least-squares estimates are presented predicting promotions from the aggregate level of constraint. The results in the first row are obtained with constraint measured with all available network data. Aspects of the data are ignored in computing constraint for the other rows as discussed in the text.

The first issue concerns contacts outside the firm. I wanted to know how social relations were coordinated with work relations. Including the important social relations outside the firm in the computation of constraint affects the exclusive access that contacts have with one another. Two contacts might have an exclusive relation within the firm, but be tied to mutual friends outside the firm. Ceteris paribus, it is better to have the data on outsiders than not, but the results in the second row of Table 4.7 are similar to those in the first row, indicating that little evidence of hole effects would have been lost if the sociometric choices had been restricted to relations within the firm.

The second issue concerns the strength of relations with each contact. Respondents were asked to sort their relations into categories of especially close, close, less close, and distant. The results in the third row of Table 4.7 are obtained with these distinctions ignored. All relations with contacts are set to the maximum strength ($z_{ij} = 1$). The evidence of hole effects on fast promotion is not much affected, but the hole effects on early promotion are noticeably weaker. Still, the connection between constraint and early promotion for high-ranking men remains strong (-5.0 t-test). Under severe time pressure to shorten interviews, it would be possible to delete the question on relation closeness and still anticipate strong evidence of hole effects.

The third issue involves a more serious temptation and a more debilitating compromise. It concerns the strength of the relations between contacts. Respondents were asked to sort relations between each pair of contacts into categories of especially close, distant ("in the sense that they are total strangers or do not enjoy one another's company"), and somewhere in-between. This is a time-consuming task, so it is tempting to look for ways to simplify it.

One possibility is to ask respondents only to indicate which pairs of contacts are distant. This option focuses on the most probable structural holes in a network. The results in the fourth row of Table 4.7 show what happens if constraint is measured with distant relations set to 0 and all other relations set to 1. The hole effects are all weaker, but the effects on fast promotion are not much affected and the effects on early promotion are still strong.

The results in the bottom row of the table show what happens if constraint is measured with especially close relations set to 1 and all others set to 0. Hole effects on fast promotion are weaker, the hole effect on early promotion for all managers disappears, and the hole effect on early promotion for high-ranking men is weaker though still significant. The message is clear, and consistent with the structural hole argument. What matters in predicting promotions is not the structure of strong relations between contacts so much as the structure of missing or hostile relations between contacts. The latter more clearly indicate structural holes in the manager's network. It is possible to delete the task of identifying especially close relations, but it is essential to obtain data on distant relations between contacts.

Appendix B: Causal Order

I now have empirical evidence of association between the holes in a manager's network and the timing of his or her promotions relative to similar managers. Managers rich in structural holes get promoted faster and at a younger age. The established association between holes and promotion makes causal order a serious question for future research. Early, fast promotion might be the cause, not the result, of a manager's network. Do the information and control benefits possible in a network give an advantage to a manager? Or, do advantaged managers build networks rich in information and control benefits? If one wishes to disentangle these questions, precise data are needed. The key is to find out how much of the association between structural holes and promotion happens before promotion. I suggest data, argue that promotion causes network structure, and conclude that the evidence in this chapter better fits the structural hole argument.

MORE PRECISE EVIDENCE

The arrows in Figure 4.17 trace a manager from her last promotion, at age a_1, through the survey, to her next promotion, at age a_2, through another observation, to her subsequent promotion at age a_3. The figure puts the data for this study in the context of more precise data. The survey of managers for this study obtained network data, and personnel records defined the date of each manager's last promotion. The network data defined constraint, age at promotion to current rank defined early promotion, and time in current rank defined fast promotion. The p_1 network predicts the t_1 and a_1 promotion times in Figure 4.17, relative to the times for other managers.

There are two problems with the inference. First, I don't know the manager's actual time in rank (t_2). I know how long it has been since his or her last promotion (t_1). The fast promotion variable is correct in tagging slow promotions; managers who have been in their current rank for a long time have been overlooked for promotion. But recently promoted managers could either be on their way up or at the beginning of a long stay at their current rank. My crude control for this was to set aside managers recently promoted (see note 10 and the second point after note 6).

Second, I have to assume that the volume of structural holes in a manager's network is stable over time to presume that constraint in the p_1 network in Figure 4.17 is the constraint that existed before the p_1 promotion. This is not to say that individual contacts continue over time. The people relevant for one project can be completely different for another project. But the social structure the manager fosters in his or her network can be quite stable. A person who only feels comfortable with a small circle of trusted advisors surrounded by weak ties to key people outside the circle, for example, can re-populate the structure with different people for different projects and still maintain a close circle of advisors structure. Network structure depends on the manager's interpersonal skills and preferences, and so endures past the specific contacts with whom the manager has relations at any one point in time. Managers with networks rich in structural holes are unlikely later to build a network bereft of holes, just as a fundamentally conservative person is unlikely suddenly to decide to become a radical liberal. I don't mean to take this too far. Managers can change their preferences and skills if they have to, or if they are trained to. They are not the market producers whose transaction networks are defined by technology—to produce a car, you find a

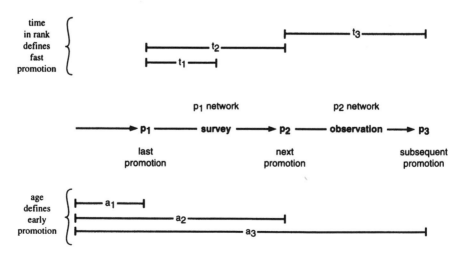

Figure 4.17 More precise evidence

steel supplier, rubber supplier, glass supplier, and so on. The stability of network structure remains an empirical question to which the answer varies from population to population by the extent to which interpersonal relations are embedded in institutional and normative structures that make it more or less difficult for individuals to adapt existing relations to their personal style.

A more precise inference could be made if I knew the date of each manager's next promotion. I would then know the full time in rank (t_2) and age at promotion (a_2). The network constraint variable is defined prior to the p_2 promotion and so couldn't have been caused by the promotion. This is a more practical research design than it might seem. Several managers have been been at their current rank for nearly a decade, and it might be a long wait for their next promotion, but I already know that their promotions are slow. I need to know who among the recently promoted managers gets promoted. The average manager has been in the same rank for 2.8 years. If I return to the study firm in four years, many of the managers will have been promoted to the next rank. Those who haven't I know are slow in getting promoted.

Still more precise inferences can be made if I observe the manager's network again about a year after the next promotion (a year seems proper to allow settling in; see note 10) and know the date of the subsequent promotion. I then have two times in rank (t_2 and t_3), age at two promotions (a_2 and a_3), and network constraint defined before both promotions. Further, I have data on the manager's network before and after a promotion. With this I can study the effects of promotion on the network.

CONSOLIDATION ARGUMENT: PROMOTION CREATES HOLES

For the sake of argument, suppose that managers can freely change both the people and the structure of their networks. The manager accustomed to the freedom of a large network of disconnected contacts, for example, might change the way he builds relations in favor of the security of a small network of closely interconnected contacts. The correlations I have presented as evidence of hole effects could now just as well be cited as evidence for an argument in which causation runs in the opposite direction. Instead of structural holes increasing the chances of early promotion, early promotion increases the likelihood of structural holes in a manager's network. It is useful to consider the evidence of this chapter in light of the counterargument to see if the evidence contradicts it, and so further supports the structural hole argument.

Time in rank is the link in my evidence most open to the reversed causation, so I'll begin there. I have shown that structural holes are associated with fast promotion where fast is measured by time in rank. But a network will change with time in rank in a way that will produce the ostensible hole effect. Managers bump into the same people from day to day. The longer they stay in the same position, the more often they'll bump into the same people. In a short time, it is rude not to say hello. Friendships develop. Friends of friends are introduced. Redundancy increases. Time in rank should increase density, and density is correlated with constraint, so time in rank should be negatively correlated with constraint, as reported in the text.

This can be termed a consolidation argument, to distinguish it from the structural hole argument. The structural hole argument is that the information and control benefits of structural holes let a manager derive higher rewards from work, early and fast promotion being illustrative rewards. The consolidation argument is the entrepreneur's nightmare— time heals all holes. Through the natural process of the accumulation of redundant ties in the networks of people who spend time in the same place with the same people, the density of ties in a manager's network should increase with the time he or she spends at the same rank (see note 4 in Chapter 1 for supporting references).

EVIDENCE FOR THE CONSOLIDATION ARGUMENT

Three results can be taken as support for this argument. First, task-oriented networks occur among the recently promoted. Managers of all kinds begin with a task-oriented network (Figure 4.12). Their networks are largely composed of contacts relevant to their immediate work group, and they socialize extensively within the group. During the first year, networks become less task-oriented, moving toward the mixed form presumably as friends of friends are added beyond the immediate work group (illustrated by the vertical drop in the dashed line from the white dots in Figure 4.12). In short, networks gradually expand from the manager's immediate work group.

Second, constraint is associated with slow promotion. Constraint increases with time in rank for managers whose networks span one or more social frontiers (-4.3 t-test). The association for insider managers is negligible (though also negative, -0.9 t-test). This fits the consolidation hypothesis. Managers whose networks span frontiers are building ties between otherwise disconnected people on opposite sides of the frontiers they span. The number of ties built increases with the time they spend in the same rank.

Third, constraint is associated with late promotion. Managers who were older at their most recent promotion tend to have fewer structural holes in their networks. With consolidation over time, older managers should have denser networks. From the 1985 General Social Survey of a national probability sample of 1,534 Americans, for example, age is strongly associated with network density (6.2 t-test, $n = 1,165, P < .001$). Speaking directly to the structural hole argument, the number of stranger relations between cited contacts is negatively associated with age (-4.9 t-test). The association between age and density is weaker for respondents who have graduated from college and are in the 27-to-64 age range, corresponding to the managers in this study population, but it is still clearly positive (2.5 t-test, $n = 402, P = .01$). Regardless of when they were last promoted, older managers should have fewer structural holes in their networks. The results in the chapter show that constraint increases with the age at which high-ranking men were promoted to their current rank.

A CLOSER LOOK AT THE EVIDENCE

On closer inspection, these points of evidence do not support the consolidation hypothesis. First, the task-oriented evidence goes sour when extended to opportunity networks. If constraint is negatively associated with fast promotion because managers gradually expand their contacts beyond the immediate work group, then managers should progress from a task-oriented to an opportunity-oriented network. But they do not. As discussed with respect to Figure 4.12, they definitely move to less task-oriented networks, but they do not move to the next step of developing opportunity-oriented networks—and constraint is only significantly decreased in the latter kind of network. This result fits the structural hole argument perfectly well in the sense that the holes in a manager's network reflect the manager's preferences and skills in maintaining a network, not the few years spent at his or her current rank.

Second, the evidence on constraint and fast promotion goes sour when constraint is broken into size and density components. If the reason for the negative association between constraint and time in rank among frontier managers is the increasing ties they are building among contacts on opposite sides of the frontiers, then the number of contacts in their networks should be expanding with time, and the average strength of relations between contacts should also be expanding. Just the opposite occurs. Recently promoted frontier managers have larger and slightly denser networks. Across the frontier managers, time in rank is negatively correlated with the number of contacts they cite (-3.8 t-test, two-tail $P < .001$), negatively correlated with the strength of relations between the contacts they cite (-2.5 t-test), and negatively, if weakly, correlated with the proportion of their contacts who are not distant from one another (-1.9 t-test, two-tail P of .06). This is consistent with the observed dense, task-oriented networks in the first years after promotion. The number of contacts cited by frontier managers decreases more quickly than density, which is why constraint is positively correlated with time in rank.[17] Again, this result fits the structural hole argument perfectly well in the sense that the holes in a manager's network reflect the manager's preferences and skills, and those with large networks rich in structural holes tend to be among the people new to their current rank because they are quickly promoted from rank to rank.

Further, the consolidation hypothesis should play out in real time. Each day on the job presents opportunities to consolidate relations between contacts. However, the association between constraint and time on the job is negligible if time is measured in calender years (-0.1 t-test). It is only significant with respect to the relative time a manager has been at his or her current rank (t-tests of -2.8 and -3.7 in Table 4.2, and -4.4 in Table 4.3 for the fast promotion variable). This too is consistent with the structural hole argument, because rates of return are the outcome of structural holes, not absolute levels of return. The argument is that holding constant differences in human capital, the person rich in structural holes will reap higher rewards from his or her network. The argument doesn't explain why field managers as a group get promoted faster than production managers, for example, or why medical doctors earn higher salaries than Ph.D.s, or why producers in one market have a higher volume of sales than other markets. It predicts that field managers with networks rich in structural holes will be promoted faster than other field managers, that medical doctors with networks rich in structural holes will earn incomes higher than other medical doctors, and that producers with transactions rich in structural holes will earn higher profit margins than other producers.

Third, related problems exist with the attempt to reinterpret constraint's association with early promotion. The first point is that the association between age and density doesn't extend to an association between age and structural holes, so the premise for the reinterpretation disappears. Above I reported the positive association between age and density in the General Social Survey results for Americans generally and for college graduates in the general age range of the study population managers. I also reported that the number of total stranger pairs of contacts decreases with age. However, this is only true if the elderly and persons with less than a college education are included in the correlation. For college-educated persons between the ages of 27 and 64—respondents more similar to the manager study population—the tendency is negligible (-0.6 t-test, $P = .55$). The association is also negligible across the managers interviewed for this study. There is no association between age and density across all 284 managers (-0.3 t-test) and no tendency for older managers to name fewer contacts (-0.4 t-test). Across high-ranking men, the managers providing the strong evidence of association between constraint and late promotion, there is a tendency for number of cited contacts to decline with age (-2.3 t-test), but there is no association with density (0.3 t-test).

Further, there is the issue of different kinds of managers relying on structural holes in different ways. Constraint and promotion age are negatively correlated for high-ranking men, but positively correlated for women and entry-rank men. If the correlation between constraint and promotion age were a result of density increasing with age through ties developing between previously disconnected contacts, then evidence of the process would be found among all managers or among certain managers especially prone to the process. There would be no reason for it to be reversed for women and entry-rank managers. Indeed, one could argue that the tendency toward denser networks should be especially strong for women and entry-rank managers, because their positions are less secure in the firm's top leadership. However, the results make perfect sense as evidence of structural holes. High-ranking men are members of the firm's top leadership. What distinguishes their early promotions is the information and control benefits their networks provide, as indicated by structural holes. Women and entry-rank men are working their way into the firm's top leadership. What distinguishes their early promotions is that they have structural holes borrowed from a strategic partner who can sponsor them at the top of the firm.

CORROBORATING EVIDENCE

Finally, there are the results from Chapter 3 to consider. The consolidation hypothesis is intuitively appealing in Chapter 4 because the networks being analyzed involve discretionary relations. The managers have considerable choice in selecting contacts, certainly in selecting whether to have a hierarchical network built around a strategic partner and kinds of contacts to be close friends in the network. It is natural to ask whether their selection was a causal factor determining their promotions or whether their promotions determined their selection. I have argued that the former seems to be the case. The question is less pertinent to the market results. The networks are defined by census data on the American economy and producers have less discretion in selecting the supplier and consumer markets in which they do business. That selection is determined for them by the kind of production technology from which they hope to turn a profit. Accordingly, few would argue that profit determines the structure of transactions in a producer market in any but the most abstract, long-term sense. The virtue of combining the evidence of hole effects for production markets with evidence of hole effects for the managers is to show that the same process seems to be operating. The structural holes that give a producer advantage in negotiating transaction price give a manager advantage in negotiating his or her work. The first leads to high profit margins, the second leads to early, fast promotions. The more obvious causal direction of effects in the case of markets lends further credibility to the causal direction of effects in the less obvious case of the managers.

Still, promotion and structural holes must reinforce one another. A manager who benefits from a structural hole can see the virtue of expanding the benefits they provide. Managers who never benefit from a structural hole might never feel the same impulse. Chickens develop from eggs, but lay the eggs of future chickens. Structural holes create advantage, but living through the advantage reinforces the impulse to build a network richer in holes for future advantage. The research questions posed by Figure 4.17 remain interesting ones.

5

Player-Structure Duality

The results in Chapters 3 and 4—examples of players' success in two very different settings—bear out the central conclusion. Structural holes are a competitive advantage. I now return to the structural hole argument to explore a broader range of hypotheses. Some illustrative data will be presented, but the emphasis is on integrating lines of work rather than on establishing empirical validity.

One of the simplifying steps I took in presenting the main argument was to ignore the complex connection between player and structure. Here I examine the connection between player and structure to show, among other things, how the structural hole argument cuts across micro-macro distinctions. I will continue to alternate between people as players and organizations as players to illustrate how structural holes are a conceptual bridge between micro and macro levels of analysis. This brief chapter provides a transition to the next two.

Structural Unit of Analysis

The causal force of structural holes is twice invisible. First, holes are invisible relations of nonredundancy, relations visible only by their absence. Second, holes don't connect the players we see. They connect invisible pieces of players. The causal force of structural holes resides in the pattern of relationships that intersect in a player's network. The intersection happens in players, but where it occurs is distinct from the causal force released by its occurrence. People and organizations are not so much the source of action as the vehicles for structurally induced action.

Micro and macro levels of analysis distinguish kinds of players in which relations intersect. Macro levels exist relative to the micro levels they contain; world systems containing nation states, markets containing organizations, organizations containing people, and so on. The distinction usually rests on the physical or legal boundaries around a unit of analysis. The boundaries indicate, for example, where a micro unit ends within the macro unit that contains it. The micro-macro distinction is significant when causal processes vary across the boundaries; organization behavior, for example, differs from the intended behavior of individuals within the organization. The boundaries around people and organizations are reliably defined for empirical research and easily communicated. Structural units of analysis cut across these boundaries.

STRUCTURAL UNITS IN A PERSON

The network elements for studying structural holes at a micro level are role behaviors coordinated within and across roles by a person. Consider the dark gray circle in Figure 1.9. You are one of the black dots in the dark gray circle, but the dot isn't all of you. It is a piece. Specifically, it is a piece of you that is redundant with structurally similar pieces of other people. One such piece is your role as a teacher, in which your network contains students, colleagues, and university administrators. The other black dots at the center of the network would be the other professors connected to the same clusters of students, colleagues, and administrators. The distribution of holes in this network defines the structural autonomy you have to determine how and what you teach. Another piece of you is your role as a scholar, in which your network contains colleagues in disciplines related to your work and contacts in foundations, government agencies, publishing, and so on. The other black dots at the center of the network would be scholars who produce similar work and so are connected to the same clusters of contacts. The distribution of holes in this network defines your structural autonomy to determine the content and distribution of your scholarly work. Still another piece of you is your domestic role. This involves another network, one composed of parents, spouse, children, and extended family. The distribution of holes in this network defines your structural autonomy to negotiate domestic relations. As a physical entity, you are an amalgam of these structural pieces as the roles you play. But structural autonomy exists for each piece of you defined by a network of others concerned with that piece.

This is the setting for the analysis in Chapter 4. I described the effects of structural holes in the network associated with a person's job. At a higher level of aggregation, structural autonomy could have been defined for the network of relations associated with a functional division, in the sense that officers in the same function stand in common relation to other divisions of the firm. Finance, for example, could have more autonomy within the firm than manufacturing. At a lower level of aggregation, jobs could have been subdivided into project networks. A respondent in the study pointed out that an active manager has several contact networks, one for each of many projects. The manager's negotiated control over a specific project is defined by the contact network for that project. A manager can be constrained in one project and autonomous in another. Still, the overlap between project networks is such that constraint in the network across projects significantly affects promotion, as illustrated in Chapter 4.

Figure 5.1 illustrates a broader disaggregation. The manager appears in domestic, work, community, and leisure roles. In the domestic sphere, he plays the role of father to his children, son to his parents, spouse to his wife. That million dollar fixer-upper house in the valley led to his becoming an accomplished carpenter in his spare time. At work, he plays a supervisory role in the corporate hierarchy, manages a new product release, and leads the team reorganizing distribution channels. In the community, he plays an active role in the church and was key in a petition drive against the chemical plant dumping waste into the stream behind his house. His leisure activities involve windsurfing and old movies.

In each role, the manager is a player in a market defined by a network of contacts related to the role. His carpenter role is a network of kindred neighbors and persons at the local hardware stores and lumber yards. His work roles are networks of the contacts described in Chapter 4 as well as project-specific contacts. His role at church is a network of other members of the church plus people in community organizations and

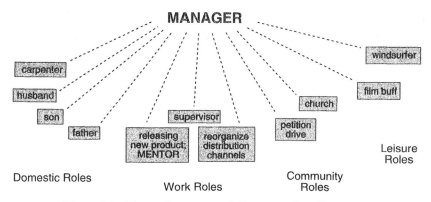

Figure 5.1   Illustrative structural disaggregation of a person

higher in the church. His role as windsurfer is a network with other windsurfers and merchants who sell windsurfing equipment.

His structural autonomy within each role is defined by the distribution of structural holes around the relationships defining each role. He could have low autonomy in his domestic roles at the same time that he has considerable negotiating room in his supervisory role at work; and he could also have low autonomy in his responsibility for the new product release, but high autonomy in his role as an expert windsurfer. Structural autonomy is not defined for the manager as a physical person. It is defined for him as a structural piece in the market at the center of the network associated with each role he plays.[1]

STRUCTURAL UNITS IN AN ORGANIZATION

Organizations are similarly disaggregated into structural units. Organizations do not enter the analysis in their entirety. Pieces of them enter as redundant organizational units. I have focused on the bedrock economic network of buying and selling. The circles in Figure 1.9 are markets and the black dots within each are redundant organizations, redundant in the sense that they are similarly positioned in economic production. The four dots in the market represented by dark gray circle at the center of the Figure 1.9 network are redundant in the sense of purchasing supplies from clusters A, E, and F and selling their products to clusters B, C, and D. Redundancy as substitutability fits neatly here. Input-output tables describe the buying and selling between clusters of redundant organizations, termed establishments. An establishment is a piece of a firm in one geographic area, producing a specific commodity. Two establishments are substitutable, and so operate in the same market, to the extent that they use similar proportions of kinds of supplies to make the product they sell. A market (or economic sector, or industry) is a cluster of substitutable establishments. This point is developed in Chapter 3 in the analysis of substitutable production markets in the topology of the American economy (Figure 3.2).

The structural disaggregation of a firm into structural pieces is illustrated in Figure 5.2 for a hypothetical firm known for its scientific and controlling instruments. The instruments market involves business with all other markets in the figure. The firm is a corporate hierarchy of ownership ties imposed on a network of market transactions. The firm operates four establishments in the Midwest that manufacture scientific and controlling instruments. The firm is vertically integrated backward and forward in the production chain through the instruments market. With vertical integration, some key market transactions for the four instruments establishments are brought into the firm. The firm has a plant in Georgia that produces a line of electrical industrial machines built around the firm's controlling instruments. It has a plant in Colorado that produces critical electronic components for the firm's instruments. The firm owns establishments in California and North Carolina that distribute its products.

The firm's structural autonomy in each of its markets is defined by the distribution of structural holes around the transactions defining each market. The firm's electronic components plant may have high autonomy while its establishments in electrical industrial machines have low autonomy. Structural autonomy isn't defined for the firm as a legal entity. It is defined for each of the firm's establishments as a structural piece of the firm at the center of a market network.

Players and Structures

Micro and macro structural units of analysis are identical in this argument. They have the same boundaries defined by an intersection of relationships. They are similarly the site for structural holes generating opportunity. The intersection is known by various names: as a role, a market, or a position in the social structure. The players in which relations intersect are any physical and legal entities: a person, an organization, or a broader aggregation of physical and legal entities. Where the

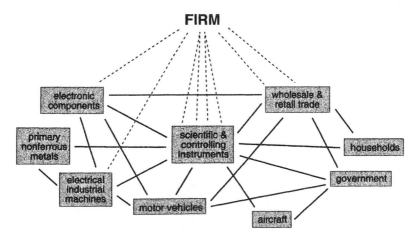

Figure 5.2 Illustrative structural disaggregation of a firm. (Dashed lines are ownership ties. Solid lines are market transactions.)

intersection occurs is irrelevant. Causation resides in the intersection of relations. Structural holes are the quality of intersecting relations here argued to cause behavior. The distribution of structural holes around the relations that intersect in a person or an organization determines the player's entrepreneurial opportunities, and so the player's competitive advantage. Structural holes create inequality between organizations as they create inequality between people. There is a pleasing unity across micro to macro levels of analysis.

It might seem that I am not cutting across the micro-macro distinction so much as narrowing it to a specific setting, macro players and micro relations. Players are macro sites that contain intersecting relations as micro elements.

The connection between player and structure is more like a symmetric duality than asymmetric levels. A player is at once a physical and legal entity and an amalgam of social structural units. The match between player and structural units is one of overlap rather than identity. Any intersection of relations is only one of many in which a player is involved. This is a point illustrated with Figures 5.1 and 5.2. At the same time, a player involved in an intersection of relations is only one of many other individuals involved in the same kind of intersection. This is the point illustrated with Figure 1.9. Across the competitive arena, each player is the site for one or more structural units of analysis, and each structural unit occurs in one or more players. A person plays many roles other than manager, and many other people play the manager role.

Escape from Attributes

A more significant point is visible through the clarified connection between player and structure. The micro-macro distinction between kinds of players is an example of the broader use of player attributes for social science explanation. The micro-macro example is benign compared with others. The qualities that free the structural hole argument from the micro-macro distinction in particular also free it more generally from the debilitating alternative of using attributes as an ersatz explanatory base.

Consider a person with income and education. The person might enjoy a high income for someone with her education. Or she might have a low income for someone with her education. Income returns to education vary across individuals. The variation can be explained in two ways.

By the structual hole argument, income returns to education depend on access to structural holes. Persons rich in entrepreneurial opportunity have higher income returns to education. Specifically, people who are the site where an important class of relationships intersects to create structural holes have opportunities to get higher income returns to education.

By another argument, the explanation may be not the intersecting relationships but, rather, the site of their intersection. The person in whom relations interact has certain attributes. The attributes can be physical qualities, or socially assigned labels, or legal labels, but they are all player attributes, because they describe the player in which relations intersect rather than the intersecting relations. At the beginning of Chapter 4, I discussed research showing that managers enjoy higher income returns to education than do workers. I described the work as an illustration of hole effects. Managers have more structural autonomy than workers, so managers should have higher rates of return to education. I followed that interpretation with empirical research showing how rates of return vary across managers with differences in relative autonomy. Still, there are manager career tracks such that anyone can get a higher income return to education if he can just acquire the role label of manager.

There will be empirical support for the attribute explanation even if the outcome is structurally induced. Consider the illustration in Figure 5.3. Intersecting relations define a position in the social structure. The form of those intersecting relations generates an outcome for the players occupying the position. For example, greater access to structural holes generates higher income returns to education. The positions that players oc-

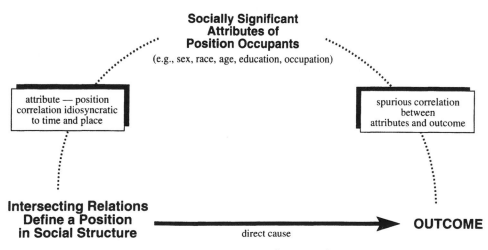

Figure 5.3 Social structure, attributes, and outcomes

cupy are often correlated with player attributes: age, sex, race, and so on. Some positions contain a high proportion of young, highly educated females, others contain a high proportion of old, poorly educated males. Until recent years in Europe and the United States, for example, mature white males tended to occupy the positions of greatest structural autonomy. The correlation between attributes and position in social structure creates a correlation between attributes and the structurally generated outcome. The correlation is spurious. It would disappear if the social structural condition responsible for the outcome were held constant. Without structure held constant, the correlation is empirical support for an attribute explanation of the outcome.

The three-way association in Figure 5.3 is a familiar part of everyday life. We use that familiarity to interpret what people with specific attributes are likely to do and say. The map between attributes and social structure is an ethnomethodological calculus for understanding social life. One person has the attributes of someone it would be dangerous to meet in a dark subway entrance. Another person has the attributes of someone it would be fun to meet in the dark. More, we like to personalize competition with the attributes of combatants. The abstract concept seems to gain substance when understood as a contest in which certain kinds of people or kinds of organizations have an advantage. The classic American hero is a strong, solitary figure, confident in his or her abilities, who overcomes hardships, gets the job done, is able to solve others' problems when they need help: a steely-eyed tower of strength staring hard at the horizon's possibilities. Here are the Clint Eastwoods of the cinema, the Ludlum protagonist of popular fiction. Here are the Charles Lindberghs, the Amelia Earharts, of recent history.

This colloquial understanding is the substance of prejudice and the seedbed for social science. In the early stages of work on a phenomenon, attributes are often used to describe variation. Attributes are easy to see and familiar to everyone in the audience. The ostensible effects of attributes are therefore easy to communicate. In sociology, income differences are often correlated with age, sex, race, and education to assess how much these attributes contribute to income differences. In anthropology, initial fieldwork on a society depends on attributes to describe it: sex, costume, age, wealth, and so on.

As in everyday life, when attributes are used as causal variables in social science, they are typically used as a surrogate for social structural data. Sociologists don't search for sex differences to attribute the differences to biology. Where sex differences are detected, they are used to identify kinds of positions to which women have been assigned in a male-oriented society.

It is easy to forget the causal importance of relations. Status-defining attributes are more easily detected and communicated. Without direct measures of structural qualities, social science explanation often relies on the inferior, but available, attributes. Linton (1936:257–258) cautioned against this problem when he made the distinction between role and status. The results described above comparing workers and managers can be seen repeated in comparisons of men and women, blacks and whites, and many others. Measurement is ordinal and based on attributes as summary colloquial codes representing patterns of relations. The exact mechanism by which the intersection of relations associated with the attributes creates unequal returns to education is obscured from direct inspection.

This inelegance becomes a problem when attempts are made to generalize attribute explanations across study populations or over time. The problem is that the connection between attributes and social structure changes across populations and over time. How frequently the connection changes and how much it changes is an empirical question. The point is that the connection isn't causal. It is a correlation, as in Figure 5.3, idiosyncratic to when and where observations are recorded for analysis.

In a cross-sectional analysis, rates of return will vary across people with similar attributes as a function of their position in social structure. For example, the manager of a disorganized work force could play his subordinates off against one another, thus exploiting his work relations with them to his own advantage. The manager of a well-organized work force would be less able to do this; in fact, he could be dominated by the interests of the workers he ostensibly manages. The second manager has less autonomy than the first. Though both have authority over subordinates, the first can exercise that authority to suit his own interests. Returns to education for the first manager will be higher.

Over time, rates of return associated with an attribute will vary as a function of the attribute's distribution across positions in social structure. Research results on the attributes associated with inequality are journalistic descriptions of a study population at a moment in time. They only generalize to other populations or other moments in time when the same correlation occurs between attributes and social structure. For example, sex differences in income between American men and women must have been greater at the turn of the century than now, because firms are now constrained to employ men and women as comparable workers. Then, women could be assigned to low-autonomy positions despite their work qualifications. Comparing the incomes of men and women is a statement of fact for a specific population at a specific moment. But the structural conditions creating job autonomy, and so higher income, have their effect now as in the past. Explaining the income-gender difference over time is a matter of explaining how women entered the high-autonomy jobs earlier reserved for men.

The escape from attributes requires conceptual and research tools to look past the player attributes associated with significant structural forms to see the forms themselves. The result is stronger, more cumulative theory and research. The structural hole argument is illustrative. Relations that intersect to create structural holes give a player entrepreneurial opportunities to get higher rates of return. The kinds of players in whom the relations intersect is an empirical curiosity irrelevant to the explanation. Competition is not about being a player with certain physical attributes; it is about securing productive relationships. Physical attributes are a correlate, not a cause, of competitive success. Holes can have different effects for people with different attributes or for organizations of different kinds, but that is because the attributes and organization forms are correlated with different positions in the social structure. The manner in which a structural hole is an entrepreneurial opportunity for information and control benefits is the bedrock explanation that carries across player attributes, populations, and time.[2]

No Escape

Two arguments can be cited in response. One is to say that the attributes of the player where relations intersect affect the player's response. In its crudest form, this position holds that people with certain racial or gender or other physical attributes respond differently than other people to an entrepreneurial opportunity. A more palatable form is to argue that people with certain beliefs respond differently. The psychological and cultural explanations of entrepreneurial behavior cited in Chapter 1 are an example. These beliefs in player attributes as a causal force are typically advanced without benefit of thinking or data about the pattern of relations in which the player is involved. In Chapter 1, I described how the motivation to be an entrepreneur is in large part recovered by knowing the extent to which a player is involved in a network rich in entrepreneurial opportunity. I put it to you: If someone argues that race, sex, age, education, or some other player attribute causes an outcome, examine their explanation of how the attribute has its effect. Thinking back to Figure 5.3, how much of the explanation is intrinsic to the attribute as opposed to a structure of intersecting relations in place when the attribute acquired its ostensible causal force? To what extent is race a cause apart from the structure of relations associated with a particular race? To what extent is gender a cause apart from the structure of relations in which women perform? To what extent is education a cause apart from the structure of relations with which it is correlated? Putting aside obvious physical shortcomings—a man can't bear children, for example, regardless of his position in the social structure—you will find behind a successful attribute explanation an implicit statement about the manner in which players are or were involved in relationships.

A more sophisticated argument is to say that attributes are important if other people act as though they are. Even if attributes have no part in the structural processes generating outcomes, they are significant if other people respond to them so as to distort structural processes. This response is compellingly articulated by DiMaggio (1992). The women in Chapter 4 are an illustration in two ways. On the surface, women have better promotion chances than men. They are significantly younger than men promoted to the same manager rank in the same divisions. Under the surface, the process by which women get promoted early is different. Structural holes enhance the promotion chances of high-ranking men, but a woman who builds an opportunity-oriented network rich in structural holes can expect promotion delays. She only moves ahead when teamed with a strategic partner at the top of a hierarchical contact network. Access to structural holes is still an advantage, but she has to get to them through a strategic partner.

This only serves to illustrate the escape from attributes. Attributes aren't ruled out as a useful guide for discovering structural processes. They are ruled out as an explanation. I make extensive use of manager attributes to detect significant structural conditions in Chapter 4, but the attributes aren't in the final explanation. Given the observed difference between men and women in the Chapter 4 study population, I looked for kinds of men with hole effects similar to those observed for women. The similar men were in entry-rank positions. This led to the idea that both kinds of managers were breaking through a political boundary and would benefit from a strategic partner on the other side to help them break through. That led to the discovery of the hierarchy effects and institutional holes. That discovery was turned around in Figure 4.15 to define a manager breaking through a political boundary as anyone for whom the constraint of a hierarchical network can be beneficial. Such managers tended to be women and entry-rank men, but all women and entry-rank men do not fall into the category and some high-ranking men do. A high-ranking man moving from the sales division to the manufacturing division, for example, benefits from a strategic partner in manufacturing to sponsor him to key players in manufacturing. Managers aren't distinguished by sex or rank in the summary results presented in Figure 2.9. Rather, the structural autonomy model measures the advantages of structural holes for anyone, with an adjustment for the advantages of incurring some constraint from a strategic partner when breaking through a political boundary. In a different study population, or the same study population observed at a different time, the persons breaking through the political boundary can be different—blacks moving up to positions traditionally held by whites, whites moving up to positions traditionally held by Asians, young people moving up to positions traditionally held by older people. The final conclusion in Chapter 4 is relevant here. The network a manager decides to build should be chosen for its particular advantage, not for the kind of manager who has most often benefited in the past from its advantage.

Summary

The unit of analysis in which structural holes have their causal effect is the same at a macro or micro level of analysis. It is the network of relations that intersect in a player. The intersection is known by various names: as a role, a market, or a position in social structure. The players in which relations intersect are any physical and legal entities: a person, an organization, or a broader aggregation of physical and legal entities. Where the intersection occurs is irrelevant. Causation resides in the intersection of relations. Structural holes are the quality of intersecting relations here argued to cause behavior. The distribution of structural holes around the relations that intersect in a person or organization determine the player's entrepreneurial opportunities, and so the player's competitive advantage. Structural holes create inequality between organizations as they create inequality between people.

The connection between player and structure is more like a symmetric duality than asymmetric levels. A player is at once a physical and legal entity and an amalgam of social structural units. The match between player and structural units is one of overlap rather than identity. Any intersection of relations is only one of many in which a player is involved.

This is a point illustrated with Figures 5.1 and 5.2. At the same time, a player involved in an intersection of relations is only one of many other individuals involved in the same kind of intersection. This is the point illustrated with Figure 1.9. Across the competitive arena, each player is the site for one or more structural units of analysis, and each structural unit occurs in one or more players. A person plays many roles other than manager, and many other people play the manager role.

A more significant point is visible with the clarified connection between player and structure. The micro-macro distinction between kinds of players is an example of the broader use of player attributes for social science explanation. The micro-macro example is relatively benign. The qualities that free the structural hole argument from the micro-macro distinction in particular also free it more generally from the debilitating alternative of using attributes as an ersatz explanatory base.

The escape from attributes requires conceptual and research tools to look past the player attributes associated with significant structural forms to see the forms themselves. The result is stronger, more cumulative theory and research. The structural hole argument is illustrative. Relations that intersect to create structural holes give a player entrepreneurial opportunities to get higher rates of return. The kinds of players in whom the relations intersect is an empirical curiosity irrelevant to the explanation. Holes can have different effects for people with different attributes or for organizations of different kinds, but different effects occur because the attributes and organization forms are correlated with different positions in social structure. The manner in which a structural hole is an entrepreneurial opportunity for information and control benefits is the bedrock explanation that carries across player attributes, populations, and time. The task for the analyst is to cut past the spurious correlation between attributes and outcomes to reach the underlying social structural factors that cause the outcome. It is this escape from attributes, in the definition of structural holes and in the causal processes of hole hypotheses, that makes the structural hole argument a powerful conceptual bridge across micro and macro levels of analysis.

Motivation for the micro-macro bridge is threefold. First, there is intellectual satisfaction in a single explanation that transcends levels of analysis. Also, there are advantages of more accurate and generalizable theory associated with the escape from attributes. Third, there is the value added to research at both levels of analysis if precise comparisons can be made between results at each level. People and organizations have complementary strengths and weaknesses as research sites. The virtues of studying organizations include the more reliable and more available data on them. Moreover, motivational variables are less of an issue and there is a relatively clear distinction between constraint-generating market relations and embedding corporate ties. These strengths are the qualities most problematic in studying people. Selecting the right wording for a question that seeks to elicit network relations from respondents is always open to debate, because it is so difficult to distinguish kinds of relations from one another. Motivational controls are more an issue, and what is a constraint-generating relation in one context can be a discretionary embedding tie in another context.

The reliability of organizational data comes at a cost. Market relations are strongly determined by production technologies. To make a specific product, certain supplies are needed and certain kinds of customers buy the product. People are more varied, both in the structure of their roles and in the mutability of role relations. But the broader diversity of structural conditions they bring to the analyst comes at the cost of greater difficulty in measuring interpersonal relations. Theory that spans the distinction between micro and macro levels of analysis can be used to generalize the necessarily limited research results available from either level of analysis.

6

Commit and Survive

The central idea in this chapter is that the information and control benefits of structural holes responsible for higher rates of return also free players to try diverse ways to get those higher rates of return. I derive hypotheses about player heterogeneity and survival within markets, then ground the hypotheses in market interface and population ecology arguments. In prior chapters, I have described how structural holes are responsible for different rates of return in different markets. In this chapter, I describe how structural holes are responsible for heterogeneity and survival within markets and how they can be used to integrate arguments in two of contemporary sociology's significant contributions to understanding market competition.

Holes and Heterogeneity

The control benefits of structural autonomy are both an opportunity and an assurance. Autonomous players can worry less about being forced out of their roles. Their greater control over the relations defining their roles means they are freer to explore alternative ways of performing the relations. People can be less concerned about getting the role "right." Firms can be less nervous about reorganizing to try alternative organization forms. With inertia working against change and the energy it demands, structural autonomy will increase the time that specific behaviors and players survive in their roles. Firms can continue past practices without worrying about the behavior optimum for their market. With an eye to the rigidity of personal styles and organization forms once adopted, the prediction can be stated in another way—a greater variety of role performances will be accepted as adequate performances of a high-autonomy role and a greater variety of organization forms will survive in a high-autonomy market.

There is more to these hypotheses than a quantitative extension of time. There is a qualitative shift in the meaning of time. Spending a long time in certain roles is a result of competitive failure. The managers in Chapter 4 are an illustration. Time in other roles is a result of successful competition.

Consider the illustration in Figure 6.1. The horizontal axis is time in a role. The vertical axis is the achievement represented by time in the role. Entry is a time for celebration—a person just appointed to a new job, a student entering a graduate program, a new corporate player in a market. Time passes. The flush of achievement fades, and the new entrant becomes a typical player in the role. The individual reaches the socially expected duration for the role (Merton, 1984). Past the socially expected duration (SED), the achievement represented by continuing in the role moves in the two directions indicated in Figure 6.1.

The dashed line in Figure 6.1 illustrates a negatively sanctioned SED. Spending more than the socially expected duration in the role indicates repeated failure in competitions to move ahead. As discussed in Chapter 4, for example, continuing time in the same rank means that a manager is being passed over for promotion. Time in rank past the SED should

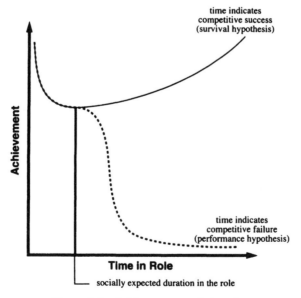

Figure 6.1   Achievement and duration

be correlated with the lack of structural holes in a network as it is in Chapter 4. This is a familiar example of a negatively sanctioned SED, but others come easily to mind. Examples from academic life are spending more than the usual time in graduate school or spending too long on that book manuscript that you've been meaning to finish for years. Examples from everyday life are the invalid who is "sick" longer than the socially accepted time for his illness, the athlete too long on the bench, or even something as simple as taking too long to travel between two points.[1]

The solid line in Figure 6.1 illustrates a positively sanctioned SED. Spending more than the socially expected duration in the role indicates repeated success in competitions. Time in rank past the SED should be correlated with the volume of structural holes in a network. This is the domain of the survival hypothesis. Later in this chapter, for example, I will present data on the extent to which firms at the top of their market can stay at the top for a long time. A firm that stays at the top of its market for twenty years has successfully competed against the other firms striving for market leadership. Other examples would be the senator who stays in office, the CEO who lasts as CEO (without owning the firm), or the scientist whose work continues to be widely used by peers.

This reasoning yields two hypotheses. The commit hypothesis is that players with little structural autonomy conform more closely to the behavior characteristic of their location in the social structure. Survival involves a commitment to the characteristic behavior. The corollary survival hypothesis is that higher rates of change, new players replacing old, will occur where there is little structural autonomy, precisely because there is little room for error. At a micro level, the more constrained of two roles should show: (a) less varied styles of performing the role and (b) shorter durations of time in the role. At a macro level, the more constrained of two markets should show: (a) less varied organization behavior and (b) higher mortality rates.

Interface and the Commit Hypothesis

The market model proposed by Harrison White (1981a, 1981b, 1988), developed with Eric Leifer (Leifer, 1985; Leifer and White, 1988), and later elaborated as the commit interface in White's (1992, chap. 2) general treatment of identity and control provides a powerful framework for expressing the commit hypothesis and linking it to data. The hypothesis could be discussed more simply as a conformity hypothesis. However, the theoretical power of the hypothesis is greatly extended by developing it within White's interface argument.

THE TWO SIDES TO A TRANSACTION
The model begins with producer and customer evaluating the cost and value of having y units of an item produced at quality level n. From the producer's side of the transaction, the cost of producing y units at quality level n—$C(y,n)$—is defined by the following production function (for example, White, 1988:240):

$$C(y,n) = qy^c/n^d,$$

where q is a constant term. Cost is presumed to increase with volume ($c > 1$). From the customer's side of the transaction, the value of having y units of the market item produced at quality level n—$S(y,n)$—is defined by an analogous production function:

$$S(y,n) = ry^a n^b,$$

where r is a constant term. Customers are presumed to value having a large volume of units produced ($a > 1$).

For the sake of argument, I will ignore variations in quality. This robs the model of some richness, but simplifies the task of linking it with the structural hole argument. The same link could be developed with or without a consideration of quality variation, but it is simpler without. In ignoring variations in quality, I presume that products below a threshold level of quality are unacceptable to customers and that products above the threshold are viewed as equally acceptable. With n in the above equations set to 1 as the acceptable level of quality, producer and customer perceptions reduce to the following:

$$C(y) = qy^c \quad \text{and} \quad S(y) = ry^a.$$

The relative magnitudes of the exponents are the core of the model. Producer perceptions of cost can increase more quickly or more slowly with volume than customer perceptions of value's increase with volume.

The point is illustrated in Figure 6.2. The vertical axes represent producer perceptions of cost and customer perceptions of value. The horizontal axes represent production volume. In an aluminum plant, for example, volume would refer to the number of pot lines in production. In book publishing, it would refer to thousands of copies produced in a standard print run.

From the producer's side of the transaction, cost can be viewed as a balance between economies of scale and overhead. Economies of scale are the savings obtained by producing a large volume in a continuous process. The savings include lower prices of supplies purchased in large quantity, the flexibility of having suppliers dependent on the producer's purchases, and avoiding idle capital in the form of empty buildings and dormant equipment. Overhead costs include the employees needed for production, real estate, and an expanded distribution system. Overhead increases with production volume. Larger producers need more employees in manufacturing, in the field roles of sales and service, and in the corporate roles of finance, personnel, marketing, and general administration. Larger producers have offices in central, more expensive locations. They have larger, and more, buildings at separate geographical locations. Larger producers need complex distribution systems to get their product from its multiple manufacturing sites to scattered points of customer purchase.

The exponent c describes the balance between economies of scale and overhead. In the graph to the left in Figure 6.2, three balances are given. If economies of scale offset the increasing overhead of higher production

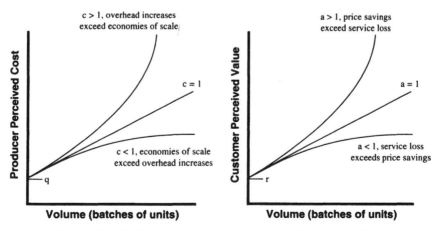

Figure 6.2   Producers and customers evaluate increased volume

volume, then c equals 1. The linear cost function describes producer perceptions. If overhead increases faster than economies of scale, then c is greater than 1. The increasing cost function in Figure 6.2 describes producer perceptions. These are products in which unit cost is stable despite the number of units produced. Heavy industry metal presses are an example. At the other extreme, if overhead increases more slowly than economies of scale, then c is less than 1. The decreasing cost function in Figure 6.2 describes producer perceptions. These are products that cost little to produce and sell once facilities are in place to make the initial units. Book publishing is an example.

From the customer's side of the transaction, value can be viewed as a balance between price and service. Unit price usually goes down as volume goes up. Just the opposite happens with service. When you are one of only a few customers, you get a high level of service. For heavy industry metal presses, a team of people visits you from the manufacturer to help you plan your financing and the most productive location for the new press. When you are one of many customers, producers can't afford such personal service. The value of the exponent a can be viewed as a customer's evaluation of the balance between price savings and service with increasing volume. The graph to the right in Figure 6.2 provides an illustration. When service evaporates faster than prices go down, a is less than 1. The decreasing value function describes customer perceptions. Large businesses' perceptions of microcomputer mail-order vendors are an example. When prices decrease without a comparable erosion of service, a is greater than 1. The increasing value function describes customer perceptions. Home and small business perceptions of mail-order microcomputer vendors are an example.

TRANSACTION AS INTERFACE

The market transaction is an interface between producer and customer. It brings together the two graphs in Figure 6.2. Figure 6.3 illustrates possible outcomes.

The best outcome is a declining cost function combined with an increasing value function ($c < 1$ in the left-hand Figure 6.2 graph combined with $a > 1$ in the right-hand graph). In such transactions the producer can enjoy high profit margins, because costs decline with increasing volume (for example, White, 1988:245–246), and high customer satisfaction, because price savings are greater than the erosion in service.

An unhappy alternative is to find an increasing cost function combined with a decreasing value function ($c > 1$ in the left-hand Figure 6.2 graph combined with $a < 1$ in the right-hand graph). To make a profit on producing large volumes, the producer has to keep price high and the customer doesn't see value in the balance between price and service. In setting volume, the producer runs a risk of profit loss and dissatisfied customers. The probable result is that large-volume producers will stay out of the market, leaving it to small specialty producers providing highly personal customer service.

Routine business refers to transactions combining the linear cost and linear value functions in Figure 6.2. The producer sees economies of scale offsetting increasing overhead ($c = 1$). The customer sees price savings offsetting losses in service ($a = 1$).

MARKET

The above description concerns transactions between customers and an individual producer. A market typically contains multiple producers. To aggregate up to the market level, I have to refine the term "producer." Producers here are products. When a firm produces only one product, the firm is a producer in the analysis. More typically, one firm produces multiple products, and in this analysis the organization responsible for

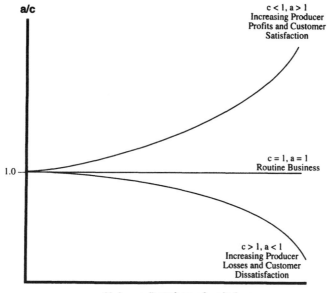

Figure 6.3 Producers and customers define their transaction

each product is a producer. For example, IBM produces mainframes, minicomputers, and microcomputers. Its microcomputer division produces a series of product models ranging from inexpensive entry-level machines based on an antique Intel chip to expensive machines based on recent Intel chips. Each kind of machine is a product, with a volume of units produced and a level of revenue generated.

Let $W(y)$ be the dollars of a product sold in a given time period. A market can be characterized, as in Figure 6.4, by the distribution of income, $W(y)$, across volumes of each product produced in the market. Each dot in Figure 6.4 is a product. The line through five products sold in a market is the market schedule (for example, White, 1988:240). Producers are expected to scan this schedule for alternative combinations of cost (economies of scale versus overhead) and value (price and service) viable in the market. Survival in the market involves a producer commitment to the market's schedule.

The shape of the $W(y)$ function indicates the kind of transactions that characterize the market interface between producers and customers. The high profit, high customer satisfaction transactions described by the top line in Figure 6.3 generate the increasing $W(y)$ function at the top of

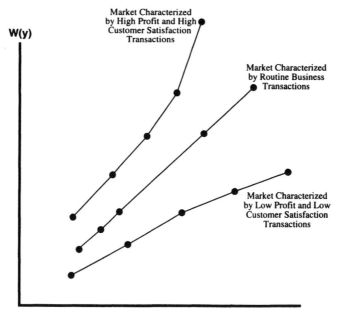

Figure 6.4   Market schedules from kinds of transactions

Figure 6.4. This is a positive market of profitable producers and satisfied customers, more so for the highest-volume producers. The microcomputer industry in the 1980s is an illustration.

The low profit, low customer satisfaction transactions described by the bottom line in Figure 6.3 generate the decreasing $W(y)$ function at the bottom of Figure 6.4 (compare Leifer, 1985:449). This is a negative market of producers facing profit losses and dissatisfied customers, more so for the highest-volume producers. The American automobile industry in the early 1970s is an illustration.

The routine business transactions described by the line in the middle of Figure 6.3 generate the linear $W(y)$ function in the middle of Figure 6.4. This is the market schedule expected in a perfectly competitive market (Leifer, 1985:445–446). Income is a linear function of volume.

MARKET COMMITMENT AND STRUCTURAL AUTONOMY

Producers vary from their market's schedule at their peril. If they fail to match the value perceptions of customers, they run the risk of losing the customers. It is in producers' own interest to show a commitment to the market schedule. When producers are in a strong position in bargaining with customers, however, they can survive even if they deviate from their market's schedule. Structural autonomy measures the extent to which producers are in such a position.

Taking the market schedule as the behavior characteristic of a market, the commit hypothesis is that producers in high-autonomy markets conform less closely to their market schedule. Autonomous producers have more flexibility in conforming to customer perceptions of price and service value. They have the flexibility of operating across more diverse production runs, ranging from small runs of expensive products to large runs in which economies of scale can yield considerable profit. In low-autonomy markets, producers operate close to a minimum profit margin and so have a rigid sense of how many units to produce at the going market price. In Figures 6.3 and 6.4, the commit hypothesis is that the vertical spread of data around the horizontal line in Figure 6.3 increases with the structural autonomy of producers, and that the spread of dots in Figure 6.4 around whatever schedule characterizes a market increases with the structural autonomy of producers.

ILLUSTRATIVE EVIDENCE

To provide illustrative evidence, I will use the aggregate markets in Chapter 3 as a frame of reference. I have no product-specific volume or sales data to estimate the schedule in each market, but the commit hypothesis should hold across levels of aggregation. Within microcomputer firms, a market schedule can be constructed across kinds of machines. At a higher level of aggregation, a market schedule could be constructed across mainframes versus minicomputers versus microcomputers. At a still higher level of aggregation, a market schedule could be constructed across computers versus other kinds of equipment within the accounting and office equipment market.

In other words, there is a use for pairing markets in the aggregate input-output tables and the many product categories within them distinguished in the four-digit Standard Industrial Classification (SIC). Within the aggregate food market, for example, there are 47 four-digit SIC product categories ranging from sausages, to cheese, to frozen food, to cereal breakfast foods, to dog and cat food, to beet sugar, to chewing gum, to malt beverages, to roasted coffee, to macaroni and spaghetti. The three market schedules in Figure 6.4 are distinguished by the link between net income and volume. Net income increases with volume in the positive market and decreases with volume in the negative market. To measure a market schedule slope, the net income in a market subcategory can be regressed across total sales in the subcategory. Residual variance around the regression line indicates the extent to which products deviate from the aggregate market schedule. The commit hypothesis predicts that this residual variance increases with market structural autonomy.

Illustrative evidence is presented in Table 6.1. Columns of the table distinguish three categories of markets. Given a 99.9% confidence interval around the average level of structural autonomy in an aggregate market (see the top graph of Figure 2.9), low-autonomy markets are below the confidence interval and high-autonomy markets are above the confidence interval. Total dollars of sales for each of the 443 four-digit SIC product categories within the 52 aggregate manufacturing markets come from the 1977 *Census of Manufactures* published by the U.S. Department of Commerce. These 443 product categories are the units of analysis in Table 6.1. Net income is measured by dollars of value added in a product category minus the dollars of labor costs. The ratio of this net income measure over total sales is the price-cost margin reported in Table 6.1, analogous to the price-cost margin computed from input-output data as a profit indicator in Chapter 3.

These results support the commit hypothesis in two ways. First, variation in profit margins increases with structural autonomy. Variation is measured in the first panel of Table 6.1 by the difference between minimum and maximum price-cost margins and the standard deviation of price-cost margins. The standard deviation of price-cost margins across four-digit SIC product categories in low-autonomy markets is 5.1 cents. This increases to 11.1 cents in high-autonomy markets. The Bartlett test for homogeneous variation in price-cost margins across product categories in low versus average versus high autonomy markets is clearly rejected with a 44.69 chi-square statistic ($P < .001$ with 2 d.f.). In short, the vertical spread of data around the horizontal line in Figure 6.3 increases with structural autonomy.

Second, variation in net income around market schedules increases with structural autonomy. In the variation in net income section of Table 6.1, the increasing standard deviation shows the increasing range of production volumes in high-autonomy markets (75.66 chi-square with 2 d.f., $P < .001$). More to the point of the commit hypothesis, the standard deviation in net income adjusted for total sales increases with structural autonomy (250.30 chi-square with 2 d.f., $P \ll .001$). The variation around total sales has two components: variation around whatever market schedule characterizes a market and variation between market schedules. Re-

Table 6.1 Evidence of the commit hypothesis

	Market structural autonomy			Bartlett test
	Low	Average	High	
Four-digit product categories	143	193	107	
Variation in price-cost margin (cents net income/dollar of sales)				
Minimum	14.8¢	10.2¢	3.2¢	
Maximum	46.7¢	54.1¢	59.5¢	
Standard deviation	6.1¢	7.7¢	11.1¢	44.69
Variation in net income (in billions of 1977 dollars)				
Standard deviation	0.750	1.421	1.610	75.66
Adjusted for total sales	0.164	0.590	0.793	250.30
Adjusted for total sales and market group	0.157	0.571	0.756	259.45
R^2 from total sales	0.952	0.829	0.760	

Note: Results are computed across the 443 four-digit SIC product categories within the 52 aggregate manufacturing markets. Sales data are taken from the 1977 *Census of Manufactures.* The Bartlett tests for homogeneous variances across the three categories of market structural autonomy are chi-square statistics with 2 degrees of freedom. All are significant well beyond a .001 level of confidence.

sults adjusted for total sales and market group in the next line in Table 6.1 are a more precise estimate of the first component. Six market groups can be distinguished in the American economy (where markets are more interdependent within than between groups; Burt, 1991b). Net income and total sales vary significantly between the groups. With market groups held constant, the standard deviation in net income around total sales increases with structural autonomy (259.45 chi-square with 2 d.f., $P \ll$ .001). The last row of the table summarizes in a more familiar form. The squared correlation between net income and total sales decreases with structural autonomy, from 95.2% of net income variation predicted by total sales in low-autonomy markets down to 76.0% predicted in high-autonomy markets. In short, the spread of dots in Figure 6.4 around whatever schedule characterizes a market increases with structural autonomy.

The spread is easier to see in Figure 6.5. Four-digit SIC product categories are plotted in the graphs. Products in high-autonomy markets are displayed at the top.[2] The horizontal axes indicate total dollars of product sold in 1977, in billions of dollars. The vertical axes indicate the net income from each product. Dollars of net income increase with dollars of total sales. The regression lines in the two graphs show similar profit margins across products (slightly higher across products in the high-autonomy markets). A dollar of sales on average yields 28 cents in net income.

The important point is the difference between the two graphs. The distributions of product data around the regression lines in the two graphs are quite different. At the bottom of Figure 6.5, the 143 product categories in low-autonomy markets are tightly distributed around the regression line. The squared correlation shows that all but 2.8% of the variation in product net income can be predicted from the total volume of product sales. This corresponds to Leifer's (1985:445–446) prediction of what should happen in perfectly competitive markets. The low-autonomy markets are the most competitive, and producers conform more closely and uniformly to a simple linear market schedule.

In contrast, the product categories in high-autonomy markets vary widely from the regression line. Net income increases with total sales in the graph at the top of Figure 6.5, but the increase is inconsistent. Variation in net income that cannot be predicted from the volume of sales— less than 3% in low-autonomy markets—increases to 36.2% in the high-autonomy markets. The graph shows that the weaker aggregate connection between product net income and sales volume in high-autonomy markets is weakest at high volumes. For product categories involving two billion dollars in sales or less (at the left of the graph), there is a 0.759 squared correlation between net income and sales volume. This drops to 0.461 at higher sales volumes, leaving 53.9% of the variation in product net income unexplained by sales volumes in the high-autonomy markets.

Even allowing for the compromises I made to get to the results in Table

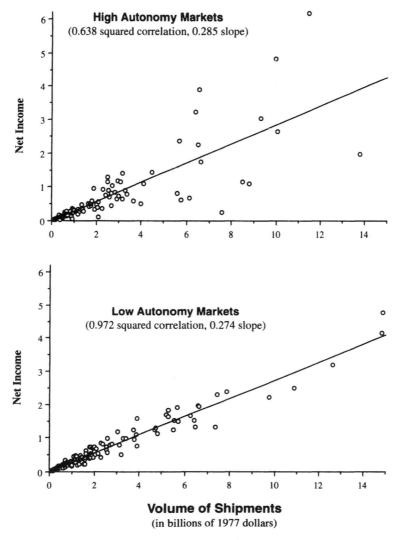

Figure 6.5 Variation around market schedules in high and low autonomy markets

6.1 and Figure 6.5, there is clearly a fruitful connection between the market interface mechanism and the distribution of structural holes around the transactions in which the interface is played out. With no more than the few concepts and variables already discussed, there are many hypotheses to explore.[3] The evidence presented is sufficient for the purposes here: The lower the structural autonomy of players in a market, the greater their commitment to the market schedule characteristic of their market.

Population Ecology and the Survival Hypothesis

Where there is empirical evidence for the commit hypothesis, there will be evidence for the corollary survival hypothesis. If low-autonomy producers cleave to their market schedule because of constrained transactions, then they are more likely to die if they deviate from the schedule. Market viability is a central theme in the interface metaphor.

Nevertheless, I turn to population ecology—developed by Michael Hannan and John Freeman (1977, 1989) and elaborated with Glenn Carroll (1983, 1984, 1985; Hannan and Carroll, 1992)—as a powerful framework for expressing the survival hypothesis and linking it to data. I have two reasons. The first is to further illustrate the generality of the structural hole argument by using it to derive hypotheses within diverse lines of theorizing. Second, population ecology provides a well-established methodology and a rich body of empirical results explicitly relevant to the survival hypothesis.

MARKET NICHE

Population ecology and structural hole theory have a fundamental point of contact in their units of analysis. For both, the unit of analysis is a set of structurally equivalent producers, termed a population niche in the first line of work and a market role in the other. The unit of analysis is a pattern of connections to segments in a differentiated resource environment. This point is elaborated in Burt and Talmud (1992). The generic concept can be illustrated with the image in Figure 6.6. There is a producer in a differentiated resource environment, surviving on the first, fourth, and last kinds of resources.

In the structural hole argument, resources are keyed to relations between players, and kinds of resources are defined by clusters of redundant players similarly positioned in the environment. Producer i is connected to the resources of a specific cluster q by relationship u_{iq} that increases with the cluster q resources used by producer i. The usage relations, u_{iq}, are the lines in Figure 6.6 to kinds of resources in the environment. The usage relations I examine in Chapter 3 are based on the dollars of goods exchanged between production markets. In Chapter 4 they are based on manager sociometric ties to significant contacts. Producers are competitors in the same market to the extent that they use the same resources, in other words, to the extent that they have identical patterns of relations to each potential source of resources (compare Figure 6.6 to Figure 1.9). Such individuals are structurally equivalent. The degree of their equivalence is measured by the Euclidean distance between their relation patterns, such as

$$d_{ij} = \left[\sum_q (u_{iq} - u_{jq})^2 \right]^{1/2}, \qquad q \neq i, j,$$

where zero distance between i and j indicates that they have identical relations with each resource segment q. This is similarly the criterion defining boundaries between segments in the environment. Two producers are competitors in the same market to the extent that they are structurally equivalent in their dependence on kinds of resources, and kinds of resources are defined by the benefits provided by structurally equivalent players. Applied to input-output data on dollars of goods exchanged between markets, the above equation defines two producers i and j as competitors in the same market to the extent that they make similar purchases from the same supplier markets and similar sales to the same customer markets (see Figure 3.2). The same criterion defines competitors within each supplier market and competitors within each customer market. Chapter 3 contains a more detailed discussion.

This network image of market corresponds to the niche in population

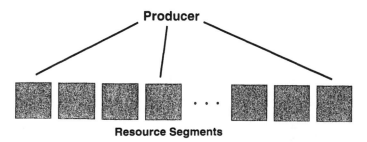

Figure 6.6 Producer in differentiated resource environment

ecology. Hannan and Freeman (1989:50) write: "The niche of a population consists of combinations of resource abundances and constraints in which members can arise and persist." In social structural terms, the niche of a population is a pattern of variably constrained relationships providing the resources that sustain the population's members. So stated, population niches correspond to the markets analyzed as network locations in the social structure of the economy.

The similarity is clearer when Hannan and Freeman (1989:103–104) explicitly define competition between populations. Using their terminology, $u_i(z)$ is a measure of the intensity with which population i utilizes a particular resource at level z. Partitions between resources in Figure 6.6 distinguish kinds of transactions in the resource environment. The lines correspond to the $u_i(z)$ to indicate the extent to which producers in population i feed on each segment of the environment. Hannan and Freeman use transaction size for illustration. In construction, for example, contracts range from a few hundred dollars for household construction to billions of dollars for constructing dams or highways. The population of construction firms that specialize in the former is distinct from the population specializing in the latter. Different populations of organizations specialize in competing for transactions of a certain size, general contractors specializing at the low end and large multinational firms specializing at the high end. The competition between populations i and j is a function of the extent to which they feed on the same resources, which Hannan and Freeman (1989:104) define in theory as:

$$\alpha_{ij} = \frac{\int u_i(z)u_j(z)\,dz}{\int u_i^2(z)\,dz}.$$

With respect to Figure 6.6, this measures the extent to which population j feeds on population i's resources. Hannan and Freeman (1989:104) explain: "This expression tells the probability that a member of population i will encounter a member of population j at a particular resource position averaged over all resource positions divided by the probability that it will encounter a member of its own population at each position. Thus, the competition coefficient tells the probability of inter-population interaction in resource acquisition relative to intra-population interaction." Competition increases with the extent to which a member of one population using a resource is likely to encounter a member of the other population using the resource. Resource segments could be nations (Carroll, 1981), occupational groups (Hannan and Freeman, 1984), categories of demographic or professional attributes (McPherson, 1983; McPherson and Smith-Lovin, 1988), or kinds of corporate strategies (Brittain and Wholey, 1988).

Structural equivalence is especially clear in Miller McPherson's (1983:524–537) empirical estimates of alpha coefficients. His concern is organizations recruiting new members. The resource environment is defined by potential recruits. The environment is stratified in terms of certain player attributes (such as age, sex, etc.). The boxes in Figure 6.6 could be levels of education, age categories, men versus women, or combinations of these attributes or others. The niche in which an organization operates is defined by the kinds of people to whom it appeals (for example, younger well-educated women or older men with little education). Two organizations operate in the same niche to the extent that they recruit the same kinds of people. Such organizations are structurally equivalent with respect to the defined resource segments.

There are differences between the structural hole boundary between markets and the ecology boundary between niches, but both are clearly examples of structural equivalence. The connection between structural equivalence, input-output sectors, and markets has been long recognized by network analysts, but that work developed with closer ties to the sociology of organizations and industrial economics than to population ecology. DiMaggio (1986) was the first to call the structural equivalence analogy to the attention of population ecologists (for example, Hannan and Freeman, 1989:52–53). Hannan and Freeman (1989:52) wonder about the stability of equivalence boundaries defined at the level of individual firms, but market boundaries are defined in terms of transactions between classes of structurally equivalent establishments, not between firms, and available evidence shows these to be quite stable in recent decades (for example, Burt, 1988a). Data are not available to test stability across the broader time periods often covered by population ecology analyses (for example, the mid-1800s through today); but it is reasonable to ask whether the boundaries around markets, defined by technology production requirements, are any less stable than the population boundaries implicit in the archival compilations of firms by market used in ecology analyses. The more important point is that the boundary around the theoretical unit of analysis in each approach is a boundary defined by structural equivalence.

RESOLVING DIFFERENCES

Although the differences between population ecology and structural hole theory are minor in comparison with the similarities, there are three to note. Two are obvious, concerning distinctions between resource segments in the environment and normalizing differences in the connections to segments. The third is less obvious, concerning the role of boundaries in the arguments.

Resource Segments in the Environment

For the structural sociologist, resources are keyed to relations between players in the environment. The clusters q in the definition of market boundaries are clusters of structurally equivalent players similarly positioned in the flow of resources. Resource segments in the environment are defined by the same boundaries that define the producer's market. The relative significance of each resource segment for the survival and prosperity of producers is defined by the structure of relations surrounding producer relations with players in the resource segment.

Distinctions between segments are less clearly defined a priori in population ecology. The analyst is encouraged to identify resources critical to survival, typically one broadly defined class of resources, and segments are defined by whatever criterion seems proper. Hannan and Freeman (1989:103–104) use the scale or scope of transactions to illustrate distinctions between resource segments without suggesting that it is the only criterion. Still, this is too simplistic an image of differentiation. Results such as those presented in Chapter 3 show that the pattern of transactions with kinds of suppliers and customers is strongly associated with producer performance.

That differentiation is already implicit in the empirical definitions of populations for population ecology analysis. Incorporating it into the definition of niche is completely consistent with, and improves the reality of, population ecology theory. At the same time, the population ecology differentiation by kind of transaction does no violence to the network definition of market boundaries. The following equation combines both kinds of differentiation to define the boundaries around a market niche:

$$d_{ij} = \left[\sum_q \sum_k (u_{iqk} - u_{jqk})^2 \right]^{1/2}, \qquad q \neq i, j,$$

where k is the scale at which a transaction is conducted (or some other criterion used to define classes of transactions) and u_{iqk} is the usage relation from producer i to resource segment q in the kth category of i-q relationships. In the aggregate transaction between construction firms and lumber companies, for example, some construction firms specialize in small volumes of high-quality wood for residential projects and other construction firms specialize in projects that call for a large volume of low-quality wood for large-scale construction. In the above definition, two establishments operate in the same market to the extent that they buy and sell with the same kinds of suppliers and customers (same q) in the same kinds of transactions (same k).

The key point is that a single logic of differentiation is involved. Structural equivalence cuts across levels of aggregation. It slides across levels of aggregation, from boundaries around kinds of suppliers or customers as establishments similarly positioned in the flow of goods between markets down to boundaries around kinds of transactions similarly positioned in the volume of flow.

Normalizing Resource Flows
In addition to differing in their numerators, as we have just seen, the two definitions also differ in the denominator. The population ecology definition is normalized by volume of producer business (with the probability that an organization will encounter a member of its own population in each resource segment). A similar normalization is used in input-output analysis to define input coefficients: sales from market i to market j divided by total purchases by market j. This is a proper normalization for tracing the flow of dollars across markets, but when incorporated in a definition of structural equivalence, it homogenizes important distinctions between markets. The problem is that total producer volume is so large that it obscures differences in the patterns of transactions with supplier and customer markets. The primary quality recovered is the distinction between markets that do business with a single other market and those that do business with several markets. A clearer picture of market boundaries is obtained if transactions are measured relative to the largest volume of business producers transact with any one supplier or customer market (as for Figure 3.2). Both points are discussed and illustrated in Burt and Carlton (1989).

Causal Force
Although the causal propositions of population ecology and structural holes are defined for the same market niche unit of analysis, they draw

causal force from different aspects of the unit. This difference can be discussed as a contrast between static and dynamic analysis (to stress the virtues of ecological analysis) or as a contrast between comparative and case study analysis (to stress the virtues of structural hole analysis). Polemics aside, the fact of this third difference between the approaches is that they draw causal inferences from different comparisons.

As argued in Chapter 1 and illustrated in Chapters 3 and 4, the structural hole argument defines player advantage in negotiating market transactions for comparisons across markets. Causal inference is made from covariation across markets between market prosperity and the structure of the market's relations with suppliers and customers. Market boundaries define distinctions for comparative analysis.

Population ecology is less concerned with comparisons between markets than patterns of growth within markets. Market boundaries define a population for case study over time. Competition is measured by the extent to which growth in the members of one population occurs at the expense of another population. Correlated growth indicates that the two populations are competitors feeding on the same resources—whatever those resources are. The point is illustrated by the alpha coefficient in the Lotka-Volterra population growth model describing expected change in the number of organizations within population i (dN_i) during a given time interval (dt):

$$\frac{dN_i}{dt} = r_i N_i \left[\frac{K_i - (N_i + \alpha_{ij} N_j)}{K_i} \right],$$

where r_i is the per capita number of new organizations expected in the time interval with everything else held constant (intrinsic growth rate), N_i is the existing number of organizations in the population (population density), and K_i is the equilibrium number of organizations that can survive on the resources available to the population (niche carrying capacity). The term in brackets adjusts growth for the extent to which the existing population is close to the carrying capacity of available resources. When the population is smaller than the carrying capacity (N_i near zero relative to K_i), abundant resources mean unconstrained growth. When the population is close to the carrying capacity (N_i about equal to K_i), growth is severely constrained. The existing population stretches available resources to their limit. If some other population j feeds on the same resources, their numbers have to be added to the size of population i. This is the function of the alpha coefficients. The size of population i

is the number in the population, N_i, plus the number in population j, to the extent that j feeds on i's resources, $a_{ij}N_j$.

In short, population ecology infers competition from the conditions of differential growth that result from competition; structural hole analysis infers competition from the network conditions that generate competition. This clarification is an important one for two reasons. First, it explains the greater rigor with which resource segments are defined a priori for structural hole analysis. Distinctions between segments are a key component in the causal variables for such analysis. Population ecology doesn't have the same requirement, and so is less preoccupied with the problem. Second, the different analytical uses of market boundaries are independent of the boundaries themselves. Market and niche are similarly defined by structural equivalence criteria, whether one draws comparisons between markets or studies a niche over time. Population ecology and structural hole analysis differ in what they do with their units of analysis but correspond in their structural equivalence definition of the units.

POPULATION ECOLOGY PREDICTS SURVIVAL WITHIN A MARKET

I now have population ecology and structural hole propositions based on the same unit of analysis: a population of structurally equivalent players where equivalence is defined by similar patterns of relations to kinds of resources. To derive structural hole hypotheses within the population ecology framework, I need to be more explicit about the kinds of empirical results taken as evidence in a population ecology analysis.[4]

Population ecology offers a variety of insights about factors that affect survival rates within a market's population. The liability of newness is a central insight both because of its consistency with population ecology reasoning about selection processes and because of the strong empirical support that early analyses provided. Simply put, young organizations have higher mortality rates than old ones. Stinchcombe (1965) introduced the idea with the argument that new organizations are more fragile: fragile in the lack of trust between suppliers and customers that develops over time and fragile in having to institutionalize new organization roles and socialize new employees. The summary argument in population ecology is couched in the idea of structural inertia. The longer that an organization can survive, the more widely it becomes known among investors, suppliers, and customers for its reliability and accountability, and the greater its ability to reproduce the roles, authority, and communication structure that define the form of the organization (for example, Hannan and Freeman, 1989:70–77, 245–247).

Empirically, the liability of newness is measured with the gamma parameter in Makeham's extension of Gompertz's mortality model:

$$r(t) = \alpha + e^\beta e^{\gamma(t)},$$

where $r(t)$ is the mortality rate at age t, α is an intercept term defining the mortality rate at old age, β is an adjustment to capture the mortality rate at birth (birth mortality), and γ describes change in the mortality rate from birth to old age. Freeman, Carroll, and Hannan (1983:696–699) provide a succinct introduction to the model adapted to population ecology. A Weibull model is in some ways preferable to Makeham's (Hannan and Freeman, 1989:188–189, chap. 10), but the simpler Makeham model is sufficient here. Applications to diverse populations consistently show strong negative estimates of γ (for example, Carroll, 1983; Freeman, Carroll, and Hannan, 1983). Mortality rates decline with age.

Competition is more explicit in density dependence analyses. Competition remains implicit, as just explained with respect to the Lotka-Volterra model, but is keyed to an empirical condition—the number of players in a market. Births and deaths are patterned by competition and legitimacy.

The graph at the top of Figure 6.7 shows how competition and legitimacy change with the number of players in a market. The number of players is discussed as density (not to be confused with the more traditional image of dense social interaction), and density dependence refers to changes in competition and legitimacy wrought by changing density (for example, Hannan and Freeman, 1989:131–141, especially pp. 133–134; Hannan and Carroll, 1992). Density increases on the Figure 6.7 horizontal axes.

Competition intensifies as an increasing number of players live on the available resources. This is indicated by the solid line in the top graph of Figure 6.7. The line increases sharply at the right of the graph as the number of competitors begins to strain the limit of available resources.

The dashed line describes the legitimacy, or social acceptance, of behavior. With an increasing number of individuals performing a role in the same way, social acceptance of their performance increases. Linking population ecological and institutional approaches to organizations, Hannan and Freeman discuss this as the legitimacy of the prevailing organizational form (Hannan and Freeman, 1989:132). The dashed line flattens out as the prevailing form is widely accepted.

The graph is a useful heuristic, but no more than that. The theory does not predict absolute levels of competition or legitimacy. It predicts the relative importance of competition and legitimacy at different levels of density: legitimacy at low density, competition at high density. More specifically, mortality rates are expected to have a nonmonotonic association with density in a model predicting mortality from the number of players in a market and the number squared (Hannan and Freeman, 1989:135–139, especially the bottom of p. 137). The mortality rate, for example, declines as density increases from a near-zero level. This is the effect of legitimacy. Then, as the number of players approaches the limit that can be supported, competition eliminates the weaker ones. The mortality rate increases.

My concern here is not density dependence effects but the population ecology logic of competition. That logic can be keyed to the structural

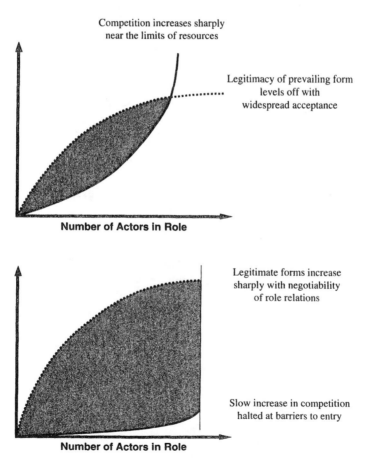

Figure 6.7   Competition and legitimacy

hole argument to provide a bridge between the two approaches, and significant value added for both.

STRUCTURAL AUTONOMY PREDICTS SURVIVAL DIFFERENCES ACROSS MARKETS

The situation illustrated in the graph at the top of Figure 6.7 describes a low-autonomy market role, one characterized by intense competition among the constituent players for participation in constrained relations providing low rates of return. In the extreme, this is the image of a perfectly competitive market. The situation for high-autonomy players is illustrated in the graph at the bottom of Figure 6.7. The solid line describing competition increases more slowly, then stops. The dashed line describing legitimacy increases more sharply.

Competition increases more slowly for two reasons. First, there are more resources available from the higher rates of return that can be obtained. Structural holes allow entrepreneurs to set a higher market price for their performances, which allows more people to survive in the role. Structural holes among suppliers and customers allow entrepreneurial firms to set a higher market price for their commodity, which allows more establishments to survive in the market. Second, competition in high-autonomy markets is managed more through the social organization of players. Workers are organized through unions, elites are organized through ties of social obligation, establishments are organized through large parent firms. The result of the two processes is that the number of players can expand faster than competition intensifies. Competition stops at some point when the autonomous players establish barriers to new entrants; medical schools put a quota on the number of new doctors, for example, or large tobacco and auto firms define the number of brands or establishments that the market can support at existing favorable profit margins.

The steeper increase in legitimacy results from the same processes. People connected with a high-autonomy role—not in it, but connected to the people performing it—have less influence over the role's performance. They are more in a position of putting up with the preferences of the autonomous people performing the role. Where acquiescence is acceptance, the social acceptance of whatever performances appear in a high-autonomy role increases quickly as illustrated by the dashed line at the bottom of Figure 6.7. With relations more negotiable, and players varying by random chance, more legitimate variation can be expected in more autonomous roles and markets. The more people successfully perform a role in varied ways, the more socially acceptable it will be to perform the role in varied ways. The more organization forms observed to survive in a market, the more legitimate these forms will be as ways of doing business in the market.

In sum, structural autonomy increases the shaded area between the competition and legitimacy curves in a density dependence graph. Both the commit hypothesis and the survival hypothesis can be seen in the connection. The commit hypothesis portrays the greater diversity of legitimate performances allowed for increasingly autonomous players. The larger shaded area between competition and legitimacy in high-autonomy markets (bottom of Figure 6.7) contains more varied behaviors than the smaller shaded area in low-autonomy markets (top of Figure 6.7). One aspect of that greater variation is the connection firms make between product volume and income, and the evidence in Table 6.1 and Figure 6.5 shows increasing product variation with increasing structural autonomy. In other words, variation around the market schedule in the interface model corresponds to the shaded area between the competition and the legitimacy curves. The market interface model is a stronger vehicle for pursuing the commit hypothesis, because it is more articulate about the way in which producer and customer perceptions combine to create the greater product variation observed with increasing structural autonomy.

The population ecology framework is a stronger vehicle for pursuing evidence of the survival hypothesis, because it is more articulate about the manner in which survival changes over time. The odds of a player's finding somewhere to survive within the shaded area in the bottom graph of Figure 6.7 are higher than in the top graph. The area indicates capacity to support a large number of diverse performances: many people performing a role in varied ways or many heterogeneous organizations. Structural autonomy is analogous to niche carrying capacity in population ecology (Hannan and Freeman, 1989:100, 131–132). Carrying capacity is more precisely a consequence of structural autonomy. Higher-autonomy markets can carry a larger load of players. Structural autonomy is more directly analogous to niche width in population ecology. In their first empirical analysis of niche width, Freeman and Hannan (1983:1118) introduce the concept as "a population's tolerance for changing levels of resources, its ability to resist competitors, and its response to other factors that inhibit growth. A population which has wide tolerance, meaning that it can reproduce in diverse circumstances, is said to have a broad niche." The more negotiable transactions in which high-autonomy players operate are a buffer against the normal selection processes presumed to kill off weaker competitors. The structural origins of this greater negotiability lie in the broader diversity of relations available to autonomous players (compare Hannan and Freeman, 1989:105, on measuring niche width in terms of the diversity of products and industrial categories in which an organization is a player).

With respect to the survival model in population ecology analysis, therefore, structural autonomy is a covariate. Holding constant mortality rate (γ) and the rate toward which it asymptotically declines (α), organizations in structurally autonomous markets are born with better chances of surviving to old age:

$$r(t) = \alpha + e^{(\beta + \beta_a A)} e^{\gamma(t)},$$

where the effect of structural autonomy, β_a, is expected to be negative, reflecting the lower mortality rates of organizations in high-autonomy markets (compare Carroll, 1985, for a similar specification of concentration in his analysis of niche width effects). In other words, structural autonomy explains differences in the mortality curves of organization populations in different markets.

ILLUSTRATIVE EVIDENCE

Illustrative evidence is presented in Figure 6.8. The units of analysis are aggregate manufacturing markets. Markets are arranged on the horizontal axis in Figure 6.8 by their structural autonomy in 1967. The autonomy data for 1967 are taken from Burt (1988a) and displayed in the profit margin metric of pennies of profit expected from the average dollar of sales. These vary from a minimum of half a cent in the manufacture of radios, televisions, and communication equipment to a maximum of 20 cents in tobacco. The vertical axis describes turnover from 1967 to 1977 among the twenty leading firms in each market. Given the twenty firms with the most extensive sales in 1967, how many of them are replaced by new firms by 1977? Turnover ranges from a minimum of 4 new firms in food processing and drugs to a maximum of 17 new firms in electric lighting. The turnover data are taken from an inventive paper by Shin-Kap Han (1990) describing the volatility of corporate leadership within manufacturing markets despite dramatic stability in the aggregate structure of transactions defining the markets.

The survival hypothesis predicts lower turnover in high-autonomy markets. With one caveat, this is precisely what is observed. The bold line in the graph describes the regression of turnover across levels of structural autonomy. As autonomy goes up, turnover goes down (-3.4 t-test, 35 d.f., $P < .001$; see Han, 1990, for details on controls for size and market stability).

The caveat is that a strong connection with a government customer can override the market effect. Markets dependent on government consumption are indicated by hollow dots in Figure 6.8. Across the 14 dependent markets, there is no association between turnover and structural autonomy (0.7 t-test, 12 d.f.)—as indicated by the nearly horizontal thin regression line through the hollow dots. This is especially interesting because many markets dependent on government purchases are low-autonomy markets (to the left in Figure 6.8), such as the furniture market. High-autonomy markets dependent on government purchases lie within

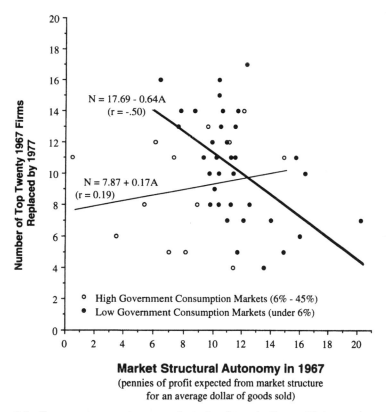

Figure 6.8   Turnover among top manufacturing firms declines with increasing structural autonomy. (Trade with government agencies decreases turnover in low-autonomy markets.)

the distribution described by the aggregate association between turnover and structural autonomy. In other words, once a firm gets into the government contract stream, its market leadership position is protected from the normal vicissitudes of operating in a highly competitive, severely constrained market.

Structural Autonomy and Survival
The empirical evidence in Figure 6.8 illustrates three points. First, there is significant covariation with structural autonomy. As predicted by the survival hypothesis, there is less turnover in more autonomous markets. Market leaders survive longer as leaders in more autonomous markets.

Analytical Shift: Replication versus Hypothesis Tests
Second, the evidence highlights an analytical shift that makes structural hole and population ecology analysis powerfully complementary. Population ecology tests hypotheses with comparisons over time between organizations in the same market. This describes birth and death processes within any one of the dots in Figure 6.8. Analyses of more than one market are treated as replications.

Just the opposite is true of structural hole analyses. Hypotheses are tested by comparing players in different markets. This describes differences across the dots in Figure 6.8. The data within dots merely have to be comparable across dots, for example, the single largest firm, four largest firms, or the twenty largest firms as in Figure 6.8. Comparisons of different people in the same role or of different organizations in the same market are the substance of replication. With a large research budget, population data could be obtained for an ecological analysis in each of many markets to compare birth and death processes across markets. Systematic comparisons across markets are possible in a population ecology analysis, but they would be difficult as such research is currently practiced. The structural hole survival hypothesis offers less description within markets, but more across markets (with fewer data).

Consider Carroll's (1983:320–325) results on the liability of newness in 52 organization populations. The multiple populations are replications. For example, "the estimates of α_0 in the constant rate model range from $-.799$ to -2.30, but they tend to cluster around -1.50." The interesting question from the structural hole perspective is how estimates vary between markets. Figure 6.9 is a graph of Carroll's (1983:321–324) estimates of β in the Makeham model across levels of market structural autonomy. Forty-nine of Carroll's 52 estimates are presented. The three excluded populations are two outside the United States and one for which Carroll has no parameter estimates.

These data are not as systematic a comparison as the data in Figure 6.8. Over half of the populations in Figure 6.9 are drawn from two markets (24 from the wholesale and retail market, 10 from printing), and the populations are often confined to a single city. Market structural autonomy is defined for the 1960 to 1980 time period (taken from the top of Figure 2.9) while the organization mortality data refer to populations typically observed in earlier time periods.

Still, the results are intriguing. As predicted by the survival hypothesis, the 0.49 correlation in Figure 6.9 between market autonomy and the estimates of β shows that birth mortality declines as structural autonomy increases (3.2 *t*-test with 34 d.f., *P* = .003, for the 36 populations with less than 30% censoring). Censoring weakens estimation, as Carroll emphasizes (1983:315, 325). The hollow symbols in the graph are organization populations in which a large proportion of deaths are unknown, cen-

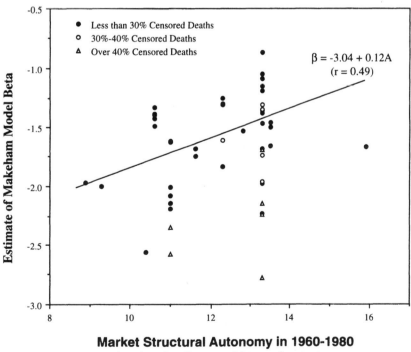

Market Structural Autonomy in 1960-1980
(pennies of profit expected from market structure
for an average dollar of goods sold)

Figure 6.9   Structural autonomy increases birth survival

sored. The hollow symbols mostly lie below the regression line; censoring causes underestimated values of the birth mortality rate.

Comparative Population Ecology

This illustration of the comparative emphasis in structural hole analysis brings me to my third point. The complementary analytical differences between the approaches is potentially powerful in the stage it sets for comparative population ecology analysis.

The simplest line of work is to study how effects within populations vary across populations. The evidence in Figure 6.8 is suggestive, showing higher survival rates in increasingly autonomous markets. More interesting questions ask how known population ecology effects vary across markets in their sensitivity to structural autonomy. This is the point illustrated in Figure 6.9, showing a significant decline in the birth mortality parameter as structural autonomy increases. Alternatively—given the fact that the firms in Figure 6.8 are all well-established market leaders—the structural autonomy effect specified as a birth mortality covariate might instead be a factor in old age mortality:

$$r(t) = e^{(\alpha + \alpha_a A)} + \beta e^{\gamma(t)},$$

where a negative value of α_a would indicate the decreased mortality rate of old firms in structurally autonomous markets. There is some evidence of this from Carroll's (1983) estimates. Across the 36 organization populations with low censoring (solid dots in Figure 6.9), Carroll's estimates of α decrease as market structural autonomy increases, but the association is weak (-1.5 t-test) and the data distribution is more discontinuous than in Figure 6.9. Alternatively, the structural autonomy effect could be a change in the rate at which firms overcome the liability of newness:

$$r(t) = \alpha + \beta e^{(\gamma + \gamma_a A)(t)},$$

where a positive value of γ_a would indicate the extent to which firms in structurally autonomous markets are less subject to the liability of newness. A further alternative is for autonomy to be a covariate in all three parameters, simultaneously decreasing the mortality rate at birth, at old age, and its change over the life cycle. Judging from secondary analysis of Carroll's estimates, structural autonomy is a covariate that dampens birth mortality, β, and old age mortality, α. I find no association between autonomy and Carroll's estimates of γ ($r = 0.043$ across the 36 populations marked by solid dots in Figure 6.9). A direct test of these alternatives requires estimation across organization populations rather than secondary analysis as in Figure 6.9.[5]

Interesting theoretical steps toward comparative population ecology have been laid with niche width studies. In such studies, a population of organizations is divided into two subpopulations and parameter estimates are compared across the subpopulations. The above is the same idea, but structural autonomy provides a continuous, quantitative covariate for comparing survival rates across populations.

The two subpopulations in niche width studies are defined by a distinction between firms that focus on a narrow segment of the customer market (specialists) versus firms that try to appeal to a broad range of customers (generalists). Available evidence on their comparative mortality is based on building the comparison into the birth mortality rate (β_a, above) and is mixed (Hannan and Freeman, 1989:321, 326), but Carroll (1985) provides suggestive results. As a few large generalist firms come to dominate a market, they kill off other large generalist firms and create opportunities for specialist firms to focus on narrow segments of customers with demands unmet by the generalist firms. The result is that market concentration, a significant component in structural autonomy, is expected to increase the mortality rates of generalists and decrease the mortality rates of specialists. Carroll (1985) shows that concentration increases the mortality rates of generalist newspapers while it decreases the mortality rates of specialist newspapers. Similar results describe the survival chances of microbreweries and brew pubs (Carroll and Swaminathan, 1992). Once there are only a few generalist competitors within the market, however, the results in Figure 6.8 suggest that they will enjoy relatively low mortality rates at the same time that stable opportunities are created for specialists.

Summary

In prior chapters, I described how structural holes are responsible for different rates of return in different markets. In this chapter, I have described how they are responsible for variably heterogeneous and durable rates within markets and how they can be used to integrate arguments in two of contemporary sociology's significant contributions to understanding market competition.

The idea is that the information and control benefits of structural holes responsible for higher rates of return also free players to try diverse ways of getting those higher rates of return. I derive hypotheses about player heterogeneity and survival within markets. The commit hypothesis is that low-autonomy players conform more closely, under threat of being excluded from relationships, to behavior characteristic of their location in social structure. The corollary survival hypothesis is that higher rates of change, new players replacing old, occur where there is little structural autonomy precisely because there is little room for error. At a micro level, the more constrained of two roles will show: (a) less varied styles of performing the role and (b) shorter durations in the role. At a macro level, the more constrained of two markets will show: (a) less varied organization behavior and (b) higher mortality rates. Across micro to macro levels of analysis, in short, the structural holes that increase the rate of return typical of a location in social structure increase the diversity and durability of behaviors by which players obtain the higher rate of return.

The commit hypothesis is an occasion to develop a bridge between the structural hole argument and the interface model of markets. The interface model describes players evaluating one another over the interface between producers and customers. Their joint evaluations create a visible and accepted line of association, a market schedule, between production volume and revenues. Producers vary from their market's schedule at their peril. If they fail to match the value perceptions of customers, they run the risk of losing the customers. With the market schedule defining the behavior characteristic of a market, the commit hypothesis is that producers in high-autonomy markets conform less closely to their market schedule. Autonomous producers have more flexibility in conforming to customer perceptions of price and service value. They have the flexibility of operating across more diverse production runs, ranging from small runs of expensive products up to large runs in which economies of scale can yield considerable profit. I conclude with illustrative evidence on American markets. Both variation in profit margins (Table 6.1) and variation in net income around market schedules (Figure 6.5) increase with structural autonomy. The lower the structural autonomy of players in a market, the greater their commitment to the market schedule characteristic of their market.

The survival hypothesis is an occasion to develop a bridge to population ecology analysis. The network image of a market is analogous to the population ecology image of a niche. Structural autonomy is analogous to niche width. The greater the structural autonomy of a market, the wider the niche, and the more likely that diverse organization forms can survive in the market niche. Specifically, structural autonomy decelerates the growth of competition associated with an increasing number of players in a market and accelerates legitimacy. Competition increases more slowly for two reasons. There are more resources available from the higher rates of return that can be obtained, and competition is more managed through the social organization of players. The result is that the number of players in a market can expand faster than competition intensifies. The steeper increase in legitimate ways of producing the market's product results from the same processes. With relations more negotiable and individuals varying simply by random chance, more legitimate variation can be expected in more autonomous markets. The more players successfully perform in varied ways, the more socially acceptable it will be to perform in varied ways. The more organization forms are observed to survive in a market, the more legitimate these forms are as ways of conducting business in the market. Illustrative evidence on American markets shows that market leaders survive longer as leaders in more autonomous markets (Figure 6.8) and that structural autonomy decreases the mortality of organizations new to the market (Figure 6.9). The lower the structural autonomy of a market, the greater the odds of players being forced out of the market.

7

Strategic Embedding and Institutional Residue

Economic and sociological understandings of the division of labor are similar in that they both trace the phenomenon to the density of connections between people and the volume of their markets.[1] But two approaches—each involving economists and sociologists, though economists more in the first and sociologists more in the second—have evolved to describe the social and emotional organizations within which we transact exchanges.

One approach focuses on the friction inherent in conducting the exchanges and explains ways in which social and emotional organizations integrate trade partners to lessen the friction. Corporations are described in terms of the ways they facilitate imperfectly competitive market transactions. Personality is described in terms of mechanisms that help a person manage the emotions of difficult relationships.

The second approach focuses on the fact that once people have performed a transaction, the performance is a template for their next performance. Norms and customs emerge to legitimate the known script. This approach describes social and emotional organizations, perhaps built initially to lessen exchange friction, as entities with lives of their own that introduce their own friction into the day-to-day life of transactions. Corporations are described in terms of how law, management behavior, and culture shape the way in which business is transacted. Personality is a predisposition to act in certain ways.

There are many ways to phrase the distinction. Organization is consequence or cause, equilibrium or process, rational or irrational, friction-free or friction-ful. The key criterion between the approaches is whether organization is described as a mechanism facilitating underlying exchange or an entity in its own right defining exchange. Over time, the two are adjacent parts of the same puzzle.

I mention the two approaches and their intimate connection to clarify the focus of this chapter, which concerns the social and emotional organizations players build to facilitate the doing of otherwise constrained relationships. I am mindful of frictions introduced by organization once created. Organizations are peppered with structural holes that affect behavior. Witness the effects discussed in Chapter 4 (or the extreme of a firm frozen by the holes within it; Burt and Ronchi, 1990) and the well-known examples of incrementalist and institutional factors that affect the day-to-day operation of organizations (Wildavsky, 1964; Clark and Ferguson, 1983; Zucker, 1987; Powell and DiMaggio, 1991). I limit this chapter to the causal link from constraint to strategic response because the structural hole argument provides a clear image of the link. The implications for intra-organization constraint and subsequent strategic response should be as obvious in theory as they are diverse and complex in fact.

This chapter provides the third of the three views developed on the player-structure duality: views of player differences between, within, and around markets as positions in social structure. In Chapters 1 and 2, I described how structural holes are responsible for rates of return varying between markets. In Chapter 6, I described how structural holes are responsible for heterogeneity and survival within a market. In this chapter, I describe how structural holes are responsible for social and emotional organization as a kind of residue that accumulates in the wake of entrepreneurial players navigating around the constrained relations that define a market. When the constrained player is an organization, the structural hole argument is a revised theory of the firm: the firm is the social residue of managers who are trying to ease the constraint of certain market transactions. When the constrained player is a person, the argument is a description of personality as the emotional residue of a person who is trying to manage the loss of control in constrained relationships. From the corporate to the personal, today's institutions are the residue of yesterday's entrepreneurial efforts.

The Other Tertius

Tertius strategy has two sides. The first side concerns developing the information and control benefits of structural holes. That is the domain of the two *tertius* strategies in Chapter 1 (summarized in the columns of Table 7.1). The first strategy puts redundant contacts into play against one another. These are contacts in competition for the same relationship—two suitors after the same bride or two buyers after the same purchase. The second strategy puts nonredundant contacts into play against one another. These are contacts from separate clusters, in competition because of conflicting demands on the same player in separate relationships—a science professor's course demands, for example, being played by a student against the course demands of a humanities professor.

THE OTHER SIDE

Players who can see the reward of an entrepreneurial opportunity probably have the wit to see the potential benefit of opportunity lost to constraint. *Tertius* is a strategic player. Part of strategy is setting up the playing field. Where structural holes do not exist, they can be manufactured, or the constraint of their absence can be neutralized. This is the other side to *tertius* strategy—navigating around the constraint of missing holes—and the domain of the strategy hypothesis in the structural hole argument.

There is a literature, largely in political science, on defining issues to get preferred decisions. The network contains everyone entitled to vote

Table 7.1   The two sides to *tertius* strategy

Other side: Manage the constraint of an absent hole	One side: Develop the information and control benefits of an existing structural hole	
	Redundant contacts in play	Nonredundant contacts in play
Withdrawal	Withdraw from a contact in favor of his competitor	Withdraw from a contact's cluster to focus network resources in other clusters
Expansion	Add a contact's competitor to the network	Add a new cluster to the network
Embedding	Establish second relationship with contact, giving the player more control	Establish second relationship with either or both contacts, giving the player more control

on the issue, and a voting rule, usually majority rule, aggregates votes into a decision. Decisions by committees and legislative bodies, where there is a clear definition of the players entitled to vote and the rule aggregating votes into a decision, are typical research sites. By strategically combining and highlighting certain aspects of an issue into motions, voter constituencies can be mobilized to support a preferred decision. William Riker and Peter Ordeshook (1973) provide a textbook introduction to this literature. Riker (1986) provides a delightful collection of stories about illustrative strategic actions.

The insights from this literature are useful to understanding strategy in groups more broadly defined, where it is not clear who has a vote or how votes will be aggregated into a decision. Edward Laumann and David Knoke (1987) provide detailed illustration in their analysis of American energy and health policy. The content of issue conflict evolves in a predictable, destructive symbiosis with the structure of relations among players (for example, Coleman, 1957; Burt, 1981). Issues are defined strategically, but alternative definitions do not cluster a set of voters for or against a motion so much as they mobilize groups to enter the debate for or against a particular resolution of the issue. The task of issue sculpting becomes a task of network sculpting.

This is the domain of the structural hole strategy hypothesis. The distribution of structural holes in a network defines an incentive for a player to take strategic action in certain relations, action that changes the boundary around the network or its structure. The specific strategy adopted is difficult to predict because there are so many personal implementations. It is possible to predict, however, where strategic action in some form will occur and where it will not occur. The predicted strategies are distinguished by rows in Table 7.1.

WITHDRAWAL

In the first row of the table, the simplest strategy is to constrict the boundary around the network to eliminate the offending constraint. You withdraw from the high-constraint relationship. If you are negotiating between two contacts in the same cluster, this means moving a relationship to a new contact of the same kind. Examples are the person who changes jobs for a position better connected with the central administration, or the person who manages conjugal disputes by replacing partners. If you are negotiating between nonredundant contacts, withdrawal means dropping a cluster from your network to focus resources in other clusters. Examples are the upwardly mobile person who drops out of touch with old friends to develop contacts suitable to his new position, or the person, who withdraws from a frustrating, dominating boss to concentrate on personal projects or on office intrigue.

There is a clarity to withdrawal, but its use is limited. Withdrawal is usually a permanent action; you lose future benefits on the deleted relationship, though long-term benefits might seem a trivial issue when a relationship is making you miserable. On a more practical note, you might run out of contacts or, worse, end up with a gaggle of contacts who always agree with you, the "great-man" circle of sycophants. More significant, withdrawal erodes your credibility with other contacts. It might be difficult to establish a new primary contact in the cluster reached through your deleted contact. Contacts in other clusters wonder who else might be deleted for constraining you. Terms such as "opportunist" circulate. Regardless of these costs, withdrawal is often not an option when constraint is severe. Kinship, mutual friends, and corporate authority glue you to certain relationships you just have to live with.

EXPANSION

A second strategy for navigating around an absent structural hole is to expand the boundary of the network to include a new contact to compete with the offending constraint (see the middle row of Table 7.1). A structural hole is introduced to control the constraint.

Any new contact who can be played against the offending constraint will do. The new contact could be someone from within the constraint's cluster. An example is the action of feigning interest in a third party to spark jealousy, and so renewed attention, from a neglectful lover. The new contact could be more distant from the offending constraint. This is built into the matrix form of bureaucracy. The logic for the matrix is that better work will result from coordination between functions in the development of a project. Coordination is presumed to emerge from informal supervision across functions. Managers in a matrix firm are encouraged to get supervisors in functions related to their work to endorse—to "buy-in" to—projects that the manager wishes to pursue. Beyond the valuable guide this action provides to integrating work within the corporate hierarchy, it can protect an entrepreneurial manager from the constraint of a truculent supervisor. Going into the supervisor's office with a proposal already endorsed by the supervisor's peers elsewhere in the firm is different from going in with a proposal no one else has seen.

The strategy can fail for either of the two reasons in Chapter 1. You might make the new and old contacts too aware of one another. Getting together, they could find reason to cooperate in forcing you to meet their mutually agreed-upon demands. Within the matrix firm, for example, your boss and her peer could agree to a common front in managing you. Or you might provide too little incentive for the contacts to resolve their differences. People sometimes find it difficult to empathize beyond their own status group. The lover and the supervisor each know what they want and don't care that someone else exists who finds you or your ideas interesting. Your involvement with a third person could also mean losing the relationship. If the neglectful lover or the truculent supervisor has a strong reason for constraining you, your explicitly manipulative strategy could be the last straw that leads them to withdraw altogether.

EMBEDDING

A third strategy is to leave the constraint-generating network in place but to manage the offending constraint by embedding it in a second relationship over which you have more control (see the bottom of Table 7.1). The virtue of this strategy, and what makes it so frequently employed, is that it calls for no change to the underlying structure defining constraint, which is often beyond the independent control of the player trying to manage constraint.

Embedding has been a constant in the preceding chapters. Consider Figure 7.1. This is the quintuple proposed by John Commons as the fundamental unit for analyzing transactions (for example, Commons, 1924:65–69; 1950:50–52). There are two qualities emphasized in the Commons unit.

First, transactions are evaluated against the domain of alternatives possible. The unit contains the "best" two buyers for a transaction and the "best" two sellers. Between them, the four players define the optimum transaction and three second-best alternative transactions. The four players are the dots in the two clusters in Figure 7.1. A solid line connects best buyer with best seller. Given a relationship between yourself and a

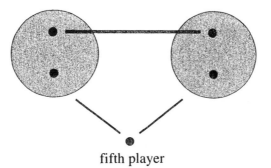

fifth player

Figure 7.1 The Commons transaction unit

contact (two primary contacts connected by the line in Figure 7.1), there is an alternative player to whom your contact could shift the relationship (a secondary contact in the cluster around you), and there is an alternative to whom you could shift the relationship (a secondary contact in the cluster around your contact). The relationship between you and your contact is evaluated against the alternative relations possible. This is the function of secondary structural holes, discussed in Chapter 1. They capture the shadow of alternatives that define the negotiability of existing relationships. Secondary holes around a contact measure the alternatives you have for replacing the contact. Holes at your end of the relationship measure the alternatives with whom you could be replaced. The contribution of the structural hole argument is its definition of the parameters of what is possible. The number of players and structure of connections within clusters, and the structure of ties among clusters (as opposed to the simple pair of clusters in Figure 7.1), define structural holes for negotiating a relationship against its alternatives.

The second quality emphasized in the Commons unit is that transactions are always embedded in a broader relationship of some kind. The broader relationship is the fifth player in Figure 7.1. This is the arbitrator to whom you and your contact turn to settle disputes. It is the governance mechanism invoked to legitimate "fair" behavior in the relationship. The concept cuts across micro to macro levels of analysis. For Commons, an economist describing the institutional foundations for market behavior, the fifth player is the capitalist legal system. At the other extreme, for Evans-Pritchard, an anthropologist describing ethnographic data, the fifth player would have been the "leopard-skin chief" mediating troubled relations between Nuer tribesmen (Evans-Pritchard, 1940:chap. 4). Between these extremes, the market transactions of Chapter 3 are embedded in rules of competitive market pricing, and the manager relations of Chapter 4 are embedded in the study firm's norms of proper behavior among employees. In Chapter 1, all is open for negotiation, subject to constraints created by the structure of interconnected relations. More generally, negotiation is subject to the further constraints of social structures in which negotiated relations are embedded. The embedding structures range in detail from specific ties between parties in the negotiated relation (Granovetter, 1985) to shared social understandings about the rules of the negotiation (such as Smith, 1989, on auctions, and Zelizer, 1989, on the social meaning of money exchanged between certain categories of people).[2]

In other words, the *tertius* discussed in Chapter 1 is never more than a second-order entrepreneur. The institution or person in the role of fifth player is the first-order entrepreneur who sets relationship expectations and outer limits. Commons summarizes the role with four verbs (for example, Commons, 1924:68, 134–142, 147–148). The fifth player enforces working rules that define what the other four players (1) may, (2) must, (3) can, and (4) cannot do in the final negotiated relationship. Respectively, these concern (1) the liberty or immunity or range of alternative behaviors you are allowed in the relationship, (2) the duty or liability or minimum you are expected to deliver in the relationship, (3) the right or power or maximum you have a right to expect from the relationship, and (4) the disability or exposure or specific behaviors prohibited to you in the relationship. Within general may-must-can-cannot rules set by the fifth player, the *tertius* in Chapter 1 negotiates a specific relationship for favorable terms.

If the fifth player is constant, like Adam Smith's invisible hand, across all relations in a competitive arena, then introducing the role adds little to an explanation of why some relations yield higher returns than others.

The situation is more interesting when there are alternative fifth players. Then a significant part of the entrepreneur's task is to select the fifth player through whom the entrepreneur has the greatest advantage. This is the substance of the embedding strategy: *tertius* navigates around the constraint on a relationship by changing the fifth player governing it. Is this transaction a favor between friends, a service between colleagues, or a business transaction? Between people, popular embedding relations are friendship, sex, joint involvement in social and professional activities, and combinations thereof. If a friendship can be developed with a source of constraint, the contact is less likely to act against your interests and more likely to act in your interests, both of which lessen the threat of the constraint.[3] The embedding can be no more than a change in the place where a relationship is negotiated. There is a difference between the front seat and the back seat for hormone-driven adolescents negotiating their ersatz conjugal tie. There is a difference between negotiating under the glare of fluorescent lights in a classroom and discussing the matter over a drink in a dark wood room with reflected light. Between organizations, embedding involves strategic alliances and vertical integration: corporate ties such as buying your own retail distribution company, buying a dedicated source of critical supplies, or entering a joint venture with a competitor who has a hold on a customer market you haven't been able to penetrate. Buying and selling, formerly transacted under competitive market pricing, are now guided by corporate authority.

Components in the fifth player's role are criteria for defining and choosing among kinds of embedding relations. Embedding shifts the default may-must-can-cannot rules in a relationship to more favorable rules. Under competitive market pricing, scarcity is the justification for high or low bids. An asking price is too high, for example, given a product's wide availability. Under embedding, high and low are determined by whatever relation is used to embed the negotiation. The asking price is too high, given our long history of doing business with one another. One or all of the may-must-can-cannot rules can be affected by embedding. Certain embeddings ensure minimum lower limits. For example, friendship puts a lower limit and certain prohibitions on the negotiation. Friends get above-market value, and you generally avoid action damaging to their interests. Other embeddings ensure stable expectations. A long-term contract between supplier and producer gives each a known flow of resources around which they can plan other transactions. Still other embeddings ensure upper limits. Ownership gives absolute control, to the extent that it is possible. When a firm vertically integrates to embed a market transaction, there is a clear upper limit: being able to impose whatever transfer price suits the broader interests of the firm and being able to close the acquired plant if it doesn't live up to expectations.

At this point, the other *tertius* is twice different from the *tertius* in Chapter 1. The first *tertius* develops the information and control benefits of a structural hole. The other *tertius* navigates around the constraint of absent holes. The first *tertius* presumes competitive market pricing as the fifth player regulating fair exchange. The other *tertius* strategically selects the may-must-can-cannot rules in which negotiation is embedded.

Strategy Hypothesis

The structural hole strategy hypothesis is a statement about where players have incentives for withdrawal, expansion, or embedding. The statement is simple: There is an incentive for strategic action in constraint relations and a disincentive in opportunity relations. The two kinds of relations were defined in Chapter 2 with respect to the hole signature of a player's network (see Figure 2.6).

Everything else constant, constraint increases the incentive for strategic action. A constraint relation is a target for strategic action because it is a large investment of player time and energy where there are few structural holes with which favorable terms can be negotiated on the investment.[4]

Constraint is balanced against opportunity. Strategic action in a relationship already rich in structural holes—even if the relation involves some constraint—could make the relationship less negotiable. Opportunity relations are a large investment of player time and energy, but are rich in structural holes. These relations the player has an incentive to protect from changes to the may-must-can-cannot rules. The prevailing rules work well.

The hypothesis can be stated more concretely for empirical research. The effort player i puts into strategic action to eliminate constraint in the relationship with contact j is a variable, w_{ij}. There are alternative measures. It could be a simple dummy variable (1 if strategic action is taken, 0 otherwise). It could be a measure of the time needed to develop an embedding relationship. It could be a measure of cost in some other form. Strategic action w_{ij} should increase with i's incentive for strategic action against j. The incentive is defined by c_{ij}, measuring j's constraint on i's opportunities, and p_{ij}, the proportion of player i time and energy spent with contact j, measuring i's direct investment in the relationship. The strategy hypothesis is that w_{ij} increases with c_{ij} and decreases with the extent to which p_{ij} dominates c_{ij}. The budget equation for strategic action in a network has an upper limit set by the player's time and energy, and is defined by the trade-off between the cost of strategic action versus the benefit of eliminating constraint (a balance between the constraint that would be eliminated and the interaction that is already unconstrained).[5]

Thinking ahead to issues of research design, note that the rows of Table 7.1 are variably suited to empirical investigation. Of withdrawal, expansion, and embedding, the last is best suited to testing the strategy hypothesis. The factors that predict embedding also predict where the other strategies occur, but testing the prediction with the other strategies calls for continuous time observation. Panel data aren't sufficient. Suppose that I observe a player's network. I locate opportunity and constraint relations to predict where strategic action should and shouldn't occur in the network. I watch the network to see where strategic action actually occurs. What I don't know at the first observation is how much time will pass before the player takes action or how long the process will take once begun. In a cross section of observed networks, some players might act quickly against constraint, some might take a long time, and some might be caught in the process of removing constraint relations. The research design problem is that withdrawal and expansion strategies destroy the causal factor responsible for them. Constraint relations managed by withdrawal disappear. Those managed by expansion are no longer constraints. The research advantage of embedding is that its residue of embedding relations and the constraints generating them continue over time. That means that it is possible to make meaningful comparisons between networks at any one moment in time.

Formal Organization as Social Residue

It is convenient to begin with organizations as an illustrative research site for the strategy hypothesis. Organizations are more attractive because the buying and selling that defines market constraint is distinct from the corporate relations created to manage it. The line between the two kinds of relations is not absolute. There are intermediate choices. Scholars responding to Williamson's (1975, 1985) analysis of market and hierarchy point to intermediate structures of hybrid contracting and authority relations (for example, Baker, 1990; Eccles and White, 1988; Powell, 1990; Schreuder, 1992; Stinchcombe, 1990:chap. 6; compare Williamson, 1992). Moreover, social norms can alleviate the need for corporate authority (Barber, 1977), even in the extreme of otherwise hostile relations between players in the market (Malinowski, 1922; Benet, 1957). This is central to Marsden and Laumann's (1977) prescient analysis of exchange embedded in social relations, Ouchi's (1980) image of the clan as an alternative to corporate authority, and Granovetter's (1985) discussion of market relations embedded in social relations. Empirical studies range from Geertz's (1979) rich anthropological account of social order in a Moroccan bazaar to more analytical network studies such as Faulkner's (1983) analysis of prominence and achievement in the music industry (and later analysis of credits in the film industry; Faulkner and Anderson, 1987), Baker's (1984) analysis of centrality and volatility in a securities market, Galaskiewicz's (1985) analysis of philanthropy and prominence in a local corporate network, Smith's (1989) analysis of auctions, Zelizer's (1989) analysis of social meanings attached to monetary exchanges, and Leifer's (1990) analysis of how social understandings between owners preserve competition in league sports.[6] I return in the next section to the more general view of corporate relations as only one example of social regulation. For the moment, my point is only that the distinction between market and corporate relations is clearer than the corresponding distinction in studying people. I can distinguish ownership ties from production buying and selling in Figure 5.2 more easily than I can tell in Figure 5.1 where the work relation between colleagues ends and their friendship begins.

THE FUNDAMENTAL QUESTION

Formal organization is the answer to a simple, fundamental production question. The setting for the question is the following: There is a producer, an entrepreneur, in charge of an organization operating in a market within a system differentiated by a division of labor. The system could be social, political, or economic. I'll focus on the economic, because these concepts are clearest from the analysis in Chapter 3. The entrepreneur's organization gets supplies from organizations in certain markets and sells its product to organizations in certain markets. The entrepreneur has a choice about how to conduct the transactions. If he conducts his buying and selling on the open market, negotiations are guided by the competitive price mechanism. If he vertically integrates his organization, for example, by buying an establishment in a key supplier market, negotiations with the internal supplier are guided by corporate authority. The choice between these options is the fundamental question for the entrepreneur. Should I conduct this transaction under the rules of competitive pricing or should I bring it into my organization to conduct it under rules defined by corporate authority?[7]

The coordination of market and corporate relations is most explicit in Jeffrey Pfeffer and Gerald Salancik's (1978) resource dependence approach to analyzing organizations and Oliver Williamson's (1975) transaction cost approach (Williamson, 1981, for an introductory review; Williamson, 1989, for a thorough review). In this, both are developments from Ronald Coase's (1937) classic statement of the theory of the firm. Coase frames his argument with two rhetorical variations on the fundamental question: Why would anyone conduct market buying and selling within a firm instead of on the open market? If there is an advantage to business within a firm, then why isn't all buying and selling conducted within a single large firm?

In response to the first question, corporate authority offers influence, stability, and privacy. Coase (1937:336–339) focuses on the advantages of being able to avoid the cost of repeatedly negotiating contracts on the open market, thereby also avoiding the uncertainty of how next year's negotiation will go and gaining privacy. The last point concerns competitors interested in doing business with the same suppliers and customers, although Coase stresses an aspect more important at the time, privacy from government agencies interested in taxing purchases and sales or, worse, regulating those transactions by price controls or rationing.

Williamson's transaction cost approach provides detailed elaboration of Coase's critical first two points. Williamson offers a framework in which he can evaluate the cost of conducting a transaction on the open market or within a corporate hierarchy (for example, Williamson, 1975: 9–10, 20–40, 254–258; compare Pfeffer and Salancik, 1978:113–187). The cost of a transaction is determined by an interaction of environmental and human factors. The environment is characterized by some level of uncertainty/complexity and the number of players it contains. If a transaction is complex and uncertain and involves a small number of market players, it might be preferable to negotiate the transaction within a corporate hierarchy. The "might be preferable" phrase depends on the human factors relevant to the transaction. People have a limited capacity to process complex information. They can make rational decisions as long as their information-processing capabilities are not overloaded (bounded rationality). Complex transactions overload these capabilities, increasing uncertainty. Small numbers of players in a transaction will be a problem if this elicits opportunistic behavior (opportunism). Further, opportunism combined with small numbers in a complex transaction can distort the flow of information among participants so that some participants do not receive critical information or receive distorted information (information impactedness). These conditions of uncertainty, complexity, small numbers, bounded rationality, opportunism, and information impactedness jointly define a general atmosphere for conducting a transaction. In the worst case, the atmosphere is nervous suspicion of Machiavellian behavior from other participants in the transaction. Bringing the transaction into the corporate hierarchy can improve the conditions for business, ideally shifting the transaction atmosphere from trade between warring factions to an exchange between friends on the same team. The corporate hierarchy is better able to control the market uncertainty of small numbers and opportunism. It provides a third party for settling disputes, audit information to improve the flow of critical information, and a higher authority to redistribute resources. Establishments can specialize in their product without worrying about market uncertainties. More generally, the corporate hierarchy can coordinate its constituent establishments to better absorb unforeseen market contingencies. As the transaction cost argument matured, the many correlated factors of opportunism, small numbers, uncertainty, and so on came to be distinguished on the one key dimension of asset specificity (for example, Williamson, 1979, 1985, 1989).[8] A transaction that requires a producer to buy assets that cannot be used for other purposes has to be controlled until the producer gets a proper return on the investment. The higher the asset specificity of a transaction, the more likely that the buyer and seller are connected by a corporate tie above and beyond their market exchange. Here again, if one stands back from the details of individual cases, the advantages of the corporate tie are as in Coase's original argument: influence, stability, and privacy.

Given the advantages of transactions within a corporate bureaucracy, why are any exchanges transacted on the open market? To use Coase's (1937:340) original question: "Why is not all production carried on by one big firm?" The answer is diseconomies of scale (Coase's "diminishing returns to management"). With an increasing number and diversity of transactions conducted within a firm, coordination costs increase—not the least of which is an increased probability of inefficient resource allocations to individual transactions. This point, referenced in a summary way by Coase (1937:340), is nicely elaborated in Lindblom's (1977:65–75) discussion of coordination by authority alone. Authority offers "strong thumbs, but no fingers." The corporate hierarchy can control transfers between establishments, but not fine-tune the coordination of many, diverse establishments.[9]

Balancing advantages and disadvantages, "a firm will tend to expand until the costs of organizing an extra transaction within the firm become equal to the costs of carrying out the same transaction by means of an exchange on the open market" (Coase, 1937:341). Costs balanced at the transaction margin define the equilibrium firm adapted to its market.

This reasoning is an attractively simple framework for studying the fundamental question of organization. It has been fruitful. The works by Coase, Pfeffer, Salancik, and Williamson lie at the heart of a voluminous and prospering literature in business, economics, and sociology.

The powerful complementarity between this reasoning and the structural hole argument can be developed in either of two ways. The stronger integration is to view constraint as a formal definition and empirical measure of the market costs that define which transactions are brought into the firm. The weaker integration is to keep the arguments separate and to use constraint as a framing device to highlight market relations likely to be fruitful sites for detailed transaction cost analysis.

STRONGER INTEGRATION: MARKET INCENTIVE
FOR CORPORATE AUTHORITY

At the beginning of Chapter 3, I described how the constraint coefficient c_{ij} measures the extent to which producers are at a disadvantage in negotiating transactions with a specific supplier or customer market (Figure 3.1). The setting is a market i producer negotiating a transaction with a supplier or customer in market j.

Producer control over the negotiation is affected by structural holes on both sides of the transaction. On the producer's side, the lack of other producers in market i increases producer control. This is the oligopoly effect created by the lack of structural holes within a market.

On the other side of the transaction, producer control is affected by structural holes beyond the market. The lack of structural holes among suppliers and customers affects the i-j negotiation in two ways, mutually reinforcing one another. First, a lack of structural holes between supplier and customer markets constrains negotiation. To the extent that market j is a large proportion of the producer's external transactions, the negotiation becomes critical. Losses in this negotiation cannot be balanced easily with gains elsewhere. To the extent that market j is itself dependent on transactions with the producer's other markets, market j establishments are likely to be owned by the same firms operating establishments in the other markets, again constraining producer price negotiation. Market j establishments are likely to have good information on the costs and profits that the producer obtains in its other markets and can claim limits on their ability to accept the producer's suggested price because of preferential transfer pricing within corporations spanning the markets. Second, a lack of secondary structural holes within supplier-customer market j constrains negotiation. Market j establishments are more likely to have a standard market price enforced by the large firms that own them. The large firms can offer long-term stability in supplies or consumption and can maintain barriers to new entrants. Moreover, the larger the firms in market j, the more likely it is that they are vertically integrated and so can exploit the lack of structural holes between markets as described in the first point.

With respect to resource dependence theory, the constraint coefficient c_{ij} measures the extent to which resources from market j are a high proportion of producer i business, and their price is uncertain and high on the open market. This is dependence in both an actuarial and a political sense (see Burt, 1983:223–235; Pfeffer, 1987, on the connection between resource dependence and the network definition of market constraint).

With producers investing in facilities and staff to service their dominant supplier and customer markets, they face large costs if those transactions change. Their dependence is akin to asset specificity in transaction cost theory (for example, Williamson, 1989:142–143) and vulnerability dependence in world system theory (for example, Baldwin, 1980:491–492). This theme can be developed to study the manner in which dependence relations between markets integrate markets into broader economic units (Burt, 1992).

With respect to transaction cost theory, the constraint coefficient most obviously captures the small numbers condition. It increases as suppliers and customers decrease. However, it is more than that. It increases as the opportunities for negotiating a favorable price decrease. The uncertainty captured is not the uncertainty of transaction complexity but the uncertainty of having little control in a transaction. The latter is the more troubling for producers. It is one thing to have to manage a large volume of information in a transaction. It is another to know that you have little control in negotiating the transaction, however much information is involved. Add to this the presumption that business partners will exploit producers if they can; then constraint captures the probability of opportunism and information impactedness because it captures the structural conditions that make it profitably possible to be opportunistic and manipulate the flow of information. Add also that firms make transaction-specific investments of personnel and facilities tailored to their dominant supplier and customer markets, and it is safe to say that the constraint coefficient is correlated across a broad range of transactions with the asset specificity criterion in transaction cost theory.

In sum, the constraint coefficient is an empirically verified measure of the cost to producers of doing business with a specific supplier or customer market under the rules of competitive pricing. The higher the constraint, the greater the incentive to replace competitive pricing with corporate authority. I do not mean that constraint captures all aspects of transaction cost in Williamson's framework or all aspects of resource dependence in Pfeffer and Salancik's framework (for example, Pfeffer, 1987:125). I mean that constraint captures significant aspects of cost and dependence in both frameworks as described in the preceding paragraphs, and has a validating association with profit margins observed in all kinds of markets as illustrated in Chapter 3. Whatever constraint measures of transaction cost and resource dependence, it is a quality that lowers the rate of return on producer investments. Constraint defines and measures the extent to which a transaction is positioned in the social structure of the economy so as to put producers at a disadvantage in negotiating the transaction.[10]

There is also a contribution to the second of Coase's questions, the question of why there isn't just one large firm. Diseconomies of scale are the usual consideration. Two further considerations emerge from the analysis of structural holes.

With ownership comes obligation. A producer establishment has the advantages of access to other establishments within its parent firm, but it also has the burden of sharing their profits and growth. Beyond having no market incentive to bring transactions with a disorganized supplier or customer sector into the corporate hierarchy, producers have a disincentive. Market pricing can be used to force the supplier or customer firms to accept prices yielding them low profit margins. If a low margin is to be endured by some establishments, better they remain outside one's own corporation. In contrast to the prediction of resource dependence theory, extensive buying and selling with a market is sometimes an opportunity instead of a dependence. Extensive trade with a poorly organized market is an opportunity to use the price mechanism to exploit structural holes within the market—an opportunity to emerge as the *tertius* in setting transaction price. Diversifying into the industry would destroy this entrepreneurial opportunity.

Second, diversification can expose a producer to severe market constraints beyond those already faced. A misleading feature of the classical theory of the firm, and my use of it above, is the evaluation of transactions independent of other transactions. This assumption is implicit in Coase's equilibrium definition of the firm and explicit in the resource dependence and transaction cost formulations built from it (for example, Williamson, 1981:559–560; but see Williamson, 1975:256, for a succinct warning about the problem). Transactions between markets exist in patterns of technologically enforced production roles. The technology available for producing a commodity involves buying supplies from certain markets and selling the commodity in certain markets. Moving the i-j market transaction into the corporate hierarchy involves more than just the one transaction; it means exposing the firm to the whole pattern of supplier-customer transactions characterizing market j. This will be a problem when new sources of constraint are added beyond the firm's current diversification. In such a situation, the firm has exposed its establishments to new, unmanaged, market constraints. The firm would be better served by a low-obligation tie such as an interlocking directorate, a tie that provides some monitoring advantages of ownership without the responsibilities.

THEORY OF THE FIRM

These considerations complete the predictions of the strategy hypothesis: There is an incentive for strategic action in constraint relations and a disincentive in opportunity relations. Where w_{ij} is a measure of corporate authority ties between markets i and j, w_{ij} increases with c_{ij} and decreases with the extent to which p_{ij} dominates c_{ij}. Where a transaction is severely constrained, the authority of a corporate hierarchy is the preferred setting for negotiating the transaction. Where constraint is low because there is no trade with a market, there is no market incentive for corporate ties, but spurious ties here do not damage the firm's profits. However, where constraint is low because of high competition within a significant supplier or customer market, the firm has a strong incentive to keep the transaction out of the corporate hierarchy in order to exploit it more efficiently through competitive pricing.

Coase's image of the equilibrium firm has a social structural definition: Begin with the producer's most severely constrained class of market transactions (maximum c_{ij} for producer i). Evaluate the costs of the transactions conducted under rules of competitive pricing against the costs if conducted under the control of corporate authority. If the difference between price and cost under corporate authority would be smaller with suppliers, or greater with customers, move the transaction into the firm by creating a suitable organizational tie to the supplier-customer market. Examples would include buying a subsidiary supplier or distributor in the market, adding to the board of directors an officer from a leading firm in the market, or creating a joint venture with a firm in the market. Move to the next most constrained class of transactions (next largest c_{ij}). Make the same evaluation. Continue down the rank order of market constraints. Where the costs of moving the next class of transactions into the firm equals the costs of conducting them on the open market, stop. The transactions now in the firm are the optimum for its market.

ILLUSTRATIVE EVIDENCE

Richly detailed evidence on transaction cost is available from case studies describing the few intermarket transactions most significant for a study industry (for example, Miles, 1982, on the tobacco industry; Stuckey, 1983, on the aluminum industry; Williamson, 1985:103–123, for review).

More systematic evidence is available in Pfeffer and Salancik's demonstration that corporate relations increase with the volume of transactions between markets (1978:157–161) and the more refined later evidence that corporate ties increase with transaction volume adjusted for concentration within supplier and customer markets (for example, MacDonald, 1985, with data on 79 manufacturing industries; Caves and Bradburd, 1988, with data on all Standard & Poor's firms operating in 83 industries—excluding transactions under 4% of producer sales; and Burt, 1983, with data on 786 firms operating across 404 transactions defining each of 322 industries).[11] Ziegler (1992) reports analogous evidence on the market basis for interlocking directorates between sectors of the German economy. Especially interesting is the evidence showing a market constraint rationale for corporate ties less often studied as a response to transaction cost, such as corporate philanthropy (Burt, 1983:chap. 6), corporate contributions to political action committees (Mizruchi, 1989, 1992), and geographic ties between firms revealed in corporate decisions to relocate (Schwartz and Romo, 1992).

Figure 7.2 contains illustrative evidence from the American economy

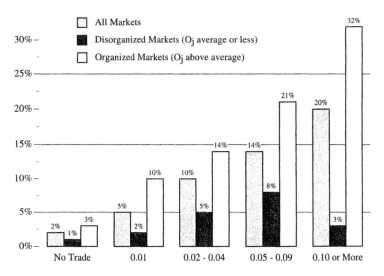

Figure 7.2   Market constraint and corporate ties. (Bars are the mean percent in 1967 of sample manufacturing establishments in producer market *i* with ownership, interlock, and indirect financial interlock ties to one or more establishments in market *j*.)

(taken from Burt, 1983:231). For a sample of firms containing the largest firms in each two-digit Standard Industrial Classification manufacturing industry in 1967, the bars in Figure 7.2 show the proportion of firms in industry i that simultaneously own an establishment in sector j, interlock with the board of any firms operating in sector j, and interlock with any financial institutions which in turn interlock with any firms in sector j. The horizontal axis in Figure 7.2 distinguishes kinds of market transactions. For this illustration, four-firm concentration ratios are divided at the mean value to distinguish oligopolistic markets (high versus low O_j). In keeping with resource dependence results, the gray bars increase from left to right in Figure 7.2 with the proportion of producer buying and selling transacted with a specific supplier-customer market. In keeping with the refinement added by constraint, this increase is directed primarily at those markets in which there are few secondary structural holes (high O_j), not at those where there are many secondary structural holes (low O_j). Extensive trade with a poorly organized market is an opportunity to use competitive pricing to exploit structural holes within the market. As predicted, corporate diversification is especially low into poorly organized markets with which extensive buying or selling occurs. This is illustrated by the bars to the right in Figure 7.2 (see Burt, 1983:chaps. 4 and 7, for more detailed evidence).

WEAKER INTEGRATION: AIMING THE TRANSACTION COST MICROSCOPE

There is value in juxtapositioning the structural hole and transaction cost arguments even if there is no effort to integrate their predictions. The structural hole definition of constraint can be used as a framing device, highlighting the places in the economy where transaction cost effects should be especially strong.

This adds value to both arguments because they lend themselves to different kinds of analyses. As I elaborated in Chapter 6, the structural hole argument gets its analytical results from comparisons across market boundaries. Evidence is presented in terms of comparisons across a large number of markets and transactions as in Figures 2.9, 3.3, 6.5, 6.8, and 7.2. For the strategy hypothesis, transactions are grouped by the incentive producers have to move the transaction into a more controlled setting.

Within a group of similarly constrained transactions, the governance structures used to embed individual transactions can vary. That variation is predicted by the parameters of transaction cost theory. For example, aluminum and tin producers are about equally constrained in their transactions with the firms that mine the ore needed to produce the two metals. Among the many transaction cost qualities captured by the structural hole definition of constraint, however, only a certain part of asset specificity is captured. It could be a large part, but this remains an unanswered empirical question to which the answer probably varies between transactions. Producers are expected to invest heavily in people and facilities to serve their primary sources of revenue. Another part of asset specificity lies beyond the constraint measure. Aluminum and tin illustrate the point. Manufacturing aluminum varies across kinds of ore. Once a plant is configured to use one kind of ore, substantial costs are involved in reconfiguring the plant for another kind. Manufacturing tin is less tied to kinds of ore. In other words, there is higher asset specificity in the ore transaction for aluminum producers than for tin producers. Hennart (1988) describes how the asset specificity underlies greater corporate integration between mining and metal production in the aluminum industry (compare Stuckey's, 1983, case study of the aluminum industry).

Transaction cost theory—usefully multidimensional for case studies— is less easily adapted to comparisons across large numbers of markets. The task of measuring site, facility, human, and corporate asset specificity in each of the 6,006 transactions among the input-output markets in Chapter 3 is intimidating from the standpoint of both the volume of data needed and the difficulty of measuring specificity for reliable comparison across the diverse transactions in the population of all markets. Transaction cost is most often described in case studies.

Transaction cost theory is like a microscope. The multiple dimensions of cost provide a close understanding of the dynamics of a specific transaction or of a class of similar transactions. Continuing the metaphor, the structural hole definition of market constraint moves the microscope to those places in the economy where the strongest evidence of the transaction cost will be observed. The higher the constraint on a class of transactions, the more likely that producers have embedded the transactions in corporate ties above and beyond their buying and selling.

Consider Figure 7.3. The horizontal axis is the market incentive for producers to embed a transaction in nonmarket governance mechanisms. The strength of the corresponding corporate ties between markets increases up the vertical axis. The horizontal axis is primarily a function of c_{ij}, and the vertical axis is w_{ij}, already described. The solid line shows the strategy hypothesis in its simplest form. Across increasingly constrained transactions, there is an increasing incentive to move the transaction into the corporate hierarchy. Firms are expected to respond to the incentive, and available research shows that they respond as expected.

Observed corporate ties, the gray area in Figure 7.3, are distributed asymmetrically around the predicted association. Firms move severely constrained transactions into the corporate hierarchy. The firm that doesn't is disadvantaged in price negotiation, and that disadvantage is a constant reminder of the incentive to move the transaction into the corporate hierarchy. The lower right of the graph is empty. But creating corporate ties where there is no market incentive for them need not disadvantage the firm in its market negotiations (assuming that the few opportunity relationships are reserved for competitive pricing). These are superfluous corporate ties. Social and political pressures beyond the market generate superfluous ties—senior managers looking for projects in which to distinguish themselves, a perception by the two parties to an agreement that it would be politically expedient and cost little to have several smaller firms join them in an agreement, public and interpersonal obligations that senior managers can discharge with a low-cost corporate tie. The result is that observations of constraint and corporate ties between markets

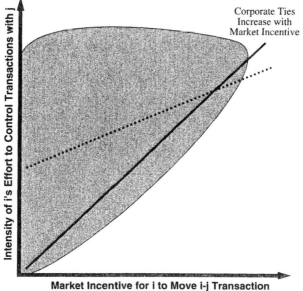

Figure 7.3   Sampling transactions for organization research. (Gray area represents data distribution, the solid line is the market effect, and the dashed line is zero-order estimate of the effect.)

have the asymmetric triangular distribution illustrated in Figure 7.3 (see Burt, 1983:151–153, for examples with respect to vertical integration and interlocking directorate ties between American markets; compare Figure 1.7 for a similar logic). This has three implications for empirical research.

First, observations in the lower right corner of the graph are especially interesting. These are constrained transactions that seem left outside the corporate hierarchy. A mechanism other than the corporate ties under study is being used to govern them. These transactions could be useful for detecting substitutable kinds of ties, or they could be sites where neoclassical or relational contracting is used instead of corporate ties as a nonmarket governance mechanism. This research focus has not yet proved useful, however, because there are so few observations to study far below the solid line.

Second, the strength of transaction cost effects will be underestimated by zero-order correlations between market constraint and corporate ties. The many superfluous corporate ties distort the connection with market constraint. Instead of the market effect given by the solid line in Figure 7.3, the zero-order correlation is given by the weaker, dashed, line. The estimation should be better with multiplex corporate ties as in Figure 7.2. The likelihood of superfluous corporate ties of different kinds occurring simultaneously is lower than the likelihood that each will occur individually. Multiplexity is a data-intensive solution. Collecting data on ties of one kind across markets—equity shares, joint ventures, interlocking directorates—is time consuming. Even ignoring the added cost of data on multiplex ties, there is no guarantee of eliminating superfluous ties.

Third, the underestimation problem is still worth noting. It highlights the importance of sampling for transaction cost research and suggests a sampling frame. A probability sample of corporate ties will represent the gray area in Figure 7.3. Because large firms are disproportionately involved in ties, quick and dirty tie samples are often defined as all ties among the N largest firms. Many sample ties will be the superfluous ties to the left in Figure 7.3. The frequency of such ties means that corporate factors other than the market will predict the ties. The resulting research will provide an accurate statistical summary of corporate ties, but shallow understanding of how they facilitate market transactions. Instead of sampling to represent all ties (the dependent variable), samples should be drawn to represent intervals on the horizontal axis (the independent variable). Explicit comparisons then can be made between ties that occur without market incentive (left of Figure 7.3) versus ties that occur where market constraint is severe (upper right of the gray area in Figure 7.3).

The latter will be the most fruitful research sites for case studies of transaction costs.

Personality as Emotional Residue

In turning to persons, I am reminded of Harry Stack Sullivan's (1953:3–4) warning about trying to communicate psychiatric concepts: Everything heard will be interpreted in two ways, neither of which will be productive. First, statements will be interpreted in terms of what readers know or half-know about their own personality and their necessarily limited experience of others. Second, statements will be interpreted by readers so as not to increase their feeling of discomfort and inadequacy in living. I add to Sullivan's warning the fact that people are more complex than organizations as a research site for the strategy hypothesis.

But firms too are prohibitively complex if everything about a firm—its structure, operation, and culture—must be described by a single explanation. The power of the structural hole contribution to the theory of the firm is its clear answer to the simple, fundamental question of coordination between market transactions and corporate hierarchy. Day-to-day corporate behavior is left unexplained. There is an analogous question for personality, and similarly, the structural hole answer is both fundamental and incomplete.

THE FIRM AS AN ILLUSTRATIVE SOCIAL CONSTRUCTION

To clarify the analogy, a more abstract view of the firm is needed. The equilibrium firm predicted by the strategy hypothesis is a network of corporate ties among establishments in different markets. Corporate ties develop to span transactions where producers are at a disadvantage under competitive market pricing.

Standing back a little further from the concrete image of an individual firm, one can see the predicted equilibrium firm as a social network of authority relations patterned to facilitate economic transactions. In this the firm has its counterpart in other kinds of economic systems. Consider the extreme example of the Kula exchange system among the Trobriand Islanders, described in Bronislaw Malinowski's (1922) classic, *Argonauts of the Western Pacific*. The Kula is a clockwise circulation of necklace valuables around a ring of islands. Necklaces are handed from individual to individual in exchange for armshells, which circulate counter clockwise around the same ring of islands. Participation in the Kula creates prestige and obligation relations in much the way Peter Blau (1964) describes social exchange more generally. Details of the exchange and questions raised by later work are summarized by Leach (1983:2–5) in his preface to a collection of more recent studies of the phenomenon. The relevant characteristic here is that trade between the islands was normally difficult because of interisland conflict. The incentive for trade was that different commodities were more often produced on one island than another, copra on one cluster of islands, for example, and canoes on another. On the occasion of exchanging Kula necklaces and armshells, active economic trade occurs. Malinowski (1922:83) describes: "The ceremonial exchange of the two articles is the main, the fundamental aspect of the Kula. But associated with it, and done under its cover, we find a great number of secondary activities and features. Thus, side by side with the ritual exchange of armshells and necklaces, the natives carry on ordinary trade, bartering from one island to another a great number of utilities, often unprocurable in the district to which they are being imported, and indispensable there."

The point is that people embed economic exchange in social relations of obligation or authority when economic exchange would be otherwise difficult. The firm as a network of authority relations predicted by the structural hole strategy hypothesis is only an example of the more general principle visible in the Trobriand Island network of Kula relations and in other economically motivated ties of social obligation (Granovetter, 1985).

ANALOGOUS VIEW OF PERSONS

The principle extends beyond economic relations. People can ease the tension of performing a constrained relationship by embedding it in other relations, real or imagined, in which they have more control. The former can be distinguished as constraint-generating relations to contrast them from the latter, embedding relations, used to manage constraint. Organizations are an attractive research site for the strategy hypothesis because market transactions as constraint generators are clearly distinct from corporate ties of ownership, joint ventures, interlocking directorates, and so on as embedding relations. The line is less clear for people individually, but kinship, work, and intimacy are probably constraint generators, while friendship and informal socializing are used as embedding relations. Kinship has an obvious obligatory quality. So do work relations based on authority, such as the relationship between supervisor and subordinate, foreman and worker, professor and student, and dean and professor. Similarly, qualities of obligation develop in long-standing friendships or other intimate relations in which personal secrets are shared. To say that these relations are constraint generators does not mean that they always generate constraint. Rather, they can generate constraint if positioned in social structure such that they are difficult to negotiate. When it would be difficult to withdraw from a relationship and the distribution of structural holes around the relationship makes it difficult to negotiate, the constraint of the relationship will be felt. Constrained relationships are the walls you bump into when you try to move. These walls have faces. They irritate. The constrained individual can be expected to respond with embedding relations to manage the constraint.

The domain of embedding relations extends beyond relations of friendship or informal socializing. At one extreme are ostensibly hostile relations that are actually embedding relations of friendship. For example, Radcliffe-Brown (1940) describes joking relations that ease constrained, uncertain relationships. The value of the joking relations he describes is such that they are an institutionalized custom. At the other extreme are the tentative opening moves that signal the first steps to an embedding relationship. Indeed, there is probably less strategic content in mature relations than there is in relations observed early in their development. Where two people find pleasure in one another's company, friendship can endure well past the original constraint incentive that initiated it. Closer to the initiation of the friendship, the constraint incentive, and so the embedding quality of the social relationship, should be more clear. The field researcher and ethnomethodologist observing newly formed groups are best prepared for this research; they watch for the tentative smile or mimicked reaction that signals the low investment I'll-be-friends-if-you're-interested opening move.

Further, embedding has strategic value beyond the limits of empirical, behavioral interaction between people. The emotions attendant to having little control in a constrained relationship can be managed with imaginary embedding relations. These imaginary relations may not be as effective as behavioral relations in managing constraint, but they can alleviate felt constraint and are a day-to-day reality for persons who don't feel able, and so are unable, to develop the behavioral embedding relations that some part of them can see they need. In some ways, these imaginary embeddings are more suited to study than are behavioral embedding relations. Through all of this, recall the distribution of embedding relations across levels of constraint in Figure 7.3. Many relations that have the potential to embed occur without constraint. The most informative site for research on embedding relations is wherever constraint is intense.

There are many reasons for the development of a behavioral relation between two people. Strategic embedding is only one. Imaginary embedding relations have a simpler etiology. They only serve to lessen the tension of performing a relationship under the constraint of having little say in the negotiation of how the relationship is performed. These imaginary relations therefore signal felt constraint and their occasional maladaptive use leaves revealing emotional boils on personality.

There is a richly documented literature on imaginary embedding relations as defense mechanisms. There are the mechanisms of projection, in which you attribute your own impulses or perceptions to another person, and identification, in which you take on characteristics of another person. There are the mechanisms of denial and dissociation, in which you cauterize the self from specific objects and relations. There are dreams, in which you perform relations in fantasy, sometimes in a heroic role that gives you an emotional release from the constrained relations you must wake to perform, sometimes in a pusillanimous role that serves to reinforce the oppression of real life. As Sullivan (1940:69) so nicely puts it: "Dreams are interpersonal phenomena in which the other fellow is wholly illusory, wholly fantastic, a projection, if you please, of certain constructive impulses, or of certain destructiveness, or of certain genital motivations, or something of that kind."

IDENTIFICATION AS AN EMBEDDING RELATION

Consider the concept of identification, for example. This is a general concept, used in many ways. When a person is severely constrained by another person, however, identification is an embedding defense mechanism like the concept discussed by Sigmund and Anna Freud.[12] Identification here refers to a person's taking on the characteristics of some object, typically a person, in his or her environment. This is an important form of attachment and, to use the Freudian phrasing, is typically directed at objects "highly cathected with libido." In the simplest examples, objects of identification are people you want to resemble: initially parents, later television heroes and rock stars, popular peers, and at some point, certain teachers and prestigious people in one's line of work. By adopting characteristic views or behaviors of a significant figure in the environment, you can rationalize perceiving yourself as similarly significant. For that moment, you rise above your actual position in the environment. With respect to the source of severe constraint, identification is an imaginary embedding relation that provides a psychic respite from being the object of constraint and replaces it with the exhilaration of being the source.[13]

Embedding qualities of identification are more apparent in abnormal situations. For example, consider Anna Freud's concept of identification with the aggressor. An identification relationship is developed with a tormentor. Frightening qualities of the tormentor are brought into the self, so that, when directed at other people, the self can feel less obviously the target. An often-mentioned example is Bettelheim's (1960) description of prisoners in Nazi concentration camps who adopted the behaviors of their guards. A contemporary example is the sympathetic relation that develops between hostages and their terrorist captors. When a person holds a gun to your head, his cause seems reasonable, even righteous.

The embedding qualities of identification are also more apparent in abnormal uses of the mechanism. In his popular review of psychoanalytic ideas, Charles Brenner (1955:114) attributes to Helene Deutsch (1934) the first systematic discussion of what would be described here as pathological embedding. Deutsch describes a class of people whose personalities are plastic adaptations built around a significant relationship. She calls them "as if" personalities because their relationship (1934:302–305) "has something about it lacking in genuineness and yet outwardly runs along 'as if' it were complete . . . These relationships are usually intense and bear all the earmarks of friendship, love, sympathy, and understanding; but even the layman soon perceives something strange . . . It is like the performance of an actor who is technically well trained but who lacks the necessary spark to make his impersonations true to life. Thus the essential characteristic of the person I wish to describe is that outwardly he conducts his life as if he possessed a complete and sensitive emotional capacity. To him there is no difference between his empty forms and what others actually experience . . . Overenthusiastic adherence to one philosophy can be quickly and completely replaced by another contradictory one without the slightest trace of inward transformation—simply as a result of some accidental regrouping of the circle of acquaintances or the like." Deutsch describes cases of "as if" personalities that developed from the lack of experience with important childhood attachments: a woman raised by nannies in severe detachment from her parents, a woman with mentally disturbed parents and a psychotic brother, and a woman with an alcoholic father who abused her mother, who the patient later discovered took pleasure in being brutalized.

BOTT ROLES

To say that the embedding qualities of identification are more obvious in abnormal uses of the defense mechanism is not to say that imaginary embedding relations are confined to the abnormal. Elizabeth Bott's (1957) close study of conjugal roles in twenty normal families illustrates the point. Bott concludes that conjugal roles are determined by the social network of relationships with people outside the marriage. As the density of the network increases, there is an increasing tendency for husband and wife to segregate their marital activities, the wife performing stereotypically female activities and the husband performing stereotypically male activities.

Segregation is described in the extreme with respect to an ideal typical family, the Newbolts (Bott, 1957:70–73): (1) husband and wife take it for granted that men have interests different from women; (2) husband controls finances, with wife given an allowance to maintain the household; (3) wife controls the household (rent, utilities, food, cooking, cleaning, etc.); (4) husband and wife deemphasize the importance of physical sexuality to a happy marriage; and (5) conjugal role activities between husband and wife are treated as the proper interest of one's friends.

Low segregation is described by the same five indicators with respect to a group of five families (Bott, 1957:79–84): (1) husband and wife question the extent to which men and women have different interests; (2) husband and wife jointly determine the family's major financial decisions; (3) husband and wife both participate in maintaining the household; (4) physical sexuality is emphasized as an important component in a happy marriage; and (5) conjugal role activities between husband and wife are deemed private, outside the proper interests of one's friends.

There are standard explanations for the role segregation. Variables such as education, occupation, parental background, and so on would be prominent in a routine sociological explanation. Bott argues, however, that the usual social and psychological variables do not account for the observed variation in segregation.

It is the structure of a couple's external network that predicts segregation. Bott (1957:60) focuses on connectivity: "The degree of segregation in the role-relationship of husband and wife varies directly with the connectedness of the family's social network." A highly connected network (Bott, 1957:65–70) is one in which: (1) relations are multiplex—friends include neighbors, relatives, and people with whom one socializes—and in particular there is extensive visiting and mutual aid from relatives, especially between the wife and her mother; (2) spouses socialize independently and with different people, the wife with female neighbors and the husband with long-time male friends; and (3) there are strong ties between friends independent of the couple, the husband's friends meeting without him and the wife's friends meeting without her. In contrast, low connectivity networks are ones in which (Bott, 1957:74ff.): (1) friends are not relatives; (2) husband and wife share the same friends and typically socialize together with their friends, going to restaurants, films, and so on; and (3) many of the couple's friends do not know one another.

Husband and wife hole signatures in an illustrative Bott role are presented in Figure 7.4 (compare with Figures 2.6 and 2.7). The couple's network, at the top of the figure, shows the wife's strong relations with her interconnected friends, especially with her mother, Jessica, and the

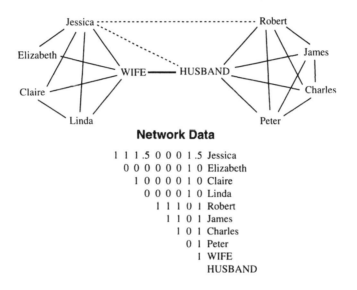

Network Data

```
1  1  1 .5  0  0  0  1 .5  Jessica
0  0  0  0   0  0  0  1  0  Elizabeth
   1  0  0   0  0  0  1  0  Claire
      0  0   0  0  0  1  0  Linda
         1   1  1  1  0  1  Robert
             1  1  1  0  1  James
                1  0  1  0  Charles
                   0  1  Peter
                      1  WIFE
                         HUSBAND
```

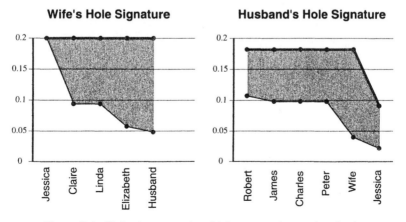

Figure 7.4 Hole signatures in a high-segregation conjugal role.

husband's strong relations with the interconnected "mates" with whom he grew up. As summarized by an informant (Bott, 1957:68–69), "Men have friends. Women have relatives" and "Women don't have friends. They have Mum." The hole signature for the wife's position in the network highlights her constrained relationship with her mother. There are no relations in this network where the wife can hide from her mother. The network is hierarchical, with "Mum" on top. The hole signature for the husband is less hierarchical. He is locked into a circle of high-constraint relations with his mates.

Spouses have little say in each other's role performance. Husband and wife have a strong relationship, but the relation's location in social structure makes it negligible. The wife's relation with her husband is the least constrained in her hole signature, the most surrounded by structural holes. When adapting to the preferences of her mother and friends, her conjugal relationship is the most open to redefinition. On the other side, the wife is a weak constraint in the husband's hole signature. When the husband adapts to the preferences of his mates, his conjugal relationship is the most open to redefinition.

The marriage is a relationship laid on top of two separate, pre-existing, high-constraint networks. Husband and wife come to this marriage as representatives of external constituencies. They have less say in the conjugal role they negotiate than in their outside constituencies. The husband performs to the audience of his mates. The wife performs to the audience of her mother and friends. Both husband and wife in such networks turn in the sex stereotypical performances deemed the proper interest of friends outside the marriage, as illustrated by Bott's indicators of high segregation.

Compare this with the hole signatures in Figure 7.5. The relations with and among the couple's contacts illustrate the low-connectivity networks in Bott's analysis. Friends are less connected with one another and are less exclusively the husband's or the wife's friends. If the network in Figure 7.4 had been deliberately transformed to look like Figure 7.5, it would be an illustration of the withdrawal and expansion strategies for managing constraint. Wife and husband have withdrawn from some high-constraint relationships and introduced new contacts connected by structural holes. Such changes are traced by Bott (1957:90, 106–108) to geographic mobility, which frees the couple from their previous high-constraint, if supportive, relationships (compare Young and Willmott, 1957). In Figure 7.5, the wife's mother isn't connected to the new friends and the husband's mates aren't an interconnected external constituency. The wife has two new friends in the neighborhood and also has friends in common with her husband. The husband has two new friends at work and shares mutual friends with his wife. These changes have reversed the position of husband and wife in each other's networks. Now they are each the strongest constraint in the other's hole signature. The conjugal role they negotiate will be more responsive to each other than to any

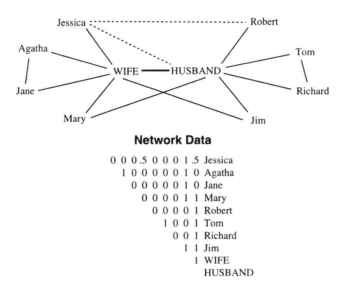

Network Data

```
0 0 0 .5 0 0 0 1 .5 Jessica
1 0 0 0 0 0 0 1 0 Agatha
0 0 0 0 0 0 1 0 Jane
0 0 0 0 0 1 1 Mary
0 0 0 0 0 1 Robert
1 0 0 1 Tom
0 0 1 Richard
1 1 Jim
1 WIFE
HUSBAND
```

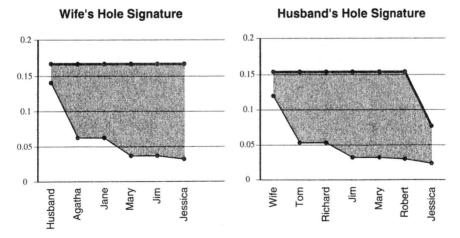

Figure 7.5   Hole signatures in a low-segregation conjugal role.

external influence. Husband and wife in such networks turn in performances less characterized by sex role stereotyping, as illustrated by Bott's indicators of low role segregation.

THE FUNDAMENTAL QUESTION

In sum, there is a fundamental question for the development of personality that is analogous to the fundamental question for the entrepreneur building a firm. The question is rarely asked explicitly, but is nevertheless informative as an analytical concept. Do I conduct this constraint-generating relationship "as is," with its known limits for negotiation, or do I embed it in another relationship that would make it easier to transact?

Framed by this question, a person is a synthesis of two networks. The foundation is a network of constraint-generating relationships—some mixture of kinship, authority, and intimacy relations. Built on top of the foundation is a network of real and imagined embedding relationships. The structure of the embedding relationships is predicted by the structure of the constraint-generating relationships. The prediction is the substance of the strategy hypothesis. The strategy hypothesis when applied to a person says that in relationships which severely constrain there is an incentive to embed the relationship in other relations over which the individual has more control. In response to felt constraint, mental images and discretionary relationships are built to manage constraint emotionally. Together, the constraints and accompanying embedding relations define a social construction visible to the analyst as personality. In orientation, this image is akin to Lewin's (1936, 1951) idea of discussing personality in terms of the surrounding field of object-specific forces shaping it. In substance, the image is allied with Sullivan's (1940, 1953) interpersonal theory of psychiatry. He describes how the growth and characteristics of personality are determined by the extent to which, and manner in which, the power motive is satisfied in relationships. This is not power as control over others so much as power as a sense of security created by having control over things that matter to the self. Relations in which security is threatened trigger anxiety to which the individual responds with a defense, and the stage is set for an adjustment to the individual's personality.

Personality is a form of organization in a complex environment. The firm is a comparatively simple person: the network of transactions among suppliers and customers defines market constraints on the producer. Corporate ties of various kinds embed constrained transactions in corporate authority to make it easier, and more profitable, to conduct what would otherwise be constrained negotiations. People are more complex. Embedding is more fluid, more varied, less visible. The foundational constraint-generating relations vary—sometimes kinship, sometimes job related, sometimes emotionally significant ties from one's past—and the embedding relations shift and vary—sometimes friendship, sometimes joking, sometimes sex, sometimes an effort to bring the source of constraint into a collaborative project, sometimes wholly imaginary relations as illustrated by the residues of identification, built to manage emotionally what cannot be managed in fact. The analogy is nevertheless instructive to establish the broad scope of the strategy hypothesis. As the firm is a social construction by players navigating around constrained market transactions, personality is an emotional construction by a person navigating around constrained relationships. The two phenomena, widely different in substance, are similarly predicted as a strategic response to constrained interaction defined by the distribution of holes in the social structure.

DOING RESEARCH

Research can move in two directions: describing how aggregate personality attributes vary with aggregate constraint or describing the transactional basis of personality.

In the first direction, kinds of personalities develop in kinds of networks. For example, David Riesman's (1950) sociological discussion of American personality develops a contrast between "inner-directed" persons, who act from internalized values, and "other-directed" persons, who act from their perception of the values of others. The two kinds of persons can both develop into "autonomous" persons, but would do so in different ways. The image of the "other-directed" person bears resemblance in the extreme to the pathologies described by Deutsch in her "as if" personalities. Riesman's (1950:142) image of the autonomous person is closely related to what I have discussed as the freedom possible from structural holes: "The autonomous are those who on the whole are capable of conforming to the behavioral norms of their society—a capacity the anomics usually lack—but are free to choose whether to conform or not."

Riesman's description of the "autonomous" person highlights the positive side of the personality associated with access to structural holes; Michael Thompson, Richard Ellis, and Aaron Wildavsky's (1990) description of the "individualist" highlights the negative side. Their classification is interesting here because it is developed in a framework related to network constraint. They distinguish ways of living, termed "cultural biases," in terms of Mary Douglas's (for example, 1970:77–92) grid-group metaphor. Their "individualist" is a person free from the constraint of socially prescribed opinion and classification (low grid) and free from the constraint of group pressure (low group). Their (1990:7–8) characterization of the "individualist" is a world view in which the rapacious exploitation of structural holes is not only legitimate but a moral obligation: "he follows a personal strategy that is both defiantly individualistic and unashamedly manipulative. He is a pragmatic materialist; he will build networks by persuading others he is a good risk; the world, he believes, is a tough place and if he doesn't get there first, somebody else will. And, anyway, it's all for the best. Though not much given to moralizing, he will, if pressed, insist that it is this unbridled competition that actually transforms the raw materials of our external world into resources we can take command of. He prospers, he tells us, if and only if he serves others. Meeting other peoples' wants in a better way than competitors is his game." They (1990:103ff.) give the type a more realistic substance when they connect it to the work of forefather structuralists such as Durkheim, Marx, Malinowski, Radcliffe-Brown, Parsons, and Merton; but the image so sharply expressed in the quote is the familiar Machiavellian personality moving through industrial, bureaucratic society.[14]

What the structural hole argument brings to such work is a formal definition and measure of the extent to which a person's social environment elicits a specific personality. It defines the conditions freeing an individual from his or her position in social structure, the specific relationships most detracting from that freedom, and so the relationships in which an otherwise "autonomous" person will play an "other-directed" role. Simply put, the volume of structural holes in a person's network should be correlated with certain personality characteristics. To name a few, the person at the center of a network rich in structural holes has: (a) greater energy and drive to build and maintain such a network, (b) higher intelligence and more symbolic (versus concrete) images of social life to maintain and report the more complex network structure, (c) less stereotypical images because of having to negotiate relations between diverse contacts, (d) more focused use of embedding relations to manage the few specific relationships in which constraint is severe (while highly constrained persons make more generalized and frequent use of embedding), and (e) more leadership attributes and higher feelings of internal control as a result of successful negotiation.

It is easy to lose sight of personality's emergent quality. Theories about personality in the aggregate usually presume an undifferentiated environment around the individual. Consider the grid-group metaphor. It is obviously related to network constraint. But in grid-group, you are classified on a single grid dimension of prescribed social norms and classifications, and a single "group" dimension of group pressure from the surrounding environment. The network details of who defines these pressures, and how, is compounded in the aggregate of how much. This is not to deny the insights from aggregate concepts. Network theory simply requires more precision. It is necessary to show how patterns of relations combine to create the causal force of the aggregate concepts. In the preceding chapters, I have shown how patterns of relations create the structural holes that enhance the negotiability of certain relationships. Aggregating constraint across a person's relations measures the group dimension in the grid-group metaphor (see Burt, 1982:173ff., 1987a, for a network rendition of the grid). In empirical research on hypotheses at the aggregate level, the results are only correlations. In the structural hole argument, personality isn't an integrated construct built as a generalized response to the surrounding environment. It is the accumulated emotional residue of managing concrete relationships with specific individuals.

The strategy hypothesis is less powerfully informative about personality in the aggregate than it is about the components in personality that develop from the constraint of specific relationships. The contribution of structural hole theory here is one of clarifying theory and setting the stage for systematic empirical research.

Consider the example of the Bott roles. Bott (1957:59) defines the condition triggering conjugal role segregation, network connectivity, as "the extent to which the people known to a family know and meet one another independently of the family." Thus strong ties among the friends of husband and wife—including strong ties between the husband's friends and the wife's friends—generate segregated conjugal roles. This interpretation only roughly describes the network data on role segregation, illustrated in Figure 7.4 and Figure 7.5. The etiology of segregated conjugal roles apparent in the data is sex-typed normative pressure on husband and wife from cohesive groups with which each socializes extensively and independently. Role segregation is generated by the pattern, not aggregate density, of connections. The absent structural holes within wife and husband networks and their abundance between the networks distinguishes the high-segregation marriage in Figure 7.4 from its opposite in Figure 7.5.[15]

Beyond clarifying the condition generating role segregation, the structural hole definition of constraint sets the stage for systematic research. Comparing hole signatures in Figures 7.4 and 7.5 across a sample of marriages would identify kinds of contacts most likely to constrain marriages. For example, how often is the wife's mother a dominant constraint? For what kinds of women is this true? To what extent does constraint on the husband's role come from relatives, or close friends, or significant co-workers? How do constraints change over the life cycle, relatives constraining the youthful performance, for example, while significant colleagues constrain the more mature performance?

More generally, the strategy hypothesis defines the places where embedding relations are expected, which in turn highlights mechanisms used to manage constraint. For the analyst, the hole signature of a person's network is a clinical disaggregation of the person's environment into variably irritating sources of constraint, defined with respect to specific individuals in the environment. As illustrated by the hypothetical signatures in Figures 2.6, 7.4, and 7.5, and the observed signatures for managers in Figure 4.7, it is immediately clear where an individual's relationships are most negotiable and most constrained. Where constraint is severe, strategic response is expected—or can be encouraged. This is the point at which empirical research describes the inventory of strategic responses used by kinds of people, in kinds of settings, with variable success. Given a constrained relationship between supervisor and subordinate, for example, what kinds of mechanisms are used to manage the constraint? When is friendship successful, and what kinds of people use it in what kinds of settings with what effects? When is an imaginary embedding relationship such as identification used and what kinds of people use it in what kinds of settings, with what effects?

Summary

This completes the three views of the player-structure duality: views of player differences between, within, and around markets as positions in social structure. In Chapters 1 and 2, I described how structural holes are responsible for rates of return varying between markets. In Chapter 6, I described how structural holes are responsible for heterogeneity and survival within a market. Here, I have described how structural holes are responsible for social and emotional organization as a kind of residue that accumulates in the wake of entrepreneurial players navigating around the constrained relationships that define a market.

The central idea is that a player who can see the advantages of an entrepreneurial opportunity can probably see advantages lost in a constrained relationship. This raises another side to the *tertius* discussed in Chapter 1. There *tertius* is a player who develops the information and control benefits of a structural hole. Here *tertius* is a strategist who navigates around the constraint of absent structural holes. The two sides to *tertius* strategy are summarized in Table 7.1. Defenses against absent holes include contracting network boundaries (withdrawal strategy), expanding network boundaries (expansion strategy), or superimposing new relations on top of constrained relationships (embedding strategy). I focus on the last as the best suited to empirical research. With embedding, the fifth player in Commons's transaction unit (Figure 7.1) comes to center stage. The fifth player is the governance mechanism that defines "fair" behavior in a relationship, the may-must-can-cannot rules defining expectations and limits on player behavior in a relationship. The substance of the embedding strategy is *tertius*'s navigation around the constraint on a relationship by changing the fifth player governing it. Embedding shifts the default rules of may-must-can-cannot to rules more favorable to the *tertius*. The task for the strategic player is to select an embedding that provides the proper level and kind of increased control.

The structural hole strategy hypothesis is a statement about where players have incentives for withdrawal, expansion, or embedding. The statement is simple: There is an incentive for strategic action in constraint relations and a disincentive in opportunity relations. The two kinds of relationships were defined in Chapter 2 with respect to the hole signature of a player's network. Everything else constant, constraint increases the incentive for strategic action. A constraint relation is a target for strategic action because it is a large investment of player time and energy where there are few structural holes with which favorable terms can be negotiated on the investment. Constraint gets balanced against opportunity. Strategic action in a relationship already rich in structural holes—even if the relation involves some constraint—could make the relationship less negotiable. Opportunity relations are a large investment of player time and energy, but are rich in structural holes. These relations the player has an incentive to protect from changes to the may-must-can-cannot conditions.

Most of this chapter is devoted to describing how the strategy hypothesis is a theory of formal organization at the same time, and in the same way, that it is a theory of personality.

Where the constrained player is an organization, the structural hole argument is a revised theory of the firm; the firm is the social residue of managers who embed constrained market transactions in contractual or authority relations. Formal organization is the answer to a fundamental production question asked by the entrepreneur: Should I conduct this transaction under the rules of competitive pricing or bring it into my organization to conduct it under rules defined by corporate authority? Coase frames the neoclassical theory of the firm with two rhetorical variations: Why would anyone conduct market buying and selling within a firm instead of on the open market? Corporate authority offers influence, stability, and privacy. Then why isn't all buying and selling conducted in one large firm? Diseconomies of scale make it inefficient. Balancing costs, "a firm will tend to expand until the costs of organizing an extra transaction within the firm become equal to the costs of carrying out the same transaction by means of an exchange on the open market" (Coase, 1937:341). Costs balanced at the transaction margin define the equilibrium firm adapted to its market. This reasoning has matured into contemporary resource dependence and transaction cost theory.

The structural hole argument speaks to the fundamental question at the heart of these theories. With respect to resource dependence theory, the constraint coefficient c_{ij} measures the extent to which resources from market j are a high proportion of producer i business, and their price is uncertain and high on the open market. This is dependence in both an actuarial and a political sense. With producers investing in facilities and staff to service their dominant supplier and customer markets, they face large costs if those transactions change. Their dependence is akin to asset specificity in transaction cost theory, and vulnerability dependence in world system theory. With respect to transaction cost theory, the constraint coefficient most obviously captures the small numbers condition. It increases as suppliers and customers decrease. However, it is more than that. It increases as the opportunities for negotiating a favorable price decrease. The uncertainty captured is not the uncertainty of transaction complexity but the uncertainty of having little control in a transaction. Add the presumption that business partners will exploit producers if they can; then constraint captures the probability of opportunism and information impactedness because it captures the conditions that make it profitably possible to be opportunistic and manipulate the flow of information. Add the fact that firms invest in personnel and facilities tailored to their dominant supplier and customer markets, and it is safe to say that constraint is correlated across transactions with the asset specificity criterion in transaction cost theory.

In sum, the structural hole constraint coefficient is an empirically verified measure of the cost to producers of doing business with a specific supplier or customer market under the rules of competitive pricing. The higher the constraint, the greater the incentive to replace competitive pricing with corporate authority. Constraint does not capture all aspects of transaction cost or all aspects of resource dependence. But constraint captures significant aspects of cost and dependence in both frameworks, and has a validating association with profit margins. Whatever constraint measures of transaction cost and resource dependence, it is a quality that lowers the rate of return on producer investments. Constraint defines and measures the extent to which a transaction is positioned in the social structure of the economy to put producers at a disadvantage in negotiating the transaction.

These considerations complete the predictions of the strategy hypothesis: There is an incentive for strategic action in constraint relations and a disincentive in opportunity relations. Where w_{ij} is a measure of corporate authority ties between markets i and j, w_{ij} increases with c_{ij} and decreases with the extent to which p_{ij} dominates c_{ij}. Where a transaction is severely constrained, the authority of a corporate hierarchy is the preferred setting for negotiating the transaction. Where constraint is low because there is no trade with a market, there is no market incentive for corporate ties. Where constraint is low because of high competition within a significant supplier or customer market, however, the firm has a strong incentive to keep the transaction out of the corporate hierarchy in order to exploit it more efficiently with competitive pricing. Illustrative empirical evidence supports the predictions (Figure 7.2), and guides for stronger transaction cost research emerge with the analogy between cost and constraint (Figure 7.3).

Coase's image of the equilibrium firm has a social structural definition: Begin with the producer's most severely constrained market transactions. Evaluate the costs of the transactions conducted under rules of competitive pricing against the costs if conducted under the control of corporate authority. If the difference between price and cost under corporate authority would be smaller with suppliers, or greater with customers, move the transaction into the firm. Move to the next most constrained transactions. Make the same evaluation. Continue down the rank order of market constraints. Where the costs of moving the next transactions into the firm equals the costs of conducting them on the open market, stop. The transactions now in the firm are the optimum for its market.

Analogous reasoning predicts the emotional organization optimum for surviving in a given network. When the constrained player is a person, the argument is a description of personality as the emotional residue that results as a person embeds constrained relationships in social obligations or psychological defense mechanisms. The firm as a network of authority relations is an example of a principle visible in other kinds of economic systems as primitive as the Trobriand Kula system: people embed economic exchange in social relations of obligation or authority when economic exchange would be otherwise difficult. The principle extends beyond economic relations. People can ease the tension of performing a constrained relationship by embedding it in other relations, real or imagined, in which they have more control. The former can be distinguished as constraint-generating relations to contrast them from the latter, embedding relations, used to manage constraint. The domain of embedding relations is diverse, going beyond the limits of behavioral relations. The emotions attendant to having little control in a constrained relationship can be managed with imaginary embedding relations. An example is the defense mechanism of identification. By adopting views or behaviors characteristic of a significant figure in the environment, you can rationalize perceiving yourself as similarly significant. For that moment, you rise above your actual position in the environment. Identification is an imaginary embedding relation that provides a psychic respite from being the object of constraint and replaces it with the exhilaration of being the source. Though the embedding qualities of identification are more obvious in abnormal uses of the defense mechanism, imaginary embedding relations are not confined to the abnormal. Bott's study of conjugal roles illustrates the point.

There is thus a fundamental question for the development of personality analogous to the fundamental question for the entrepreneur building a firm. Do I conduct this constraint-generating relationship "as is," with its known limits for negotiation, or do I embed it in another relationship that would make it easier to transact? Framed by this question, a person is a synthesis of two networks. The foundation is a network of constraint-generating relationships—some mixture of kinship, authority, and intimacy relations. Built on top of the foundation is a network of real and imagined embedding relationships. The structure of the embedding relationships is predicted by the structure of the constraint-generating relationships. The prediction is the substance of the strategy hypothesis. The strategy hypothesis when applied to a person says that in relationships which severely constrain there is an incentive to embed the relationship in other relations over which the individual has more control. In response to felt constraint, mental images and discretionary relationships are built to manage constraint emotionally. Together the constraints and accompanying embedding relations define a social construction visible to the analyst as personality.

Personality is a form of organization in a complex environment. The firm is a comparatively simple person. The network of transactions among suppliers and customers defines market constraints on the producer. Corporate ties of various kinds embed constrained transactions in corporate authority to make it easier, and more profitable, to conduct what would otherwise be constrained negotiations. People are more complex. Embedding is more fluid, more varied, less visible. The foundational constraint-generating relations vary—sometimes kinship, sometimes job related, sometimes emotionally significant ties from one's past—and the embedding relations shift and vary—sometimes friendship, sometimes joking, sometimes sex, sometimes an effort to bring the source of constraint into a collaborative project, sometimes wholly imaginary relations as illustrated by the residues of identification, built to manage emotionally what cannot be managed in fact. The analogy is nevertheless instructive to establish the broad scope of the strategy hypothesis. As the firm is a social construction by players navigating around constrained market transactions, personality is an emotional construction by a person navigating around constrained relationships. The two phenomena, widely different in substance, are similarly predicted as a strategic response to constrained interaction defined by the distribution of holes in the social structure.

Notes

Introduction

1. This paragraph owes much to Stigler's (1957) review of the evolution of competition in economic theory. He provides the simple profit question that calls for an assumption of competition. The three conditions for perfect competition are adapted from Edgeworth (1881:17–19), but I only appreciated their evolutionary significance in the context of alternatives laid out in Stigler's (1957) review. Beyond providing context, the clarity of Stigler's presentation, here and with respect to Edgeworth on marginal utility, offers a great improvement over the original. At the same time, as always, the original has value. Edgeworth's characterization of free choice in terms of no intrusive third parties is the key to the social structure of competition. Structural holes are about third parties to a relationship. Stigler's (1957:247) recoding of that to be the "complete absence of limitations upon individual self-seeking behavior" states the original thought in terms more compatible with subsequent developments in economic theory, but obscures the social structural insight in the original.

1. The Social Structure of Competition

1. I refer to people and organizations in the competitive arena as "players." Richard Swedberg has commented that I use the term to denote a very active actor, seeking out contacts and opportunities. He gently suggested that the term had a touch of frivolity that I might do well to eliminate with a more neutral term such as "actor." I have used the more neutral term in more general discussion (Burt, 1982), but for the topic of competition, I prefer the term "player." It better fits my felt-reality of the phenomenon. More than implying activity, it is a term of peer recognition: "Yes, he's a player." He's a presence in the game. If you have the motivation, resources, and skills to compete, you're a player; otherwise, you're scenery. Everyone is a player

in some arenas, scenery in most. This chapter is about the social structural conditions that give certain players a competitive advantage.

2. Coleman's (1988:S105-S108, S109-S116) argument for the importance of network closure in the transmission of human capital between generations is an illustrative alternative to Granovetter's weak tie metaphor. The weak tie metaphor is that weaker ties are most important to transmission. The work spawned by Lazarsfeld focuses on strong ties. Coleman emphasizes the importance of strong ties reinforced by other ties. Although the argument is not grounded in network models of Simmel's conflicting group-affiliation metaphor, the resemblance is obvious. For example, parents are presumed to prefer that their children obtain at least the minimal education required to graduate from high school. Relying on attribute data, Coleman (1988:S114-S115) shows that children in Catholic high schools—where parents are presumed to be closely connected with one another and other parents, and so constrain the choices of their children—have lower drop-out rates than do children in public high schools. Network analysis improves the power of such arguments, by providing: (a) concrete measures of the extent to which parents (versus others, such as peers) are structurally positioned to constrain the choices of specific children, and (b) formal theory creating more precise, testable understandings of how constraint operates. These points are both illustrated in the forthcoming argument.

3. Network contagion measures of social capital will always be a valuable addition to the application of the general definition to the situation of a specific individual. For example, a person with a poorly structured network that includes just one well-placed contact can do well through that contact's sponsorship regardless of how well the person's network as a whole is structured. We will see some evidence of this in the analysis of managers in Chapter 4. We will also see the downside. Being known as someone's minion, dependent on their sponsorship, limits the minion's attractiveness as a social capital addition in other networks. Relations require an investment of time and trust that in this case depend entirely on the sponsor's support. The minion isn't a serious player independently shaping the course of events in the arena. This makes the minion role adhesive. It holds the player with dependence on the sponsor's support. It cauterizes the development of relations with other players through which the dependence could be made more negotiable.

4. This point is significant because it contradicts the natural growth of contact networks. Left to the normal course of events, a network will accumulate redundant contacts. Friends introduce you to their friends and expect you to like them. Business contacts introduce you to their colleagues. You will like the people you meet in this way. The factors that make your friends attractive make their friends attractive because like seeks out like. Your network grows to include more and more people. These relations come easily, they are comfortable, and they are easy to maintain. But these easily accumulated contacts do not expand the network so much as they fatten it, weakening its

efficiency and effectiveness by increasing contact redundancy and tying up time. The process is amplified by spending time in a single place: in your family, or neighborhood, or in the office. The more time you spend with any specific primary contact, the more likely you will be introduced to their friends. Evidence of these processes can be found in studies of balance and transitivity in social relations (see Burt, 1982:55–60, for review) and in studies of the tendency for redundant relations to develop among physically proximate people (for example, the suggestively detailed work of Festinger, Schachter, and Back, 1950; or the work with more definitive data by Fischer, 1982, on social contexts, and Feld, 1981, 1982, on social foci). Here I ignore the many day-to-day tactical issues critical to maintaining a network.

5. The number of structural holes is not increased directly, but is likely to increase. The presumption through all this is that the time and energy to maintain relationships is limited and that the constant pressure to include new contacts will use all the time and energy available (as in the preceding note). Although structural holes are not increased directly by maximizing nonredundant contacts, they can be expected to increase indirectly through the reallocation of time and energy from maintaining redundant contacts to acquiring new nonredundant contacts (as illustrated in Figure 1.4).

6. This theme is often grouped with Durkheim's (1893) argument for the liberating effect of a division of labor, but it is useful here to distinguish the two arguments. Simmel focuses on the liberating quality of competition between multiple affiliations, which is our concern. Durkheim focuses on the liberating quality of interdependent affiliations. Integration, rather than competition, is Durkheim's theme. That theme continues in Blau's (1977) analysis of cross-cutting social circles, in which he argues that conflict between strata becomes increasingly difficult as affiliations provide people with alternative stratification hierarchies. Flap (1988) provides a network-oriented review of such work, building from anthropology and political science, to study the "crisscross" effect inhibiting violence.

7. Georg Simmel introduced this phrase in papers on the importance of group size, translated and published by Albion Small in the *American Journal of Sociology* (Simmel, 1896:393–394, 1902:174–189). A later version was translated by Wolff (Simmel, 1923:154–169, 232–234).

8. I am grateful to Anna Di Lellio for calling my attention to the Italian proverb and Hein Schreuder for calling my attention to the Dutch expression. The idea of exploiting a structural hole is viscerally familiar to all audiences, but interestingly varied across cultures in phrasing the profit obtained (an interesting site for a Zelizer, 1989, kind of analysis).

9. This point is nicely exemplified in Simmel's (1896:394) discussion of subordination comparing the freedom of two medieval subordinate positions, the bondsman ("unfree") and the vassal: "An essential difference between the mediaeval 'unfree' men and the vassals consisted in the fact that the former had and could have only one master, while the latter could accept land from

different lords and could take the oath of fealty to each. By reason of the possibility of placing themselves in the feudal relation to several persons the vassals won strong security and independence against the individual lords. The inferiority of the position of vassalage was thereby to a considerable degree equalized.''

10. The literal meaning of entrepreneur as broker continues today, but only as one of many narrow meanings in the term's more general, ambiguous meaning of anyone who sets out to accomplish or undertake a task. Before it was watered down, the term enjoyed a long history in its literal meaning as a reference to individuals who obtained their profit by coordinating the activities of others. The term comes from the French verb *entreprendre,* meaning literally "to take, grasp, or snatch" *(prendre)* from "between" *(entre).* In the mid-1500s, entrepreneurs were the men who organized and led military expeditions. Similar to the English privateer, the French entrepreneur was a private agent commissioned to coordinate the recruitment, arming, and transportation of men for a military junket with some promise of profitable booty. The reference to military projects expanded by the 1700s to refer to general contractors for large government projects. Entrepreneurs were the men who organized labor and materials for civil and military projects such as harbors, fortifications, bridges, roads, and buildings. Today's ambiguous meaning of entrepreneur as anyone who undertakes a task comes from the works of French political economists in the middle of the eighteenth century (Belidor, Cantillon, Quesnay, Baudeau, Turgot) describing individuals who undertook projects at risk of being unprofitable because of buying and selling at uncertain prices. Hoselitz (1951) provides a fascinating social etymology of the term (also Redlich, 1949, both of which appeared in the regrettably discontinued journal *Explorations in Entrepreneurial History,* produced until the late 1960s through Harvard's Research Center in Entrepreneurial History). The term's use in economics and business seems little more precise than its use in the general population (for example, see Cochran, 1968, for a quick sketch; Peterson, 1981, for a detailed review), but the literal meaning is sometimes visible. For example, see Peterson's (1981:66ff.) Schumpeterian review of entrepreneurial action as a process of bringing together in a novel way previously separate factors of production or see Kirzner's (1973, esp. pp. 75–87, 126–131, 205–211; and 1979, esp. chap. 3) comparison of his concept of entrepreneur with that of others in economic theory. There is a distinct quality of the *tertius* in Kirzner's successful entrepreneur, for example (1973:48), "Pure entrepreneurial profit is the difference between the two sets of prices. It is not yielded by exchanging something the entrepreneur values less for something he values more highly. It comes from discovering sellers and buyers of something for which the latter will pay more than the former demand.''

11. I am grateful to Richard Swedberg for giving me the benefit of his careful study of Schumpeter in calling my attention to these passages. Their broader

scope and context are engagingly laid out in his biography of Schumpeter (Swedberg, 1991). The passages can also be found in the Schumpeter selection included in Parsons et al.'s (1961:513) *Theories of Society.*

12. I am reminded of a colleague who found none of the three local banks willing to finance a mortgage on the house he wished to buy. Eventually the mortgage was financed jointly by the three banks, a mortgage my colleague obtained by going to the loan officer in each bank and indicating that each other loan officer was willing to sign off on the loan if he would. With sufficient entrepreneurial motivation, opportunities to emerge as the *tertius* can be created where they don't already exist.

13. I am begging the question of how opportunity and motivation are connected. I emphasize the causal priority of opportunity. The opposite emphasis is traditional in sociology. In his Foreword to the English version of Weber's (1905:8) analysis, R. H. Tawney put the matter succinctly: "Why insist that causation can work in only one direction? Is it not a little artificial to suggest that capitalist enterprise had to wait, as Weber appears to imply, till religious changes had produced a capitalist spirit? Would it not be equally plausible, and equally one-sided, to argue that the religious changes were themselves merely the result of economic movements?" I see no asymmetric resolution to this problem; entrepreneurial opportunity and motivation are reciprocally causal items. Kilby's (1971) edited volume and Wilken's (1979) historical comparative analysis are useful references for detailed discussion of the problem. Here I emphasize opportunity because I can analyze it in a rigorous way with network concepts and describe a great variety of empirical events. Given a rigorous concept of entrepreneurial opportunity, the next analytical step is to study motivational differences between individuals who take advantage of their opportunities and individuals who do not.

14. This sentence is the starting point for an optimization model in which the benefits of a contact are weighed against the cost of maintaining a relation with the contact, subject to a time and energy budget constraint on the aggregate of contacts in a network. The work is beyond the scope of this discussion, but I want to remove an ostensible barrier to such work and in the process highlight a scope limitation to my argument. Marks (1977) provides a cogent argument against the energy scarcity metaphor so often used to justify discussions of role negotiations. Instead of viewing roles as energy debilitating, Marks argues for an "expansion" view in which energy is created by performing roles (compare Sieber, 1974). Marks and Sieber discuss the advantages of performing multiple roles. Both are responding to the energy scarcity arguments used to motivate discussions of mechanisms by which people manage role strain (most notably, Merton, 1957; Goode, 1960). To quote Goode (1960:485), a person "cannot meet all these demands to the satisfaction of all the persons who are part of his total role network. Role strain—difficulty in meeting given role demands—is therefore normal. In general, the person's total role obligations are overdemanding." I have bor-

rowed the theme of overdemanding role obligations. The *tertius* budget constraint concerns both the time and energy cost of maintaining existing relations and the opportunity costs of contacts lost because of redundancy. However, my argument only concerns negotiations within a single role. The mechanisms used to manage role strain, such as segregating role relations in time and space, could also be used by the *tertius* to manage conflict to his or her own advantage, but I am ignoring that possibility, and so limiting the scope of my argument, to focus on the situation in which *tertius* negotiates conflicting demands that have to be met simultaneously.

2. Formalizing the Argument

1. The STRUCTURE program is available from the Center for the Social Sciences at Columbia University. The constraint results to be reported were obtained with Version 4.1, released in 1989.
2. A large literature exists on strategies for obtaining network data in various research settings. See Marsden (1990) for a general review and Burt and Minor (1983:chaps. 1–8) for illustrations of specific issues and strategies. The Network Data section of the STRUCTURE program manual also offers a detailed review with references to related literature.
3. There are several good reviews of cohesion and equivalence measures. The second half of Burt and Minor (1983) contains some. Burt (1982:chap. 2) is a quick review (from the review in the 1980 *Annual Review of Sociology*). The Clique and Equivalence sections of the STRUCTURE program manual (expanding on Burt, 1988b) provide review with software implementation.
4. I am concerned with the degree of connection between players and so sum the two relations between a pair into a single symmetric measure of connection between them. The total of i's network time and energy thus includes all relations to or from other players. This is the default in the STRUCTURE program. There is an option in the program to limit i's network to the players who are the object of a relation from i.
5. I will discuss this measure in more detail after constraint is introduced, but network analysts might wonder immediately why I am not using network density. Density, the average strength of relations in a network, is both simple and familiar. Consider three issues of increasing seriousness. First, the count of nonredundant contacts has an attractive metric that will be simple and familiar well beyond the audience of network analysts. Second, effective size is based on the concentration of density in individual contacts rather than its average distribution across all contacts. This is even more a characteristic of the constraint measure to be introduced. For example, the illustrative network to be presented in Figure 2.2 has a low density of connections among contacts (density is $0.27 = 4.0/15$) and so high efficiency (0.78), but the network contains one contact, A, who poses a disproportionate level of constraint in the network. Third, effective size increases up to a limit of the

number of observed contacts, while density varies from zero up to the limit of the strongest relationship in a network. Density holds constant differences between people in the size of their network to capture more clearly the average strength of relations. Effective size retains size differences between people, adjusted for the redundancy of their contacts.

6. I have run simulations exploring alternative ways to measure constraint. Constraint has two signature qualities: (a) it is the product of a player's investment in reaching a contact multiplied by the lack of holes around the contact, and, as illustrated in the graph at the bottom of Figure 2.3, (b) it decreases with network size and increases with density. I was most attracted to the alternative of replacing i's total investment to reach j, $p_{ij} + \Sigma_q p_{iq} p_{qj}$ in Eq. (2.4), with i's investment in direct contact with j, p_{ij}. The alternative is simpler and more intuitive. The squared expression in Eq. (2.4) reduces to the following alternative:

$$p_{ij}\left(p_{ij} + \sum_q p_{iq} p_{qj}\right), \qquad q \neq i, j.$$

By excluding indirect connections from the investment term, density is less significant in this constraint measure. Across the 17 data points in the graph at the bottom of Figure 2.3, for example, Eq. (2.4) aggregate constraint is predicted by network size (N) and density (D) with the following regression equation:

$$0.56(N^{-0.64})(1 + D)^{1.55}.$$

Compare the following equation predicting the above alternative expression as a measure constraint:

$$0.75(N^{-0.82})(1 + D)^{0.78}.$$

The effect of density is weaker. The solid line describing constraint with this measure in maximum density networks lies close to the dashed line in the graph at the bottom of Figure 2.3. The weaker role of density in defining constraint is a problem because density is a factor in the successful prediction of rates of return in the next two chapters. The above alternative measure predicts less well than the measure in Eq. (2.4). One way to increase density's effect within the alternative measure is to replace direct inter-contact connections with total connections. The idea in using p_{qj} in Eq. (2.3) is that contact q has made a large investment in his relationship with j. An alternative is to use the total proportion of q's interaction that leads to j:

$$\left(p_{qj} + \sum_k p_{qk} p_{kj}\right), \qquad k \neq q, j.$$

This varies from zero (when q has no direct or indirect connection with j), up to one (when all of q's interaction leads directly or indirectly back to j).

When it equals its maximum of one, there is no structural hole between contacts q and j to be developed by the central player i against j. Constraint is now measured by the following expression, replacing p_{qj} in the above alternative measure with $(p_{qj} + \Sigma_k p_{qk} p_{kj})$:

$$p_{ij}\left(p_{ij} + \sum_q p_{iq}\left[p_{qj} + \sum_k p_{qk} p_{kj}\right]\right), \qquad q \neq i, j; k \neq q, j.$$

The following regression equation predicts this measure of constraint from network size and density:

$$0.63(N^{-0.71})(1 + D)^{1.18}.$$

Density has a stronger role, if not as strong as in the proposed measure of constraint in Eq. (2.4). The line for this measure in maximum density networks lies about midway between the dashed and solid lines in the graph at the bottom of Figure 2.3. This measure does about as well as the Eq. (2.4) measure in empirical tests, better for some subsets of players, worse for others; so it might be a useful direction to pursue. I put it to one side here because it offers no strong improvement over, and is more complex than, the constraint measure proposed in Eq. (2.4).

7. To get the results for densities between the extremes of zero and one, I averaged relations across the present and absent ties responsible for fractional density. At the top of Figure 2.4, the contact-specific constraint is $[p + (N - 1)(p)(p)(\text{density})]^2$, and the aggregate constraint plotted in the graph is N times that amount, where N is the number of contacts, p is the proportional strength of relations $(1/N)$, and density is given for each slice in the graph. Aggregate constraint in the bottom graph is the same equation, except relations between contacts are represented by density directly: $N[p + (N - 1)(p)(\text{density})]^2$.

8. This is a fitting place to link the proposed constraint measure to prior work to avoid confusions with the prior work. I have used various constraint models to describe imperfect competition in corporate markets and to predict the structure of large firms (Burt, 1979, 1980, 1982:chaps. 7 and 8, 1983, 1988a). Burt (1988a) uses the constraint measure described here. Two others were used earlier. First, for general discussions, I used an incomplete definition grounded in Simmel's idea of conflicting group-affiliations (Burt, 1980, 1982). Constraint in these models only measures the extent to which the person at the center of the network is confined to a few contacts around whom there are no secondary structural holes. Structural holes between primary contacts are ignored. Second, for describing constraint applied to American markets, I used a group-affiliation definition fit more closely to the study population, where transactions with supplier markets generate constraint in a manner different from transactions with customer markets (Burt, 1979, 1983). My argument leading to the constraint measure here is more general in the sense

of including primary and secondary structural holes, but less attentive to the empirical detail that the two kinds of structural holes are variably significant in different kinds of relationships.

9. Defining the thin line by c_{ij} can be awkward in some networks, and in such cases it is useful to define it in a slightly different way. The constraint coefficient c_{ij} measures j's total constraint on i. To define c_{ij} in Eq. (2.7), i's investment to reach j is both i's direct investment, p_{ij}, and i's investment in other relations that lead back to j, the sum of $p_{iq}p_{qj}$. The total investment can be larger than the direct investment. The result is that c_{ij} can be larger than p_{ij}. This can happen when j is connected with every other contact and there are no other connections between contacts. In the Figure 2.7 leader hierarchy, for example, 0.29 of your network time and energy is invested in the relationship with contact C. If C's relations with contacts A and E are strengthened to 1.0, C's total constraint on you increases to 0.32 from the number in the figure. The thin line over C rises above the bold line. Aggregate constraint is still less than 1.0 and the predictions from c_{ij} are unaffected, but the hole signature idea of comparing c_{ij} to p_{ij} as a balance between constraint and investment is clumsy. An alternative is to define the thin line by direct, rather than total, constraint. Direct constraint is the lack of holes around contact j, Eq. (2.6), multiplied by the network time and energy invested in the direct connection with j, p_{ij}. This is less than or equal to the contact's total constraint on the player and never higher than p_{ij} because Eq. (2.6) has an upper limit of one. Investment to reach j indirectly through other contacts is ignored. I have used c_{ij} to define the thin line under a hole signature for four reasons; it is consistent with the discussion of constraint throughout the book, it preserves the disaggregation of total investment into constrained (C) and unconstrained ($1 - C$) portions, it provides more obvious distinctions between levels of constraint because it has a higher mean value than its alternative, and I have no networks in which c_{ij} exceeds p_{ij}.

10. Specifically, it is the vertical distance between the dots in the graph, not the area between the lines. If contacts were put immediately adjacent to one another, it would be correct to refer to area, but the graph would be unreadable. I refer to area in the text because it is easier to see in the graph.

11. The ordinary least-squares (OLS) coefficients have been scaled so that the sum of contact specific constraints has a 1.0 effect on aggregate constraint. The relative magnitudes of the OLS estimates is preserved, but displayed so that the hierarchy effects are adjustments to summed constraint. The regression model contains the equation in the text defining C plus a second equation defining aggregate constraint's association with early promotion: Early promotion $= \alpha + b_c C + e$, where e is a residual term. Substituting Eq. (2.11) for C in the regression equation gives the reduced form equation to be estimated:

$$\alpha + b_c\left(\sum_j c_{ij}\right) + b_1(H - \bar{H}) + b_2 L(H - \bar{H}) + b_3 LS(H - \bar{H}) + e,$$

where b_c is the effect of $(\Sigma_j c_{ij})$ on early promotion, b_1 is the effect of H, b_2 is the effect of LH, and b_3 is the effect of LSH. With OLS estimates of b_c, b_1, b_2, and b_3, the coefficients in the text can be computed: $\lambda_1 = b_1/b_c$, $\lambda_2 = b_2/b_c$, and $\lambda_3 = b_3/b_c$, where the correlation between early promotion and the adjusted constraint measure C is the multiple correlation in the regression model predicting early promotion from the four variables in the text. The *t*-tests reported in the text are for the reduced form effects of each hierarchy adjustment: b_1, b_2, and b_3. The adjusted constraint measure has the metric of the summed constraint measure used in Chapters 3 and 4. It has a slightly higher variance created by including hierarchy variance.

12. The two distributions of structural autonomy are not comparable across the two populations in the same way that constraint and hierarchy can be compared. Structural autonomy is the value of an outcome variable expected from structural holes. Its values reflect the outcome predicted. The mean profit margin at the top of Figure 2.9 is lower than the mean score on the early promotion variable at the bottom of the figure (0.123 versus 0.225). Therefore, structural autonomy scores in the top graph are lower than those in the bottom graph. Structural hole comparisons between the two study populations should be based on constraint. The large market networks exist at the low-constraint end of autonomy in comparison to the small, high-constraint manager networks (compare Figures 3.9 and 4.8).

13. Where PCM is the price-cost margin averaged across the four input-output tables studied in Chapter 3, the adjusted margin is PCM $- 0.152(N - .325)$, where N is a dummy variable equal to 1 for nonmanufacturing markets, 0.325 is the mean of N across all 77 markets, and 0.152 is the difference between the average manufacturing PCM and the average nonmanufacturing PCM. The natural log of the adjusted PCM is the criterion variable in the graph at the top of Figure 2.9.

14. The prediction uses three degrees of freedom with the listed variables, plus one degree of freedom for the nonmanufacturing adjustment, plus one degree of freedom for the hierarchy adjustment, leaving 72 degrees of freedom (compare Table 3.3). The *F*-test at the top of Figure 2.9 is the ratio of predicted mean squares (3.142/4) over residual mean squares (11.872/72).

15. The early promotion variable in Chapter 4 varies from negative to positive values where zero is the average age at which each kind of manager is promoted, and positive values indicate managers promoted to their current rank at an unusually young age. I need positive scores to compute logs. The early promotion variable is transformed to get the criterion variable in Figure 2.9: $Y^* = (0.5425Y + 0.2322)$, where Y is the early promotion score analyzed in Chapter 4. This shrinks the range of scores and raises them to positive values. The resulting Y^* varies from 0.038 to 0.402, the same range covered by the market profit margins in the graph at the top of Figure 2.9. Correlations between the variables discussed in the text of Chapter 4 are unaffected by this transformation, but correlations with the log of Y^* now correspond more clearly to the market results.

16. The prediction has an initial 231 degrees of freedom as explained in the note to Table 4.2, but another three are lost with the adjustment for hierarchy. The *F*-test at the bottom of Figure 2.9 is the ratio of predicted mean squares (3.213/4) over residual mean squares (32.029/228).

3. *Turning a Profit*

1. The disadvantage of analyzing more narrowly defined markets is the shifting definitions of market boundaries. Even the boundaries of the aggregate markets are redefined somewhat over time, but the changes do not interfere significantly with the estimated effects of structural holes (see Burt, 1988a, for detailed analysis). The disadvantage of the aggregate level of analysis is regression toward the mean. The more narrowly a market is defined, the more likely it is that a small number of large firms can dominate the market. In other words, measures of missing structural holes within a market, O, will increase as a smaller and smaller number of establishments are defined as operating in the market. As the range of values of O increases, variation in constraint, C, increases. In sum, the effects of structural holes measured by O and C can be studied over a broader range of conditions in more narrowly defined markets. This means that data on narrowly defined markets are better for studying structural hole effects during a single year. The data on aggregate markets used here are better for studying the broad effects of structural holes over time to guide organization research.

2. The data are taken from the 1963 transactions table (*Survey of Current Business,* 1969:30–35), the 1967 transactions table (*Survey of Current Business,* 1974:38–43), the 1972 use table (*Survey of Current Business,* 1979:62–67), and the 1977 use table (*Survey of Current Business,* 1984:52–57). These data sources are referred to hereafter as the 1963, 1967, 1972, and 1977 tables.

3. Transactions with these last two markets are largely final demand. Households make no sales to product sectors, only purchases from them. Household sales to the product markets could be introduced by including an 80th row and column for the labor market. There is no single measure of the lack of structural holes within the labor market. Although it could be introduced with market-specific measures of unionization, I have not introduced that complexity here. The 79th sector, government, does have sales to product markets through government enterprises, but the bulk of its transactions are purchases by federal, state, and local agencies for defense, education, and welfare. I treat negative dollar flows as sources of income. For example, the $1,202 million subsidy in 1967 from federal government agencies to agriculture establishments is treated as $1,202 million in sales to government.

4. My approximations cannot be checked for their accuracy across all nonmanufacturing markets, but it is heartening to see some correspondence with concentration ratios for the selected service sectors on which four-firm concentration data are available in the 1977 *Census of Services.* The *Census* data and *News Front* approximations are, 0.070 versus 0.064 for the hotel market,

0.028 versus 0.033 for the business services market, 0.089 versus 0.084 for the automobile services market, and 0.080 versus 0.081 for the amusements market, respectively.

5. There are five exceptions to these general procedures. First, the armaments market (sector 13 in the aggregate input-output table) is composed of SIC manufacturing categories, but concentration data were not released on its component SIC categories during the 1960s. I use the concentration ratio constructed from the 1972 *Census of Manufactures* to describe concentration in the 1960s. Second, if the electric, gas, water, and sanitary services market (input-output sector 68) is treated as a national market it appears unrealistically competitive (concentration of 0.09, 0.12, and 0.10 for 1967, 1972, and 1977, respectively). The government and utilities markets are assumed to be monopolies within their administratively defined jurisdictions. The highest estimated concentration ratios are close to 0.9, so I set concentration in the utilities market at the slightly higher 0.9 in government and utility markets. Third, the large diversified firms in chemical and fertilizer mineral mining (input-output sector 10) make it difficult to compare total sales in *News Front* and the *Survey of Current Business*. Total sales in the *Survey* are smaller in the 1970s than the total sales reported in *News Front;* $492 million versus $877 million in 1972 and $1,426 million versus $2,747 million in 1977. For example, sales by the four largest firms assigned to this market in *News Front* sum to $2,455 million in 1977, which defines an impossible 1.92 concentration ratio for the market. Therefore, I approximate concentration in the 1970s by dividing total sales from the four largest chemical and fertilizer mineral mining firms in *News Front* by total sales from all such firms listed in *News Front*. Fourth, concentration in the iron and ferroalloy ores market (input-output sector 5) is greatly affected in the 1970s by the presence of one enormous mining firm, American Metals Climax (AMAX). The firm is listed in *News Front* as operating in SIC 333 in 1967, which creates a dramatic increase in concentration in mining between 1967 and 1972 when AMAX is moved from manufacturing (SIC 333) to mining (SIC 106). Concentration in mining rises from 0.19 to 0.92. However, the Form 10K Reports on AMAX during this period show no change in their operations and a long history of mining ferroalloy ores (SIC 106). Therefore, AMAX is kept in the iron and ferroalloy ores market throughout the 1960s and 1970s. Fifth, and finally, Ralph Nader notwithstanding, I assume that there is no corporate organization protecting individual customers in the household market sufficient to create concentration measured to three digits (O is 0.000 in the household market).

6. The restaurant market, input-output sector 74, is an exception. In the 1963 and 1967 tables, sector 74 is the market for research and development, but no data are reported on it. Research and development transactions are incorporated into the transactions of markets performing the research and development. In the 1972 table and later, sector 74 contains restaurants (see p. 42 of the February 1979 *Survey of Current Business*). Results on the restaurant

market here are averaged across 1972 and 1977 rather than across the four points in time averaged for all other markets.

7. The 1967, 1972, and 1977 tables provide the components of value added to compute price-cost margins. The total sales figure is published at the bottom of columns in the tables. The needed data are not published with the 1963 table, but are available on p. 36 of the April 1973 *Survey of Current Business*. Value added in the input-output tables excludes all production costs, including business expenses and advertising. The restaurant market is averaged across 1972 and 1977 (see note 6).

8. Tests for nonmanufacturing slope adjustments to the effects of O and C in the linear model in the first row of Table 3.2 are negligible (t-tests of -0.1 and -0.4 respectively for slope adjustments between manufacturing and non-manufacturing, see Burt 1988a:376–377, for similar results).

9. I tried an additive adjustment for the higher profit margins in nonmanufacturing. I decreased the profit margin in each nonmanufacturing market by a constant so that the mean margin in nonmanfacturing equals the mean in manufacturing. The log of the adjusted profit margins was then predicted by log $(1 - O)$ and log (C). The results are weaker than the results in Table 3.2 (-3.0 t-tests for both hole effects). The difference between manufacturing and nonmanufacturing increases with structural autonomy as specified by the multiplicative adjustment in the text.

10. I checked for outlier effects from the ordnance and airplane markets at the extreme right of the constraint graph in Figure 3.3. Both of these markets are so dependent on purchases by the federal government that they emerge as more constrained than any other markets. However, the constraint effect is little affected by deleting these markets. The $-.30$ correlation between profit and constraint across all 52 manufacturing markets is $-.31$ excluding ordnance and airplanes. The $-.37$ correlation between profit and the log of constraint is $-.32$ excluding ordnance and airplanes.

11. I expected an interaction effect between O and C in the linear model in Table 3.2. The idea is that oligopolistic producers have a special advantage above and beyond the direct effects of O and C when negotiating price with disorganized suppliers or customers. However, this effect is weak in previous work (for example, t-tests of 2 or less in Burt, 1988a:376–377). Adding the product OC to the linear model in Table 3.2 generates a negligible 0.6 t-test. A similarly negligible effect is obtained if the model is estimated across the 306 observations over time, as in the second row of Table 3.3, with the 16 dummy variables adjusting for severe autocorrelation within markets (-0.1 t-test). The idea of an interaction effect is preserved in the final nonlinear model because $(1 - O)$ and C are multiplied by one another to predict the market profit margin.

12. Alternative strategies for pooling cross sections in a panel study are nicely laid out by Hannan and Young (1977) and Berk et al. (1979) with references to textbook treatments of the topic in the econometrics literature. The 16

markets in which autocorrelation is severe were identified by testing each of the 77 markets for autocorrelation. A dummy variable distinguishing the four observations on a single market was added to the model in the first row of Table 3.3. For 16 markets, the effect of the dummy variable is at least twice the magnitude of its standard error. The markets are sectors 2, 3, 8, 11, 12, 15, 18, 19, 21, 27, 34, 60, 61, 63, 70, and 71 in the aggregate input-output table. The controlled autocorrelation effects in the second row of Table 3.3 vary from minimum t-tests of 2.8 for the consistently high profit margin in the chemicals market (sector 27) and 2.6 for the consistently high profit margin in forestry and fish products (sector 3), up to maximum t-tests of -5.7 for the consistently low profit margin in the market for transportation equipment other than cars, trucks, and airplanes (sector 61) and 6.4 for the consistently high profit margin in real estate (sector 71).

13. Finifter (1972) provides a useful introduction to resampling methods such as the jackknife, with references to more technical treatments. The jackknife estimates in Table 3.3 are computed by creating 77 subsample estimates of each effect, where each subsample contains all but the four observations on a single market. The jackknife estimate of an effect is its weighted average across the 77 subsamples, and the standard error of the effect is defined by its variance across the subsamples. Specifically, let β be the OLS estimate of an effect based on all 306 observations (first row of Table 3.3), and let β_i be an estimate of the same effect but computed from all observations excluding the four on the ith market. The jackknife estimate of β is a weighted average of the β_i:

$$\hat{\beta} = \sum_i [N\beta - (N-1)\beta_i]/N = \sum_i [b_i]/N,$$

where N is the population of all 77 markets. The standard error of the estimate is the usual standard error of the mean, here defined by the variance of the "pseudovalues" bracketed as b_i in the above equation across subsamples:

$$s^2 = \sum_i \left(\Sigma b_i^2 - (\Sigma b_i)^2/N \right) \Big/ (N-1), \qquad s_{\hat{\beta}} = s/\sqrt{N}.$$

14. Bubble size in Figure 3.5 is defined by the absolute value of the pseudovalues generated to obtain the jackknife estimates in Table 3.3; pseudovalue b_i in note 13. Pseudovalues for β_o and β_c are tightly distributed around the aggregate estimates, but the little variation that does occur is illustrated in Figure 3.5.

15. Statistical models for estimating such effects were developed to determine the effects of geographic proximity between units of analysis (for example, factories located in similar geographic locations and therefore similarly positioned with respect to labor markets and transportation). The models were brought into sociology by network analysts, in particular Doreian (for example, 1981), and have the form $b_j = \alpha + \rho(\Sigma_i w_{ji} b_i) + e$, where b_i in this

analysis is the pseudovalue measuring the ith market's contribution to evidence of a hole effect (from the preceding two notes), ρ is a regression coefficient measuring contagion between markets, and w_{ji} is a row stochastic weight defining the extent to which market i's score on the criterion variable is contagious for market j. The standardized contagion effect will be close to 1.0 to the extent that the score in market j (b_j) resembles scores in proximate markets (b_i for which w_{ji} is high). Here, w_{ji} is high to the extent that markets j and i are structurally equivalent as defined for the market topology map in Figure 3.2 (using a value of 4 for the power function exponent v as used in Burt and Carlton's, 1989, network autocorrelation analyses of markets). The estimation of contagion effects here follows the models of structural equivalence contagion in Burt (1987a:1328ff.).

16. The stability of transaction-specific constraint for these markets is discussed in Burt (1988a) and Burt and Carlton (1989). Because household and government markets are included in a slightly different way here, I checked stability again before pooling over time. Here are the correlations among the proportional trade relations, p_{ij}, in the upper diagonal and constraint coefficients, c_{ij}, in the lower diagonal between pairs of markets in the four years:

1963	1.00	0.99	0.95	0.94
1967	0.99	1.00	0.95	0.95
1972	0.96	0.97	1.00	0.98
1977	0.94	0.95	0.98	1.00

where correlations are computed across the 5,852 ordered dyads of 76 producer markets i transacting business with 77 supplier or customer markets j. Producer markets are ignored as their own supplier or customer, and the household and government markets are not included as producers. The restaurant market is excluded from the correlations because it doesn't exist as a separate market in the 1960s (see note 6); however, the hole signature of its transaction pattern is stable between 1972 and 1977. The correlations in the above matrix between the 1960s and the 1970s are slightly lower than correlations within each decade because of SIC category redefinitions in 1972 (see Burt, 1988a); however, the correlations are all quite high.

17. The criterion for comparing markets i and j is the following Euclidean distance between their ordered proportional transactions with each other market and the constraint they face in each transaction:

$$d_{ij} = \left[\sum_k (p_{ik} - p_{jk})^2 + \sum_k (c_{ik}^* - c_{jk}^*)^2 \right]^{1/2},$$

where k refers to the rank order of markets in the hole signature, not a specific market (i.e., $k = 1$ is the first market listed in the hole signature, $k = 2$ is the second, and so on), and c_{ik}^* measures constraint normalized for each market to sum to one (i.e., $c_{ik}^* = c_{ik}/C$, so $\Sigma_k c_{ik}^* = 1$, just as $\Sigma_k p_{ik} = 1$). I have normalized constraint so distances between market hole signatures are affected by only the shape, not the aggregate level, of constraint on each market and so that distances are no more affected by differences between markets in volume of buying and selling (the p_{ik} sum to 1 for each market i) than they are affected by differences in aggregate constraint (which sum to well under 1 for each market—C varies in Table 3.1 from 0.008 to 0.421 with a mean across markets of 0.064). I cluster-analyzed the markets without the control for aggregate constraint and found clusters primarily determined by aggregate constraint. My point here is that even with a control for aggregate constraint, kinds of market constraint and opportunity distributions are primarily determined by aggregate constraint. This will be made explicit in Figure 3.9.

18. The cluster analysis of distances defined in the preceding note was carried out using Ward's (1963) algorithm provided for equivalence analyses in STRUCTURE (see note 1). The diagram in Figure 3.6 is based on the program printout. The Ward algorithm builds the hierarchical clusters using an ANOVA criterion that minimizes the sum of squares between distances to markets clustered together. It closely resembles the post-hoc covariance tests used to assess the equivalence of combined network elements (for example, Burt, 1982:73–78; Burt and Minor, 1983:chap. 13; Ziegler, 1987:70–73). Such tests for the five clusters in Figure 3.6 show acceptable to high levels of equivalence within clusters: 95.2% for the cluster of Type A signatures, 91.3% for the cluster of Type B signatures, 94.2% for the cluster of Type C signatures, 79.2% for the cluster of Type D signatures, and 66.0% for the cluster of Type E signatures. Comparing these results with Figure 3.9, you can see that the test for equivalence within a cluster decreases across clusters closer to the central concentration of markets with low aggregate levels of constraint. The Type D and Type E clusters, in particular, are affected. Within the Type D cluster, market-specific reliabilities vary from 0.99 down to 0.77, with all but three above 0.88 reliability. Within the Type E cluster, reliabilities vary from 0.95 down to 0.70, with all but seven above 0.80 reliability. The two least reliable assignments are the wood containers market (0.66 reliability) and electronic components market (0.31 reliability). Neither of these markets fit any other cluster, so they have been left as assigned in the cluster analysis to Type E.

19. There is no systematic tendency for the largest transactions to be with suppliers in one signature and customers in the others. Given the total volume of business in the producers' largest transaction, 65% of the business on average is sales to a customer market in the 16 Type B markets, 91% is sales in the 9 Type C markets, and 76% is sales in the 23 Type E markets. These differences are negligible relative to variation within the three kinds of markets (1.37 F-test with 2,45 d.f., $P = .27$). The supplier-customer differences between the three signatures are also negligible in the second-largest transaction (0.04 F-test).

4. Getting Ahead

1. The sociometric booklet was attractively produced, accompanied by a strong cover letter including the name of a corporate contact, and mailed through the firm's internal mail system. Depending on the complexity of the respondent's network, the booklet required as little as 10 minutes or as much as 40 minutes to complete. To encourage response, respondents were promised both an analysis of their network and, as a baseline against which each manager could compare his or her own network, a report describing typical networks in the firm. To assure respondents of their confidentiality, an important consideration given the potentially sensitive information requested, the return envelope was addressed directly to Columbia University. Sample managers who had not returned the booklet three weeks later were sent a reminder postcard offering to send a second booklet, and after five weeks were sent a new copy of the sociometric booklet with a final request for their participation.

2. The response categories for closeness are given quantitative values following Burt and Guilarte's (1986) use of the balance principle (friends of my friends are my friends and enemies of my friends are my enemies). Consider the triad of a manager i and two contacts j and k. If the manager is especially close to contact j, then both should be close to k if either is close, or both distant if either is distant. I tabulated the four response categories describing manager relations to contact k by the three response categories describing relations between contacts. A loglinear model can be fit to the table in which the rows and columns are quantitative response positions on a single dimension of closeness (for example, see Goodman, 1984). Fitting such a model to the manager data yields an adequate fit (4.1 chi-square with 2 d.f., $P = .13$) and the following scale values for the manager's relation with contact k: 0.656 for "especially close" relations, 0.233 for "close" relations, -0.199 for "less close" relations, and -0.690 for "distant" relations. The following scale values are obtained for the relation between contacts j and k: 0.769 for "especially close" relations, -0.148 for "less close" relations, and -0.621 for "distant" relations. These scale values are fixed relative to one another, permitting transformation that preserves their relative magnitude. They are scaled for the analysis so that "distant" relations have a value of 0 and "especially close" relations have a value of 1. Relations between contacts are scaled as follows: $z_{jk} = (s_{jk} + 0.621)/1.390$, where s_{jk} is the raw scale value given above, and 1.390 is the distance from the lowest to the highest scale value. The following quantitative values result:

    1.00 especially close
    0.34 less close
    0.00 distant (total strangers or dislike)

The "distant" relations between respondent and contact are typically with the person named in response to Question 8 in Figure 4.2. To keep this person in the manager's network while acknowledging the minimal presence of such contacts, I set the minimum strength relation to 0.01. Relations from managers to contacts are scaled as follows: $z_{ik} = (s_{ik} + 0.7)/1.356$, where s_{ik} is the raw scale value given above and 1.356 is the distance from the lowest to the highest scale value. The following quantitative values result:

1.00	especially close
0.69	close
0.37	less close
0.01	distant

There are 28 instances of missing data on relations between contacts and 7 instances of missing data on relations between the respondent and a contact. In all 28 of the first kind of missing data, the manager has a "distant" relation with one or both contacts. In six of the 7 second kind of missing data, the two contacts are "less close," and in the other instance "distant" from one another. Given this tendency for missing relations to be associated with "distant" relations, the tendency observed in the General Social Survey network data for missing relations to resemble "total stranger" relations (Burt, 1987b), and the lack of any other information, missing relations are treated as distant relations in the analysis.

3. Age was another variable kept confidential in the personnel records. Not all managers graduated from college when they were 21. Some of the older managers even graduated after they had worked in the firm for a few years. However, the linear operations to be performed on promotion age will not be affected by adding a constant (21 years) to the age variable, and the descriptive statistics on promotion age make more intuitive sense if they are expressed in terms of probable age rather than in terms of years between college graduation and promotion. The added 21 years is eliminated in the promotion age variable used as a criterion in predicting promotion from contact networks.

4. Two technical points should be noted about the computation. First, there are no significant interaction effects among the variables in Table 4.1 predicting either age variable. The most significant is between sex and seniority in predicting promotion age (recently hired women have a negligible tendency to be promoted at younger ages than do women hired some time ago; $F = 1.31$ with 1,243 d.f., $P = .25$). Second, college graduation is imputed for 37 managers. Notice in Table 4.1 that the degrees of freedom for testing promotion age differences are smaller than corresponding tests for time in rank. Of the 37 managers for whom college graduation is unknown, 25 provided no information on education. The other 12 provided a college major and professional education, but no graduation date. To get a probable promotion age for the 37 managers, I first computed their expected promotion age from the regression model used to predict known promotion ages from the

variables in Table 4.1. I regressed the known promotion ages over expected promotion age and the fast promotion variable defining social time in rank. Both predictors are known for the managers whose graduation date is unknown. I used the regression equation to predict the 37 unknown promotion ages. To be sure that the imputation is not distorting conclusions, I tested for level and slope adjustments for the managers with imputed promotion ages. Both are negligible. The 37 managers with imputed promotion ages have a negligibly lower promotion age (-0.7 *t*-test) and negligibly higher constraint effect (0.8 *t*-test).

5. I considered alternative contrasts with expected age. The ratio in the text measures the difference between age and expected age relative to the expected age. Deviations from expected age in the direction of younger or older are equally significant. If constraint primarily affects promotion by delaying it, then age/E(age) is appropriate because ages under average are compressed within the 0-1 range. Conversely, E(age)/age compresses above-average ages into the 0-1 range. This would be the better measure if the principal hole effect is a lack of constraint generating early promotion. The measure emphasizing delayed promotion is a linear transformation of the measure in the text, so it provides the same estimates of hole effects, but the negative effect of constraint on fast promotion is a positive effect on delayed promotion ([E(age) $-$ age]/E(age) $= 1 -$ age/E(age)). The measure emphasizing fast promotion is different from the measure in the text and generates weaker effects. The correlations with constraint are $-.38$ for early promotion and $-.18$ for fast promotion versus the correlations of $-.41$ and $-.31$ to be presented. The more severe drop for fast promotion reflects recent promotions as discussed in the text. Constraint predicts delayed promotion, not the demographic fact of having just been promoted.

6. Level of education is not a significant variable here because the managers are too well educated. Respondents were asked if they had any professional training beyond college graduation. Most did (77%), especially MBAs of one kind or another. Having this extra education is correlated neither with age at promotion ($r = 0.09$) nor with years at current rank ($r = -.05$).

7. The confidence interval is based on the distribution of jackknife pseudovalues for the effects in Table 4.2 (see note 13 in Chapter 3 for computations). The 284 pseudovalues for early promotion and the 284 for fast promotion have a $-.118$ mean across the combined 568 pseudovalues with a standard deviation of 1.131, and so a 0.048 standard error. The mean plus and minus twice the standard error varies from $-.02$ to $-.21$ for a 95% confidence interval, marked by the gray area in Figure 4.4.

8. These effects have been estimated from a (5 by 2) tabulation of all 3,584 contacts cited by the managers. The boundaries around age statuses were identified in a structural equivalence analysis of three networks: a network in which z_{ij} is the tendency for managers i years with the firm to cite a solid line relation to managers j years with the firm, a second network in which z_{ij}

is the tendency for them to cite a dotted line relation to managers j years with the firm, and a third network in which z_{ij} is the tendency for them to cite a thin line relation to managers j years with the firm. Methodological details on detecting age statuses are given in Burt (1991).

9. The level adjustments in Table 4.3, and those to be presented in Table 4.4, are evaluated at the mean level of constraint. For example, the slope adjustment for insider managers in Table 4.3 is the product of a dummy variable distinguishing insider managers and constraint measured as $C - .2873$, where 0.2873 is the mean value of C across all 284 managers. This means that the level adjustment for insiders measures the difference between insiders and other managers at the mean value of C (not the intercept of the regression equation where C equals 0). Allison (1977) provides a clear discussion of this issue.

10. I considered alternative cut-off points to distinguish recently promoted managers. Across the 196 managers whose networks span one or more social frontiers, constraint has a $-.30$ correlation with fast promotion (-4.3 t-test). This changes to $-.31$ (-4.6 t-test) for the 195 who have been at their current rank for 6 months or more, $-.36$ (-4.9 t-test) for the 161 at their current rank for a year or more, $-.34$ (-4.2 t-test) for the 138 at their current rank for a 1.5 years or more, $-.33$ (-3.7 t-test) for the 115 at their current rank for 2 years cr more, and $-.27$ (-2.6 t-test) for the 91 at their current rank for 2.5 years or more. The one year cut-off gives the best contrast and is reported in the text. It is unusual for managers in this study population to spend less than a year in a rank before promotion to the next higher rank.

11. The criterion for comparing managers i and j is the following Euclidean distance between their ordered proportional relations with each of their contacts and the constraint they face in each relationship:

$$d_{ij} = \left[\sum_k (p_{ik} - p_{jk})^2 + \sum_k (c_{ik} - c_{jk})^2 \right]^{1/2} ,$$

where k refers to the rank order of contacts in the hole signature, not a specific contact (in other words, $k=1$ is the first contact listed in the hole signature, $k=2$ is the second, and so on). Where manager i or j cited more contacts than the other manager, relations and constraint in the smaller network were set to zero for rank orders k beyond the cited number of contacts. The cluster analysis of distances was carried out using Ward's (1963) algorithm provided for equivalence analyses in STRUCTURE (see Chapter 3, note 1). The Ward algorithm builds the hierarchical clusters using an ANOVA criterion that minimizes the sum of squares between distances to markets clustered together. It closely resembles the post-hoc covariance tests used to assess the equivalence of combined network elements (for example, Burt, 1982:73–78; Burt and Minor, 1983:chap. 13; Ziegler, 1987:70–73).

12. The association between fast promotion and hierarchy across all managers yields a negligible -1.4 t-test. The association among managers whose net-

works span one or more social frontiers is marginally significant (-1.9 t-test), but drops to a negligible -0.5 t-test if aggregate constraint is held constant. The association for insider managers is negligible before (0.3 t-test) and after (-0.2 t-test) aggregate constraint is held constant.

13. There is a slight curve to the association in Figure 4.9 that might be taken as a nonlinear effect, as discussed earlier, but the correlation between the logs of hierarchy and early promotion is slightly weaker than the linear association reported in the text ($r = 0.256$, 2.8 t-test).

14. The distinctions are also visible in a factor analysis of the network variables. I ran a principal component analysis of 13 variables: total number of contacts cited; number of contacts cited within the firm; density; effective size; constraint; four dummy variables distinguishing the entrepreneurial, clique, and two hierarchical networks in Figure 4.13; hierarchy; the number of social relations with core work contacts; the proportion of all work contacts that are core work contacts; and the three-category contrast between opportunity- and task-oriented networks. Constraint is the dominant dimension. The first principal component describes 34% of the variance and is correlated 0.92 with constraint. It also picks up size ($r = -.81$ for total contacts, and $-.94$ for work contacts cited) and effective size ($-.78$). Spanning institutional holes defines the second dimension. The second principal component describes 17% of the variance and is correlated 0.87 with the three-category contrast between opportunity- and task-oriented networks. It picks up the variance in social relations with core work contacts ($r = -.88$) and proportion of core work contacts ($-.49$), but little else. Hierarchy defines the third dimension. The third principal component describes 16% of the variance and is correlated 0.63 with the hierarchy measure. It picks up variance in density ($r = -.66$) and some variance in the proportion of contacts drawn from the immediate work group ($r = 0.43$). It is correlated with having a hierarchical network built around someone other than the boss ($r = 0.50$) and with not having a clique network ($-.63$). The fourth principal component is small, describing 9% of the variance, and distinguishes the managers with hierarchical networks built around their boss ($r = 0.70$ with the boss hierarchy dummy variable; $-.60$ with the nonboss hierarchy dummy).

15. Managers are rank ordered in Figure 4.14 by their pseudovalues in a jackknife estimate of the correlation between constraint and early promotion. The correlation is $-.15$ across all 284 managers (first row of Table 4.2). The correlation is more positive if the managers to the left in Figure 4.14 are deleted from the estimation. The correlation is more negative if the managers to the right of the graph are deleted. See note 13 in Chapter 3 on pseudovalues in a jackknife estimate.

16. The z-score test statistics reported in this paragraph are taken from a saturated loglinear model of the three-way tabulation between rank, sex, and a dichotomous variable defined by the line between the two categories of managers in Figure 4.14.

17. Across these managers, constraint is positively correlated with density (0.24),

uncorrelated with the proportion of ties that are nonzero in a network (0.01), and the importance of exclusive access creates a strong negative correlation with size ($-.87$).

5. Player-Structure Duality

1. This is the jumping off point for a discussion of role strain following Merton (1957) and Goode (1960). The argument is not as straightforward as it might seem. Merton and Goode take strain for granted to focus their attention on mechanisms with which people manage strain. Sieber (1974) and Marks (1977) go to the other extreme of focusing on the benefits of playing multiple roles (see note 14 in Chapter 1). A structural hole line of argument lies somewhere between these extremes, describing how the distribution of holes within and between roles determines their negotiability. Some roles combine easily, even enhancing one another, because the distribution of structural holes enhances their joint negotiability. Other roles are more difficult to play off against one another and so create strain when combined.

2. The issue in these paragraphs can be discussed more precisely as a stochastic regressor problem. Physical attributes are stochastic regressors in the sense that differences in sex, race, age, and so on are imperfect indicators of underlying structural variables directly causing outcomes. You can estimate the effect directly by using network variables to predict the outcome. This is the direct causal path in Figure 5.3. Or you can estimate the effect indirectly by using physical attributes to predict the outcome, whereupon the effect is a compound coefficient. The magnitude of the compound coefficient is the product of the two correlations in Figure 5.3: the attribute-structure correlation multiplied by the attribute-outcome correlation. The compound coefficient will be weaker than the direct effect, increasingly so as the attribute-structure correlation weakens or changes between attributes.

6. Commit and Survive

1. The last of these examples is nicely illustrated by the slow walking speed of unemployed men cited by Merton (1984:271) in his discussion of socially expected durations, drawing on Jahoda, Lazarsfeld, and Zeisel's (1933) ethnography of an Austrian community.

2. Three product categories in high-autonomy markets involve a volume of sales well over the upper limit of $15 billion in Figure 6.5. If I include the three in the graph, it is difficult to see differences between the 104 other high-autonomy product categories. They are pressed into the lower left corner of the graph. The three high-volume product categories are deleted from the graph at the top of Figure 6.5 only to display more clearly product category variation between the high- and low-autonomy markets. They are included in the Table 6.1 results, and responsible for the higher prediction of net

income from total sales in high-autonomy markets (0.76 squared correlation in Table 6.1 versus 0.64 at the top of Figure 6.5).

3. Using four-digit SIC product categories to study market schedules opens a new site for empirical research on the market interface model, linking the model with more traditional market structure research. I do not have space to discuss the diverse hypotheses informing such research. I mention one, however, because it is closely connected with the discussion of market boundaries in Chapter 3. Producers in the interface model match volume and pricing to the value perceptions of customers. To the extent that producers in two markets do business in the same customer markets, they match volume and pricing to the same customer value perceptions. Therefore, they operate with the same market schedule—structurally equivalent producers should have equivalent market schedules. More concretely, the markets close together in the topology map in Figure 3.2 should have similar market schedules. This is an easily tested structural equivalence contagion hypothesis (see the discussion of Figure 3.5 or, for more diverse examples, Burt and Carlton, 1989; Galaskiewicz and Burt, 1991).

4. I will develop the idea of comparative population ecology analysis because I have evidence of structural hole effects adding a significant comparative dimension to population ecology. Burt and Talmud (1992) highlight two other implications of the market niche. First, the analogy between market and niche means that population biology models of stable eco-systems might have something useful to say about market systems. Those models describe structures of competition coefficients—the alpha coefficients in the Lotka-Volterra model—needed to ensure a stable eco-system (see Hannan and Freeman, 1989:101–102). These results have implications for the stability of market structures. Certain exchange networks should be able to survive, while certain others implode with one market coming to dominate the others. Second, the analogy between market and niche suggests that the proper organization unit for population ecology analysis is the establishment as a production entity, not the firm as a legal entity. The establishment is the organization unit directly affected by the causal processes of negotiated control that provide entrepreneurial opportunities (as explained in Chapter 5). The presumption in population ecology density effects is that firms and establishments are isomorphic; each firm owns one establishment. This presumption is explicit in the Lotka-Volterra growth model displayed in the text. The count of population members presumes roughly equivalent resource consumption. Bucks might consume more than does, but there is a basic level of food required to sustain the average deer. From this, you can predict the resource needs of a population of N deer through a specific period of time, say, through one winter. There is an analogy to establishments. A large plant requires more resources than a small one, but technology defines a range of plant sizes for optimum efficiency in producing a specific good. You can predict how much business is needed for a population of N establishments producing a specific

good to survive through a specific period of time. Firms are different. The resource needs of a firm depends on the number of establishments it operates. As the legal entity coordinating establishments, firms are free to vary widely around the optimum size and resource requirements of their establishments. Where the firm-establishment isomorphism holds, there is no problem with using the population models to predict counts of firms as counts of establishments. Where the firm-establishment isomorphism doesn't hold—as is the case for most large American firms which operate in multiple markets—the counts of establishments predicted by population models do not apply to counts of firms.

5. More precisely, the results in Figure 6.8 show that a control for dependence on government consumption should be included in whatever model is used to estimate autonomy effects. If autonomy is a covariate in birth mortality rates, for example, $r(t) = \alpha + e^{(\beta + \beta_a A)}e^{\gamma(t)}$, the exponent should be expanded to include a government consumption variable G. Then $r(t) = \alpha + e^{(\beta + \beta_a A + \beta_g G)}e^{\gamma(t)}$, where G could be a dummy variable as in Figure 6.8 (equal to 1 if a market depends on government consumption, 0 otherwise), or a continuous variable such as the proportion of market output consumed by government agencies.

7. Strategic Embedding and Institutional Residue

1. I mention this point to frame the generality of the topic at hand. I have elaborated the point elsewhere, contrasting Adam Smith's and Emile Durkheim's images of the division of labor and comparing images of the resulting social structure in anthropology, economics, and sociology (Burt, 1982: 333ff.).

2. I am using "embedding" in a narrow sense. In discussions of economic integration, the term is used more generally to refer to the embedding of economic markets within the broader society. This theme is developed in papers collected in Polanyi et al. (1957, esp. chaps. 13 and 14), reflecting themes in Parsons and Smelser's (1956) broad discussion of economic integration. Barber (1977) provides a valuable guide into this work. Also see Burt (1991b) for a contrast with structural integration of the market.

3. A strategy related to withdrawal is to segregate a relationship to a setting where it can most easily be negotiated. The relationship is transacted at a time and place where your other contacts don't see it. As far as the others are concerned, you have withdrawn from the relationship. This is commonly used to isolate severely constrained domestic relationships from work. Nuclear and extended family relations are typically transacted at a time and location outside the workplace. But a contact who poses severe constraint poses it in large part because of connections with your other contacts. These connections make it difficult to segregate the constraining contact from the

network. Segregation is a strategy best suited to negotiating constraint between separate networks (see note 1 in Chapter 5 on role strain).

4. Martin Gargiulo (1992) describes an instructive variation on constraint's role in strategy. He analyzes the political strategies of elites in a large agribusiness cooperative in Uruguay. Constraints are defined by the structure of interpersonal dependence, and embedding ties are obligation ties of political cooperation and confidential advising. The association between constraint and embedding varies with the substance of the constrained relationship. Constrained relations generally are embedded, as expected, in ties of interpersonal obligation. However, when two players have had an earlier falling out—now citing one another as the most difficult person they have had to deal with, or the person they most tried to block in a significant political controversy—the embedding tie that would go to the source of constraint instead goes to a player who constrains the source of constraint. These indirect leverage ties in Gargiulo's analysis correspond to managers in Chapter 4 who find sponsorship in their boss's boss. Gargiulo explains that where constraint is paired with conflict, interpersonal obligation is insufficient or cannot be established with a direct embedding tie. A third party has to be brought in. In other words, Commons's fifth player cannot be an implicit understanding of may-must-can-cannot conditions but has instead to be an explicit understanding enforced by a specific person (like the Nuer's leopard-skin chief).

5. This sentence is the starting point for an optimization model of strategic change within networks, adding to the model in note 14 of Chapter 1 a term balancing the cost of embedding the *i-j* relation against the incentive to eliminate constraint in the relation.

6. The social integration theme is closely related to Berkowitz's (1988; Berkowitz et al., 1979) analysis of economic production. He uses ownership and interlock ties to define corporate actors as enterprises, then defines market areas as clusters of production activities carried out within the same enterprises. The idea is that market areas defined as enterprises are a more realistic image of competitive markets than markets defined by technology requirements alone, as in input-output tables.

7. This excludes an enormous range of issues about the firm's internal structure and operation. The daunting range of issues is not only beyond the scope of this discussion but can only be touched upon in the broad, largely nonoverlapping reviews offered in sociology by Aldrich and Marsden (1988) on organizations vis-à-vis their environments and in economics by Holmstrom and Tirole (1989) on the theory of the firm. Cyert and Hedrick's (1972) review nicely positions this argument in the context of related economic literature. The contribution here falls into their category of simple extensions of the neoclassical approach. All empirical content in the proposed theory lies in the network representation of the firm's market environment (as opposed to adding

variables on behavioral or organizational issues within the firm). Succinct review of the range of forms taken by transactions and corporate ties is provided in Hall's (1982:247–265) framework for interorganizational analysis, worked out with Morrissey, and in Scott's (1987) text, especially his discussion of organization boundaries and the ties that span them.

8. Nagle (1991) provides the most comprehensive review I have seen of the argument's development. He reviews the assumptions and concepts of transaction cost economics, and traces their evolution and the increasing sophistication of related empirical research from 1971 through 1990.

9. Coase also points out that some people prefer the independence of their own small firm to a management position within a large one. The firms affected by this issue seem unlikely to be the vertically integrated firms under discussion.

10. This paragraph is adequately precise for discussing the strategy hypothesis, but inaccurate in equating cost with the constraint coefficient. More precisely, producer incentive to span market boundaries with corporate ties is affected by producer oligopoly. When the transaction with market j is moved into the more controlled setting of the corporate hierarchy, the proportion of producer trade conducted on the open market decreases. The expected increase in autonomy from a small decrease in business conducted on the open market, is negative one multiplied by the partial derivative of A with respect to p_{ij}. The distribution of constraint is so hierarchical that the largest transaction constraint is correlated 0.98 with the sum of constraint across all transactions (Figure 3.9). Focusing on that most constrained transaction, the cost of conducting the transaction on the open market can be calibrated with its contribution to producer autonomy:

$$a_{ij} = \alpha(1 - O)^{\beta_o}(c_{ij})^{\beta_c},$$

where the two effect exponents are negative, describing how producer autonomy in the transaction is increased by oligopoly (increasing O decreases the negative impact of $1 - O$) and would be increased by moving the transaction from the market into the corporate hierarchy (decreasing the negative impact of c_{ij}). Transaction-specific constraint is weighted by producer oligopoly. The more organized producers are, the more they can benefit from disorganized suppliers and customers, and the more they can benefit from getting around the constraint they face on the open market. The incentive to vertically integrate is least where producers are most competitive (see Burt, 1983:48–54, for detailed discussion).

11. The MacDonald and Caves and Bradburd articles came to my attention through a useful paper, reviewing transaction cost research in business and economics, written by Howard A. Shelanski, a graduate student in the Department of Economics at Berkeley who graciously shared his work with me.

12. The concept is developed through much of Sigmund Freud's work, but his later discussion of it in "Dissection of the Psychical Personality" (1933) draws primarily from his 1923 paper, "The Ego and the Id." Anna Freud's

use of the concept in describing identification with the aggressor is developed in her 1936 book on defense mechanisms. Brenner's (1955) review is as usual helpful (especially the three chapters on "The Psychic Apparatus").

13. Freud stresses the distinction between identification and the choice of an object. He (1933:63) writes: "The difference between the two can be expressed in some such way as this. If a boy identifies himself with his father, he wants to be like his father; if he makes him the object of his choice, he wants to have him, to possess him." The two meanings are distinguished because the former involves a change to the person's ego; the latter is a manipulation of the external environment that leaves the ego unchanged. It would be easy to confuse the two meanings in my treatment of identification as an imaginary embedding relation. The goal of controlling the source of constraint could be seen as a goal of possessing the source. This is not the intended meaning. Constraint, the lack of control in a relationship, triggers identification as a defense mechanism, but incorporating the source of constraint in the ego's personality is the strategy being invoked to manage the constraint. This may, or more likely may not, result in actually gaining control over the source of constraint.

14. This image is today more likely to be presented positively, in how-to books, than to appear in books decrying it. In the years following World War II, however, Americans were ready for stories consistent with the negative side of this image. Perhaps it was the growth in disposable income that gave us the luxury of being more reflective about our presentation of self. Perhaps it was the increased number of Americans working in large bureaucracies pursuant to the nation's growth in GNP and emergence as felt leader of the free world. In any case, books like Riesman's (1950) *Lonely Crowd* and Whyte's (1956) *Organization Man* found receptive markets. Mills (1946) provides an early, popular, extreme, and succinct illustration of the felt concern. The two points in his article are that (1) competitive entrepreneurs have been reduced to the role of "fixing" the problems of senior executives in large bureaucracies, which (2) involves, and indicates a broader condition of, selling one's self in a personality market where the self presented is manufactured to serve the interests of others. People are alienated from both their labor and the personality that they are obliged to present in order to labor (Hochschild, 1983, provides contemporary elaboration).

15. Kapferer (1973, esp. pp. 101–102) suggests some ways of formalizing the Bott analysis to clarify it, in particular emphasizing the importance of distinguishing the structure of relations within each spouse's network from the structure of relations across their networks.

References

Aldrich, Howard E., and Peter V. Marsden. 1988. Environments and organizations. Pp. 361–392 in *Handbook of Sociology,* ed. N. J. Smelser. Beverly Hills, Calif.: Sage.

Allison, Paul D. 1977. Testing for interaction in multiple regression. *American Journal of Sociology* 83:144–153.

Allison, Paul D. 1978. Measures of inequality. *American Sociological Review* 43:865–880.

Baker, Wayne E. 1984. The social structure of a national securities market. *American Journal of Sociology* 89:775–811.

Baker, Wayne E. 1990. Market networks and corporate behavior. *American Journal of Sociology* 96:589–625.

Baldwin, David A. 1980. Interdependence and power: a conceptual analysis. *International Organization* 34:471–506.

Barber, Bernard. 1977. Absolutization of the market: some notes on how we got from there to here. Pp. 15–31 in *Markets and Morals,* ed. G. Dworkin, G. Bermant, and P. G. Brown. Washington, D.C.: Hemisphere.

Barber, Bernard. 1978. Inequality and occupational prestige: theory, research, and social policy. *Sociological Inquiry* 48:75–88.

Barber, Bernard. 1983. *The Logic and Limits of Trust.* New Brunswick, N.J.: Rutgers University Press.

Barkey, Karen. 1991. Rebellious alliances: the state and peasant unrest in early seventeenth century France and the Ottoman empire. *American Sociological Review* 56:699–715.

Baron, James N., and William T. Bielby. 1980. Bringing the firms back in: stratification and the economic segmentation of work. *American Sociological Review* 45:737–765.

Benet, Francisco. 1957. Explosive markets: the Berber highlands. Pp. 188–217 in *Trade and Market in Early Empires,* ed. K. Polanyi, C. M. Arensberg, and H. W. Pearson. New York: Free Press.

Berk, Richard A., Donnie M. Hoffman, Judith E. Maki, David Rauma, and Herbert Wong. 1979. Estimation procedures for pooled cross-sectional and time series data. *Evaluation Quarterly* 3:385–410.

Berkman, Lisa F., and S. Leonard Syme. 1979. Social networks, host resistance, and mortality: a nine-year follow-up study of Alameda County residents. *American Journal of Epidemiology* 109:186–204.

Berkowitz, S. D. 1988. Markets and market-areas: some preliminary formulations. Pp. 261–303 in *Structural Sociology*, ed. B. Wellman and S. D. Berkowitz. New York: Cambridge University Press.

Berkowitz, S. D., P. J. Carrington, Y. Kotowitz, and L. Waverman. 1979. Enterprise groups. *Social Networks* 1:391–413.

Bettelheim, B. 1960. *The Informed Heart*. New York: Free Press.

Blau, Peter M. 1964. *Exchange and Power in Social Life*. New York: Free Press.

Blau, Peter M. 1977. *Heterogeneity and Inequality*. New York: Free Press.

Blin, Jean-Marie, and Claude Cohen. 1977. Technological similarity and aggregation in input-output systems: a cluster-analytic approach. *Review of Economics and Statistics* 59:82–91.

Bott, Elizabeth. (1957) 1971. *Family and Social Network*. New York: Free Press.

Boxman, Ed A. W., Paul M. De Graaf, and Hendrik D. Flap. 1991. The impact of social and human capital on the income attainment of Dutch managers. *Social Networks* 13:51–73.

Brenner, Charles. (1955) 1957. *An Elementary Textbook of Psychoanalysis*. New York: Doubleday Anchor.

Brittain, Jack W., and Douglas R. Wholey. 1988. Competition and coexistence in organizational communities. Pp. 195–222 in *Ecological Models of Competition*, ed. G. R. Carroll. Cambridge, Mass.: Ballinger.

Brooks, D. G. 1973. Buyer concentration: a forgotten element in market structure models. *Industrial Organization Review* 1:151–163.

Burt, Ronald S. 1979. A structural theory of interlocking directorates. *Social Networks* 1:415–435.

Burt, Ronald S. 1980. Autonomy in a social topology. *American Journal of Sociology* 85:892–925.

Burt, Ronald S. 1981. Spatial models of community leadership. Pp. 103–122 in *Urban Policy Analysis*, ed. T. N. Clark. Beverly Hills, Calif.: Sage.

Burt, Ronald S. 1982. *Toward a Structural Theory of Action*. New York: Academic Press.

Burt, Ronald S. 1983. *Corporate Profits and Cooptation*. New York: Academic Press.

Burt, Ronald S. 1986. A note on sociometric order in the General Social Survey network data. *Social Networks* 8:149–174.

Burt, Ronald S. 1987a. Social contagion and innovation, cohesion versus structural equivalence. *American Journal of Sociology* 92:1287–1335.

Burt, Ronald S. 1987b. A note on missing network data in the General Social Survey. *Social Networks* 9:63–73.

Burt, Ronald S. 1988a. The stability of American markets. *American Journal of Sociology* 93:356–395.

Burt, Ronald S. 1988b. Some properties of structural equivalence measures derived from sociometric choice data. *Social Networks* 10:1–28.

Burt, Ronald S. 1990a. Detecting role equivalence. *Social Networks* 12:83–97.

Burt, Ronald S. 1990b. Kinds of relations in American discussion networks. Pp. 411–451 in *Structures of Power and Constraint,* ed. C. Calhoun, M. W. Meyer, and W. R. Scott. New York: Cambridge University Press.

Burt, Ronald S. 1991. Measuring age as a structural concept. *Social Networks* 13:1–34.

Burt, Ronald S. 1992. Market integration. In *Interdisciplinary Perspectives on Organization Studies,* ed. S. Lindenberg and H. Schreuder. London: Pergamon Press.

Burt, Ronald S., and Debbie S. Carlton. 1989. Another look at the network boundaries of American markets. *American Journal of Sociology* 94:723–753.

Burt, Ronald S., and Miguel G. Guilarte. 1986. A note on scaling the General Social Survey network item response categories. *Social Networks* 8:387–396.

Burt, Ronald S., and Michael J. Minor, eds. 1983. *Applied Network Analysis.* Beverly Hills, Calif.: Sage.

Burt, Ronald S., and Don Ronchi. 1990. Contested control in a large manufacturing plant. Pp. 121–157 in *Social Networks through Time,* ed. J. Weesie and H. Flap. Utrecht, Holland: ISOR, University of Utrecht.

Burt, Ronald S., and Ilan Talmud. 1992. Market niche. *Social Networks* 14:in press.

Campbell, Karen E., Peter V. Marsden, and Jeanne S. Hurlbert. 1986. Social resources and socioeconomic status. *Social Networks* 8:97–117.

Carroll, Glenn R. 1981. Dynamics of organization expansion in national systems of education. *American Sociological Review* 46:585–599.

Carroll, Glenn R. 1983. A stochastic model of organizational mortality: review and reanalysis. *Social Science Research* 12:303–329.

Carroll, Glenn R. 1984. Organizational ecology. *Annual Review of Sociology* 10:71–93.

Carroll, Glenn R. 1985. Concentration and specialization: dynamics of niche width in populations of organizations. *American Journal of Sociology* 90:1262–1283.

Carroll, Glenn R., and Karl Ulrich Mayer. 1986. Job-shift patterns in the Federal Republic of Germany: the effects of social class, industrial sector, and organizational size. *American Sociological Review* 51:323–341.

Carroll, Glenn R., and Anand Swaminathan. 1992. The organizational ecology of strategic groups in the American brewing industry from 1975 to 1990. *Industrial and Corporate Change* 1:65–97.

Caves, Richard E. 1982. *American Industry: Structure, Conduct, Performance.* Englewood Cliffs, N.J.: Prentice-Hall.

Caves, Richard E., and Ralph M. Bradburd. 1988. The empirical determinants of vertical integration. *Journal of Economic Behavior and Organization* 9: 265–279.

Clark, Terry N., and Lorna C. Ferguson. 1983. *City Money.* New York: Columbia University Press.

Clevenger, T. S., and G. R. Campbell. 1977. Vertical organization: a neglected element in market structure-profit models. *Industrial Organization Review* 6:60–66.

Coase, Ronald H. (1937) 1952. The nature of the firm. Pp. 331–351 in *Readings in Price Theory,* ed. G. J. Stigler and K. E. Boulding. Chicago: Richard D. Irwin.

Cochran, Thomas C. 1968. Entrepreneurship. Pp. 87–90 in *International Encyclopedia of the Social Sciences,* vol. 5. New York: Macmillan.

Cole, Stephen. 1992. *Making Science.* Cambridge, Mass.: Harvard University Press.

Coleman, James S. 1957. *Community Conflict.* New York: Free Press.

Coleman, James S. 1964. *Introduction to Mathematical Sociology.* New York: Free Press.

Coleman, James S. 1988. Social capital in the creation of human capital. *American Journal of Sociology* 94:S95-S120.

Collins, Norman R., and Lee E. Preston. 1968. *Concentration and Price-Cost Margins in Manufacturing Industries.* Berkeley: University of California Press.

Collins, Norman R., and Lee E. Preston. 1969. Price-cost margins and industry structure. *Review of Economics and Statistics* 51:271–286.

Commons, John R. (1924) 1968. *Legal Foundations of Capitalism.* Madison: University of Wisconsin Press.

Commons, John R. 1950. *The Economics of Collective Action.* New York: Macmillan.

Cook, Karen S., and Richard M. Emerson. 1978. Power, equity, and commitment in exchange networks. *American Sociological Review* 43:721–739.

Cook, Karen S., Richard M. Emerson, Mary R. Gillmore, and Toshio Yamagishi. 1983. The distribution of power in exchange networks: theory and experimental results. *American Journal of Sociology* 89:275–305.

Coser, Rose Laub. 1975. The complexity of roles as a seedbed of individual autonomy. Pp. 237–263 in *The Idea of Social Structure,* ed. L. A. Coser. New York: Harcourt, Brace, Jovanovich.

Cyert, Richard M., and Charles L. Hedrick. 1972. Theory of the firm: past, present, and future—an interpretation. *Journal of Economic Literature* 10: 398–412.

Davis, S. M., and P. R. Lawrence. 1977. *The Matrix Firm.* Reading, Mass.: Addison Wesley.

De Graaf, Nan D., and Hendrik D. Flap. 1988. With a little help from my friends. *Social Forces* 67:453–472.

Deutsch, Helene. (1934) 1942. Some forms of emotional disturbance and their relationship to schizophrenia. *Psychoanalytic Quarterly* 11:301–321.

DiMaggio, Paul. 1986. Structural analysis of organizational fields: a blockmodel approach. Pp. 335–370 in *Research in Organizational Behavior,* ed. B. Staw and L. Cummings. Greenwich, Conn.: JAI Press.

DiMaggio, Paul. 1992. Nadel's paradox revisited: relational and cultural aspects of organizational structures. In *Networks and Organizations,* ed. N. Nohria and R. G. Eccles. Boston: Harvard Business School Press.

Doeringer, Peter B., and Michael J. Piore. 1971. *Internal Labor Markets and Manpower Analysis.* Lexington, Mass.: Heath.

Doreian, Patrick. 1981. Estimating linear models with spatially distributed data. Pp. 359–388 in *Sociological Methodology, 1981,* ed. S. Leinhardt. San Francisco: Jossey-Bass.

Douglas, Mary. (1970) 1973. *Natural Symbols.* London: Barrie and Jenkins.

Durkheim, Emile. (1893) 1933. *The Division of Labor in Society.* Translated by G. Simpson. New York: Free Press.

Eccles, Robert G., and Harrison C. White. 1988. Price and authority in inter-profit center transactions. *American Journal of Sociology* 94:S17-S51.

Edgeworth, F. Y. 1881. *Mathematical Psychics.* London: C. Kegan Paul.

Evans-Pritchard, E. E. 1940. *The Nuer.* New York: Oxford University Press.

Faulkner, Robert R. 1983. *Music on Demand.* New Brunswick, N.J.: Transaction.

Faulkner, Robert R., and Andy B. Anderson. 1987. Short-term projects and emergent careers: evidence from Hollywood. *American Journal of Sociology* 92:879–909.

Feld, Scott L. 1981 The focused organization of social ties. *American Journal of Sociology* 86:1015–1035.

Feld, Scott L. 1982. Social structural determinants of similarity. *American Sociological Review* 47:797–801.

Festinger, Leon, Stanley Schachter, and Kurt W. Back. 1950. *Social Pressures in Informal Groups.* Stanford: Stanford University Press.

Finifter, Bernard M. 1972. The generation of confidence: evaluating research findings by random subsample replication. Pp. 112–175 in *Sociological Methodology, 1972,* ed. H. L. Costner. San Francisco: Jossey-Bass.

Fischer, Claude S. 1982. *To Dwell among Friends.* Chicago: University of Chicago Press.

Flap, Hendrik D. 1988. *Conflict, Loyalty, and Violence.* New York: Verlag Peter Lang.

Flap, Hendrik D., and Nan D. De Graaf. 1989. Social capital and attained occupational status. *Netherlands Journal of Sociology* 22:145–161.

Flap, Hendrik D., and F. Tazelaar. 1989. The role of informal social networks on the labor market: flexibilization and closure. Pp. 99–118 in *Flexibilization of the Labor Market,* ed. H. Flap. Utrecht: ISOR, University of Utrecht.

Freeman, John H., Glenn R. Carroll, and Michael T. Hannan. 1983. The liability of newness: age dependence in organizational death rates. *American Sociological Review* 48:692–710.

Freeman, John H., and Michael T. Hannan. 1983. Niche width and the dynamics of organizational populations. *American Journal of Sociology* 88:1116–1145.

Freeman, Linton C. 1977. A set of measures of centrality based on betweenness. *Sociometry* 40:35–41.

Freud, Anna. (1936) 1946. *The Ego and the Mechanisms of Defense.* Trans. C. M. Baines. New York: International Universities Press.

Freud, Sigmund. (1923) 1960. *The Ego and the Id.* Trans. J. Riviere; rev. and ed. J. Strachey. New York: Norton.

Freud, Sigmund. (1933) 1965. *New Introductory Lectures on Psychoanalysis.* Trans. J. Strachey. New York: Norton.

Galaskiewicz, Joseph. 1985. *Social Organization of an Urban Grants Economy.* New York: Academic Press.

Galaskiewicz, Joseph, and Ronald S. Burt. 1991. Interorganization contagion in corporate philanthropy. *Administrative Science Quarterly* 36:88–105.

Galbraith, Kenneth J. 1952. *American Capitalism: The Concept of Countervailing Power.* New York: Houghton Mifflin.

Gargiulo, Martin. 1992. Two-step leverage: social networks and managerial strategies in a cooperative agribusiness. Ph.D. dissertation, Department of Sociology, Columbia University.

Geertz, Clifford. 1979. Suq: the bazaar economy in Sefrou. Pp. 123–313 in *Meaning and Order in Moroccan Society,* ed. C. Geertz, H. Geertz, and L. Rosen. New York: Cambridge University Press.

Goode, William J. 1960. A theory of role strain. *American Sociological Review* 25:483–496.

Goodman, L. A. 1984. *The Analysis of Cross-Classified Data Having Ordered Categories.* Cambridge, Mass.: Harvard University Press.

Granovetter, Mark S. 1973. The strength of weak ties. *American Journal of Sociology* 78:1360–1380.

Granovetter, Mark S. 1974. *Getting a Job.* Cambridge, Mass.: Harvard University Press.

Granovetter, Mark S. 1981. Toward a sociological theory of income differences. Pp. 11–47 in *Sociological Perspectives on Labor Markets,* ed. I. Berg. New York: Academic Press.

Granovetter, Mark S. 1983. The strength of weak ties: a network theory revisited. Pp. 201–233 in *Sociological Theory, 1983,* ed. R. Collins. San Francisco: Jossey-Bass.

Granovetter, Mark S. 1985. Economic action and social structure: the problem of embeddedness. *American Journal of Sociology* 91:481–510.

Hall, Richard H. 1982. *Organizations: Structure and Process.* Englewood Cliffs, N.J.: Prentice-Hall.

Han, Shin-Kap. 1990. Unstable firms in stable markets: 1967–1977. Paper presented at the 1990 Sunbelt Social Networks Conference.

Hannan, Michael T., and Glenn R. Carroll. 1992. *Dynamics of Organizational Populations.* New York: Oxford University Press.

Hannan, Michael T., and John Freeman. 1977. The population ecology of organizations. *American Journal of Sociology* 82:929–964.

Hannan, Michael T., and John Freeman. 1984. Internal politics of growth and decline. Pp. 177–199 in *Environments and Organizations,* ed. M. W. Meyer et al. San Francisco: Jossey-Bass.

Hannan, Michael T., and John Freeman. 1989. *Organizational Ecology.* Cambridge, Mass.: Harvard University Press.

Hannan, Michael T., and Alice A. Young. 1977. Estimation in panel models: results on pooling cross-sections and time series. Pp. 52–83 in *Sociological Methodology, 1977,* ed. David R. Heise. San Francisco: Jossey-Bass.

Heinz, John P., and Edward O. Laumann. 1982. *Chicago Lawyers: The Social Structure of the Bar.* New York: Russell Sage Foundation.

Hennart, Jean-François. 1988. Upstream vertical integration in the aluminum and tin industries. *Journal of Economic Behavior and Organization* 9:281–299.

Hochschild, Arlie R. 1983. *The Managed Heart.* Berkeley: University of California Press.

Holmstrom, Bengt R., and Jean Tirole. 1989. The theory of the firm. Pp. 61–133 in *Handbook of Industrial Organization,* vol. 1, ed. R. Schmalensee and R. Willig. New York: North-Holland.

Homans, George C. 1950. *The Human Group.* New York: Harcourt, Brace and World.

Hoselitz, Bert F. 1951. The early history of entrepreneurial history. *Explorations in Entrepreneurial History* 3:193–220.

Jahoda, Marie, Paul F. Lazarsfeld, and Hans Zeisel. (1933) 1971. *Marienthal: The Sociography of an Unemployed Community.* Chicago: Aldine-Altherton.

Kanter, Rosabeth M. 1983. *The Change Masters.* New York: Simon and Schuster.

Kapferer, Bruce. 1973. Social network and conjugal role in urban Zambia: towards a reformulation of the Bott hypothesis. Pp. 83–110 in *Network Analysis: Studies in Human Interaction,* ed. J. Boissevain and J. C. Mitchell. Paris: Mouton.

Kilby, Peter, ed. 1971. *Entrepreneurship and Economic Development.* New York: Free Press.

Killworth, Peter D., and H. Russell Bernard. 1978. The reverse small-world experiment. *Social Networks* 1:159–224.

Kirzner, Israel M. 1973. *Competition and Entrepreneurship.* Chicago: University of Chicago Press.

Kirzner, Israel M. 1979. *Perception, Opportunity, and Profit.* Chicago: University of Chicago Press.

Laumann, Edward O., and David Knoke. 1987. *Organization State: Social*

Change in National Policy Domains. Madison: University of Wisconsin Press.

Lazarsfeld, Paul F., Bernard Berelson, and Hazel Gaudet. 1944. *The People's Choice.* New York: Columbia University Press.

Leach, Jerry W. 1983. Introduction. Pp. 1–26 in *The Kula: New Perspectives on Massim Exchange.* New York: Cambridge University Press.

Leifer, Eric M. 1985. Markets as mechanisms: using a role structure. *Social Forces* 64:442–472.

Leifer, Eric M. 1990. Market and authority in league sports. *American Journal of Sociology* 96:655–683.

Leifer, Eric M., and Harrison C. White. 1988. A structural approach to markets. In *The Structural Analysis of Business,* ed. M. Schwartz and M. Mizruchi. New York: Cambridge University Press.

Lewin, Kurt. 1936. *Principles of Topological Psychology.* New York: McGraw-Hill.

Lewin, Kurt. 1951. *Field Theory in Social Science.* Ed. D. Cartwright. New York: Harper & Row.

Lin, Nan. 1982. Social resources and instrumental action. Pp. 131–145 in *Social Structure and Network Analysis,* ed. P. V. Marsden and Nan Lin. Beverly Hills, Calif.: Sage.

Lin, Nan, and Mary Dumin. 1986. Access to occupations through social ties. *Social Networks* 8:365–385.

Lin, Nan, Walter M. Ensel, and John C. Vaughn. 1981. Social resources and strength of ties. *American Sociological Review* 46:393–405.

Lindblom, Charles E. 1977. *Politics and Markets.* New York: Basic Books.

Linton, Ralph. 1936. *The Study of Man.* New York: D. Appleton-Century.

Lustgarten, S. H. 1975. The impact of buyer concentration in manufacturing industries. *Review of Economics and Statistics* 57:125–132.

MacDonald, James M. 1985. Market exchange or vertical integration: an empirical analysis. *Review of Economics and Statistics* 67:327–331.

Malinowski, Bronislaw. 1922. *Argonauts of the Western Pacific.* London: George Routledge & Sons.

Markovsky, Barry, David Willer, and Travis Patton. 1988. Power relations in exchange networks. *American Sociological Review* 53:220–236.

Marks, Stephen R. 1977. Multiple roles and role strain: some notes on human energy, time, and commitment. *American Sociological Review* 42:921–936.

Marsden, Peter V. 1983. Restricted access in networks and models of power. *American Journal of Sociology* 88:686–717.

Marsden, Peter V. 1987. Core discussion networks of Americans. *American Sociological Review* 52:122–131.

Marsden, Peter V. 1990. Network data and measurement. *Annual Review of Sociology* 16:435–463.

Marsden, Peter V., and Jeanne S. Hurlbert. 1988. Social resources and mobility outcomes: a replication and extension. *Social Forces* 67:1038–1059.

Marsden, Peter V., and Edward O. Laumann. 1977. Collective action in a community elite: exchange, influence resources, and issue resolution. Pp. 199–250 in *Power, Paradigms, and Community Research,* ed. R. J. Liebert and A. Imershein. Beverly Hills, Calif.: Sage.

McClelland, David C. 1961. *The Achieving Society.* Princeton: Van Nostrand.

McClelland, David C. 1975. *Power.* New York: Irvington.

McPherson, Miller. 1983. An ecology of affiliation. *American Sociological Review* 48:519–532.

McPherson, Miller, and Lynn Smith-Lovin. 1988. A comparative ecology of five nations: testing a model of competition among voluntary associations. Pp. 85–109 in *Ecological Models of Organizations,* ed. G. R. Carroll. Cambridge, Mass.: Ballinger.

Merton, Robert K. (1957) 1968. Continuities in the theory of reference group behavior. Pp. 335–440 in *Social Theory and Social Structure.* New York: Free Press.

Merton, Robert K. 1984. Socially expected durations: a case study of concept formation in sociology. Pp. 262–283 in *Conflict and Consensus,* ed. W. W. Powell and R. Robbins. New York: Free Press.

Miles, Robert H. 1982. *Coffin Nails and Corporate Strategies.* Englewood Cliffs, N.J.: Prentice-Hall.

Mills, C. Wright. 1946. The competitive personality. *Partisan Review* 13:433–441.

Mizruchi, Mark S. 1989. Similarity of political behavior among large American corporations. *American Journal of Sociology* 95:401–424.

Mizruchi, Mark S. 1992. *The Structure of Corporate Political Action.* Cambridge, Mass.: Harvard University Press.

Murray, S., J. Rankin, and D. Magill. 1981. Strong ties and job information. *Sociology of Work and Occupations* 8:119–136.

Nagle, Donald. 1991. A historical review of transaction cost economics: a framework for understanding organizational boundaries. Unpublished paper, Graduate School of Business, Columbia University.

Nohria, Nitin. 1991. Structural equivalence as an occasion for the production of trust. Paper presented at the Euro-American conference "Boundaries and Units."

Ouchi, William T. 1980. Markets, bureaucracies, and clans. *Administrative Science Quarterly* 25:129–142.

Parsons, Talcott, Edward Shils, Kaspar D. Naegele, and Jesse R. Pitts. 1961. *Theories of Society.* New York: Free Press.

Parsons, Talcott, and Neil J. Smelser. 1956. *Economy and Society.* New York: Free Press.

Peterson, Richard A. 1981. Entrepreneurship and organization. Pp. 65–83 in *Handbook of Organizational Design,* vol. 1, ed. P. C. Nystrom and W. H. Starbuck. New York: Oxford University Press.

Petersen, Trond, Seymour Spilerman, and Svenn-Åge Dahl. 1989. The structure of employment terminations among clerical employees in a large bureaucracy. *Acta Sociologica* 32:319–338.

Pfeffer, Jeffrey. 1987. Bringing the environment back in: the social context of business strategy. Pp. 119–135 in *The Competitive Challenge: Strategies for Industrial Innovation and Renewal,* ed. D. J. Teece. Cambridge, Mass.: Ballinger.

Pfeffer, Jeffrey, and Gerald R. Salancik. 1978. *The External Control of Organizations.* New York: Harper & Row.

Polanyi, Karl, Conrad M. Arensberg, and Harry W. Pearson, eds. 1957. *Trade and Market in the Early Empires.* New York: Free Press.

Powell, Walter W. 1990. Neither market nor hierarchy: network forms of organization. Pp. 295–336 in *Research in Organizational Behavior,* vol. 12, ed. B. Staw. Greenwich, Conn.: JAI Press.

Powell, Walter W., and Paul DiMaggio, eds. 1991. *New Institutionalism in Organizational Analysis.* Chicago: University of Chicago Press.

Radcliffe-Brown, A. R. (1940) 1965. On joking relationships. Pp. 90–104 in *Structure and Function in Primitive Society.* New York: Free Press.

Redlich, Fritz. 1949. The origins of the concepts of "entrepreneur" and "creative entrepreneur." *Explorations in Entrepreneurial History* 1:1–7.

Riesman, David, with Nathan Glazer and Reuel Denney. 1950. *The Lonely Crowd.* New York: Doubleday Anchor.

Riker, William H. 1986. *The Art of Political Manipulation.* New Haven: Yale University Press.

Riker, William H., and Peter C. Ordeshook. 1973. *An Introduction to Positive Political Theory.* Englewood Cliffs, N.J.: Prentice-Hall.

Rosenbaum, James E. 1984. *Career Mobility in a Corporate Hierarchy.* New York: Academic Press.

Schreuder, Hein. 1992. Coase, Hayek, and hierarchy. In *Interdisciplinary Perspectives on Organization Studies,* ed. S. Lindenberg and H. Schreuder. London: Pergamon Press.

Schumpeter, Joseph A. (1912) 1961. *The Theory of Economic Development.* Trans. R. Opie. Cambridge, Mass.: Harvard University Press.

Schwartz, Michael, and Frank P. Romo. 1992. The structural embeddedness of business decisions. In *Explorations in Economic Sociology,* ed. R. Swedberg. New York: Russell Sage Foundation.

Scott, W. Richard. 1987. *Organizations: Rational, Natural, and Open Systems.* Englewood Cliffs, N.J.: Prentice-Hall.

Shepherd, William G. 1970. *Market Power and Economic Welfare.* New York: Random House.

Sieber, Sam D. 1974. Toward a theory of role accumulation. *American Sociological Review* 39:567–578.

Simmel, Georg. 1896. Superiority and subordination as subject-matter of sociology, II. Trans. A. Small. *American Journal of Sociology* 2:392–415.

Simmel, Georg. 1902. The number of members as determining the sociological form of the group, II. Trans. A. Small. *American Journal of Sociology* 8:158–96.

Simmel, Georg. (1922) 1955. *Conflict and Web of Group Affiliations.* Trans. K. H. Wolff and R. Bendix. New York: Free Press.

Simmel, Georg. (1923) 1950. *The Sociology of Georg Simmel.* Trans. K. H. Wolff. New York: Free Press.

Smith, Charles W. 1989. *Auctions.* New York: Free Press.

Spilerman, Seymour. 1977. Careers, labor market structure, and socioeconomic achievement. *American Journal of Sociology* 83:551–593.

Spilerman, Seymour. 1986. Organizational rules and the features of work careers. Pp. 41–102 in *Research in Social Stratification and Mobility,* ed. R. Robinson. Greenwich, Conn.: JAI Press.

Spilerman, Seymour, and Tormod Lunde. 1991. The effects of educational attainment on promotion prospects. *Amer. Journal of Sociology,* 97:689–720.

Stigler, George J. (1957) 1965. Perfect competition, historically contemplated. Pp. 234–267 in *Essays in the History of Economics,* ed. G. J. Stigler. Chicago: University of Chicago Press.

Stinchcombe, Arthur L. 1965. Social structure and organizations. Pp. 142–193 in *Handbook of Organizations,* ed. J. G. March. Chicago: Rand-McNally.

Stinchcombe, Arthur L. 1979. Social mobility in industrial labor markets. *Acta Sociologica* 22:217–245.

Stinchcombe, Arthur L. 1990. *Information and Organizations.* Berkeley: University of California Press.

Stuckey, J. A. 1983. *Vertical Integration and Joint Venture in the Aluminum Industry.* Cambridge, Mass.: Harvard University Press.

Sullivan, Harry Stack. (1940) 1953. *Conceptions of Modern Psychiatry.* New York: Norton.

Sullivan, Harry Stack. 1953. *The Interpersonal Theory of Psychiatry.* Ed. H. S. Perry and M. L. Gawel. New York: Norton.

Swedberg, Richard. 1991. *Schumpeter—A Biography.* Princeton: Princeton University Press.

Thompson, Michael, Richard Ellis, and Aaron Wildavsky. 1990. *Cultural Theory.* San Francisco: Westview Press.

Tuma, Nancy B. 1985. Effects of labor market structure on job shift patterns. Pp. 327–363 in *Longitudinal Analysis of Labor Market Data,* ed. J. J. Heckman and B. Singer. New York: Cambridge University Press.

Ward, J. H. 1963. Hierarchical grouping to optimize an objective function. *Journal of the American Statistical Association* 58:236–244.

Weber, Max. (1904–05) 1930. *The Protestant Ethic and the Spirit of Capitalism.* Trans. T. Parsons. New York: Charles Scribner's Sons.

White, Harrison C. 1970. *Chains of Opportunity.* Cambridge, Mass.: Harvard University Press.

White, Harrison C. 1981a. Where do markets come from? *American Journal of Sociology* 87:517–547.

White, Harrison C. 1981b. Production markets as induced role structures. In *Sociological Methodology, 1981,* ed. S. L. Leinhardt. San Francisco: Jossey-Bass.

White, Harrison C. 1988. Varieties of markets. In *Structural Sociology,* ed. B. Wellman and S. D. Berkowitz. New York: Cambridge University Press.

White, Harrison C. 1992. *Identity and Control: A Structural Theory of Social Action*. Princeton: Princeton University Press.

White, Harrison C., Scott Boorman, and Ronald L. Breiger. 1976. Social structure from multiple networks, I, Blockmodels of roles and positions. *American Journal of Sociology* 81:730–780.

Whyte, William F. 1956. *Organization Man*. New York: Simon and Schuster.

Wildavsky, Aaron. 1964. *The Politics of the Budgetary Process*. Boston: Little, Brown.

Wilken, Paul H. 1979. *Entrepreneurship*. Norwood, N.J.: Ablex.

Williamson, Oliver E. 1975. *Markets and Hierarchies*. New York: Free Press.

Williamson, Oliver E. 1979. Transaction-cost economics: the governance of contractual relations. *Journal of Law and Economics* 22:3–61.

Williamson, Oliver E. 1981. The economics of organization: the transaction cost approach. *American Journal of Sociology* 87:548–577.

Williamson, Oliver E. 1985. *The Economic Institutions of Capitalism*. New York: Free Press.

Williamson, Oliver E. 1989. Transaction cost economics. Pp. 135–182 in *Handbook of Industrial Organization*, vol. 1, ed. R. Schmalensee and R. Willig. New York: North-Holland.

Williamson, Oliver E. 1992. Comparative economic organization: the analysis of discrete structural alternatives. In *Interdisciplinary Perspectives on Organization Studies*, ed. S. Lindenberg and H. Schreuder. London: Pergamon Press.

Wright, Erik O. 1978. Race, class, and income inequality. *American Journal of Sociology* 83:1368–1397.

Wright, Erik O., and Luca Perrone. 1977. Marxist class categories and income inequality. *American Sociological Review* 42:32–55.

Wright, Erik O., Cynthia Costello, David Hachen, and Joey Sprague. 1982. The American class structure. *American Sociological Review* 47:709–726.

Young, Michael, and Peter Willmott. 1957. *Family and Kinship in East London*. London: Routledge & Kegan Paul.

Zelizer, Viviana A. 1989. The social meaning of money: "special monies." *American Journal of Sociology* 95:342–377.

Ziegler, Rolf. 1987. Positionen in sozialen raumen, die multivariate analyse multipler netzwerke. Pp. 64–100 in *Methoden der Netzwerkanalyse*, ed. F. U. Pappi. Munich: Oldenbourg.

Ziegler, Rolf. 1992. Market, power and cooptation: accounting for corporate networks. In *Interdisciplinary Perspectives on Organization Studies*, ed. S. Lindenberg and H. Schreuder. London: Pergamon Press.

Zucker, Lynne G. 1987. Institutional theories of organization. *Annual Review of Sociology* 13:443–464.

Index

311